BUICK RIVIERA
PERFORMANCE PORTFOLIO
1963-1978

Compiled by R M Clarke

ISBN 1 85520 5351

BROOKLANDS BOOKS LTD.
P.O. BOX 146, COBHAM,
SURREY, KT11 1LG. UK
sales@brooklands-books.com

Brooklands Books

MOTORING
B.B. ROAD TEST SERIES
Abarth Gold Portfolio 1950-1971
AC Ace & Aceca 1953-1983
Alfa Romeo Giulietta Gold Portfolio 1954-1965
Alfa Romeo Giulia Coupés 1963-1976
Alfa Romeo Giulia Coupés Gold Port. 1963-1976
Alfa Romeo Spider 1966-1990
Alfa Romeo Spider Gold Portfolio 1966-1991
Alfa Romeo Alfasud 1972-1984
Alfa Romeo Alfetta Gold Portfolio 1972-1987
Alfa Romeo Alfetta GTV6 1980-1986
Alvis Gold Portfolio 1919-1967
AMX & Javelin Muscle Portfolio 1968-1974
Armstrong Siddeley Gold Portfolio 1945-1960
Aston Martin Gold Portfolio 1948-1971
Aston Martin Gold Portfolio 1972-1985
Aston Martin Gold Portfolio 1985-1995
Audi Quattro Gold Portfolio 1980-1991
Audi Quattro Takes On The Competition
Austin A30 & A35 1951-1962
Austin-Healey 100 & 100/6 Gold Port. 1952-1959
Austin-Healey 3000 Ultimate Portfolio 1959-1967
Austin-Healey Sprite Gold Portfolio 1958-1971
Berkeley Sportscars Limited Edition
BMW 6 & 8 Cyl. Cars Limited Edition 1935-1960
BMW 1600 Collection No. 1 1966-1981
BMW 2002 Gold Portfolio 1968-1976
BMW 6 Cylinder Coupés & Saloons Gold P. 1969-1976
BMW 316, 318, 320 (4 cyl.) Gold Port. 1975-1990
BMW 320, 323, 325 (6 cyl.) Gold Port. 1977-1990
BMW 3 Series Gold Portfolio 1991-1997
BMW 5 Series Gold Portfolio 1981-1987
BMW 5 Series Gold Portfolio 1988-1995
BMW 6 Series Gold Portfolio 1976-1989
BMW 7 Series Performance Portfolio 1977-1986
BMW Alpina Performance Portfolio 1967-1987
BMW Alpina Performance Portfolio 1988-1998
BMW M Series Gold Portfolio 1976-1997
BMW Z3 & Z3M Limited Edition
Borgward Isabella Limited Edition
Bricklin Gold Portfolio 1974-1975
Bristol Cars Gold Portfolio 1946-1992
Buick Performance Portfolio 1947-1962
Buick Muscle Portfolio 1963-1973
Buick Riviera Performance Portfolio 1963-1978
Cadillac Allanté 1986-1993
Cadillac Automobiles 1949-1959
Cadillac Automobiles 1960-1969
Cadillac Eldorado Performance Portfolio 1967-1978
Checker Limited Edition
Chevrolet 1955-1957
Impala & SS Muscle Portfolio 1958-1972
Corvair Performance Portfolio 1959-1969
El Camino & SS Muscle Portfolio 1959-1987
Chevy II & Nova SS Muscle Portfolio 1962-1974
Chevelle & SS Muscle Portfolio 1964-1972
Caprice Limited Edition 1965-1976
Chevrolet Muscle Cars 1966-1971
Chevy Blazer 1969-1981
Camaro Muscle Portfolio 1967-1973
Chevrolet Camaro & Z-28 1973-1981
High Performance Camaros 1982-1988
Chevrolet Corvette Gold Portfolio 1953-1962
Chevrolet Corvette Sting Ray Gold Port. 1963-1967
Chevrolet Corvette Gold Portfolio 1968-1977
High Performance Corvettes 1983-1989
Chrysler 300 Gold Portfolio 1955-1970
Imperial Limited Edition 1955-1970
Valiant 1960-1962
Citroen Traction Avant Gold Portfolio 1934-1957
Citroen 2CV Ultimate Portfolio 1948-1990
Citroen DS & ID 1955-1975
Citroen DS & ID Gold Portfolio 1955-1975
Citroen SM 1970-1975
Shelby Cobra Gold Portfolio 1962-1969
Cobras & Cobra Replicas Gold Portfolio 1962-1989
Crosley & Crosley Specials Limited Edition
Cunningham Automobiles 1951-1955
Datsun 240Z & 260Z Gold Portfolio 1970-1978
Datsun 280Z & ZX 1975-1983
DeLorean Gold Portfolio 1977-1995
De Soto Limited Edition 1952-1960
Charger Muscle Portfolio 1966-1974
Dodge Viper Performance Portfolio 1990-1998
ERA Gold Portfolio 1934-1994
Excalibur Collection No.1 1952-1981
Facel Vega 1954-1964
Ferrari Limited Edition 1947-1957
Ferrari Limited Edition 1958-1963
Ferrari Dino 308 & Mondial Gold Portfolio 1974-1985
Ferrari 328 348 Mondial Ultimate Portfolio 1986-94
Fiat 500 Gold Portfolio 1936-1972
Fiat 600 & 850 Gold Portfolio 1955-1972
Fiat Pininfarina 124 & 2000 Spider 1968-1985
Fiat X1/9 Gold Portfolio 1973-1989
Fiat Abarth Performance Portfolio 1972-1987
Ford Consul, Zephyr, Zodiac Mk. I & II 1950-1962
Ford Zephyr, Zodiac, Executive Mk. III & IV 1962-1971
Ford Cortina 1600E & GT 1967-1970
High Performance Capris Gold Portfolio 1969-1987
Capri Muscle Portfolio 1974-1987
High Performance Fiestas 1979-1991
Ford Escort RS & Mexico Limited Edition 1970-1979
High Performance Escorts Mk. I 1968-1974
High Performance Escorts Mk. II 1975-1980
High Performance Escorts 1980-1985
High Performance Escorts 1985-1990
High Perf. Sierras & Merkurs Gold Port. 1983-1990
Ford Thunderbird Performance Portfolio 1955-1957
Ford Thunderbird Performance Portfolio 1958-1963
Ford Thunderbird Performance Portfolio 1964-1976
Ford Automobiles 1949-1959
Ford Fairlane Performance Portfolio 1955-1970
Ford Ranchero Muscle Portfolio 1957-1979
Edsel Limited Edition 1957-1960
Falcon Performance Portfolio 1960-1970
Ford Galaxie & LTD Limited Edition 1960-1973
Ford GT40 Gold Portfolio 1964-1987
Mustang Muscle Portfolio 1967-1973
Ford Torino Limited Edition 1968-1974
Ford Bronco 4x4 Performance Portfolio 1966-1977
Ford Bronco 1978-1988
Goggomobil Limited Edition
Holden 1948-1962
Honda S500 • S600 • S800 Limited Edition 1962-1970
Honda CRX 1983-1987
International Scout Gold Portfolio 1961-1980
Isetta Gold Portfolio 1953-1964
ISO & Bizzarrini Gold Portfolio 1962-1974
Jaguar and SS Gold Portfolio 1931-1951
Jaguar C-Type & D-Type Gold Portfolio 1951-1960
Jaguar XK120, 140, 150 Gold Portfolio 1948-1960
Jaguar Mk. VII, VIII, IX, X, 420 Gold Port. 1950-1970
Jaguar Mk. 1 & Mk. 2 Gold Portfolio 1959-1969
Jaguar E-Type Gold Portfolio 1961-1971
Jaguar E-Type V-12 1971-1975
Jaguar S-Type & 420 Limited Edition 1963-1968
Jaguar XJ12, XJ5.3, V12 Gold Portfolio 1972-1990
Jaguar XJ6 Series I & II Gold Portfolio 1968-1979
Jaguar XJ6 Series III Perf. Portfolio 1979-1986
Jaguar XJ6 Gold Portfolio 1986-1994
Jaguar XJS Gold Portfolio 1975-1988
Jaguar XJ-S V12 Ultimate Portfolio 1988-1996
Jaguar XK8 Limited Edition
Jeep CJ-5 & CJ-6 1960-1976
Jeep CJ-5 & CJ-7 4x4 Perf. Portfolio 1976-1986
Jeep Wagoneer Performance Portfolio 1963-1991
Jeep J-Series Pickups 1970-1982
Jeepster & Commando Limited Edition 1967-1973
Jeep Cherokee & Comanche Pickups P. P. 1984-1991
Jeep Wrangler 4x4 Performance Portfolio 1987-1999
Jeep Cherokee & Grand Cherokee 4x4 P. P. 1992-1998
Jensen Interceptor Gold Portfolio 1966-1986
Jensen - Healey Limited Edition 1972-1976
Kaiser - Frazer Limited Edition 1946-1955
Lagonda Gold Portfolio 1919-1964
Lamborghini Countach & Urraco 1974-1980
Lamborghini Countach & Jalpa 1980-1985
Lancia Aurelia & Flaminia Gold Portfolio 1950-1970
Lancia Fulvia Gold Portfolio 1963-1976
Lancia Beta Gold Portfolio 1972-1984
Lancia Delta Gold Portfolio 1979-1994
Lancia Stratos 1972-1985
Land Rover Series I 1948-1958
Land Rover Series II & IIa 1958-1971
Land Rover Series III 4x4 Perf. Portfolio 1971-1985
Land Rover 90 110 Defender Gold Portfolio 1983-1994
Land Rover Discovery 1989-1994
Land Rover Story Part One 1948-1971
Fifty Years of Selling Land Rover
Lincoln Gold Portfolio 1949-1960
Lincoln Continental Performance Portfolio 1961-1969
Lincoln Continental 1969-1976
Lotus Seven Gold Portfolio 1957-1973
Lotus Elan Gold Portfolio 1962-1974
Lotus Elan & SE 1989-1992
Lotus Europa Gold Portfolio 1966-1975
Lotus Elite & Eclat 1974-1982
Lotus Elise Limited Edition
Marcos Coupés & Spyders Gold Portfolio 1960-1997
Matra Limited Edition 1965-1983
Mazda Miata MX-5 Performance Portfolio 1989-1997
Mazda Miata MX-5 Takes On The Competition
Mazda RX-7 Gold Portfolio 1978-1991
McLaren F1 Sportscar Limited Edition
Mercedes 190 & 300 SL 1954-1963
Mercedes G-Wagen 1981-1994
Mercedes S & 600 1965-1972
Mercedes S Class 1972-1979
Mercedes 230 • 250 • 280SL Gold Portfolio 1963-1971
Mercedes SLs & SLCs Gold Portfolio 1971-1989
Mercedes SLs Performance Portfolio 1989-1994
Mercury Limited Edition 1947-1959
Mercury Comet & Cyclone Limited Edition 1960-1970
Cougar Limited Edition 1967-1973
Messerschmitt Gold Portfolio 1954-1964
MG Gold Portfolio 1929-1939
MG TA & TC Gold Portfolio 1936-1949
MG TD & TF Gold Portfolio 1949-1955
MGA & Twin Cam Gold Portfolio 1955-1962
MG Midget Gold Portfolio 1961-1979
MGB Roadsters 1962-1980
MGB MGC & V8 Gold Portfolio 1962-1980
MGB GT 1965-1980
MGC & MGB GT V8 Limited Edition
MG Y-Type & Magnette ZA/ZB Limited Edition
MGF Limited Edition
Mini Gold Portfolio 1959-1969
Mini Gold Portfolio 1969-1980
Mini Gold Portfolio 1981-1997
High Performance Minis Gold Portfolio 1960-1973
Mini Cooper Gold Portfolio 1961-1971
Mini Moke Gold Portfolio 1964-1994
Morgan Three-Wheeler Gold Portfolio 1910-1952
Morgan Plus 4 & Four 4 Gold Portfolio 1936-1967
Morris Minor Collection No. 1 1948-1980
Shelby Mustang Muscle Portfolio 1965-1970
High Performance Mustang IIs 1974-1978
Mustang 5.0L Muscle Portfolio 1982-1993
Mustang 5.0L Takes On The Competition
Nash & Nash-Healey Limited Edition 1949-1957
Nash-Austin Metropolitan Gold Portfolio 1954-1962
NSU Ro80 Limited Edition
NSX Performance Portfolio 1989-1999
Oldsmobile Automobiles 1955-1963
Oldsmobile Muscle Portfolio 1964-1971
Cutlass & 4-4-2 Muscle Portfolio 1964-1974
Oldsmobile Toronado 1966-1978
Opel GT Gold Portfolio 1968-1973
Opel Manta Limited Edition 1970-1975
Packard Gold Portfolio 1946-1958
Pantera Gold Portfolio 1970-1989
Panther Gold Portfolio 1972-1990
Barracuda Muscle Portfolio 1964-1974
Pontiac Limited Edition 1949-1960
Pontiac Tempest & GTO 1961-1965
GTO Muscle Portfolio 1964-1974
Firebird & Trans-Am Muscle Portfolio 1967-1972
Firebird & Trans-Am Muscle Portfolio 1973-1981
High Performance Firebirds 1982-1988
Pontiac Fiero Performance Portfolio 1984-1988
Porsche 356 Gold Portfolio 1953-1965
Porsche 912 Limited Edition
Porsche 911 1965-1969
Porsche 911 1970-1972
Porsche 911 1973-1977
Porsche 911 SC & Turbo Gold Portfolio 1978-1983
Porsche 911 Carrera & Turbo Gold Port. 1984-1989
Porsche 911 Gold Portfolio 1990-1997
Porsche 911 Takes On The Competition 1990-1997
Porsche 914 Ultimate Portfolio
Porsche 924 Gold Portfolio 1975-1988
Porsche 928 Performance Portfolio 1977-1994
Porsche 928 Takes On The Competition
Porsche 944 Gold Portfolio 1981-1991
Porsche 968 Limited Edition
Porsche Boxster Limited Edition
Railton & Brough Superior Gold Portfolio 1933-1950
Range Rover Gold Portfolio 1970-1985
Range Rover Gold Portfolio 1986-1995
Range Rover Takes on the Competition
Reliant Scimitar 1964-1986
Renault Alpine Gold Portfolio 1958-1994
Riley Gold Portfolio 1924-1939
R. R. Silver Cloud & Bentley 'S' Series Gold P. 1955-65
Rolls Royce Silver Shadow Ultimate Portfolio 1965-80
Rolls Royce & Bentley Gold Portfolio 1980-1989
Rolls Royce & Bentley Limited Edition 1990-1997
Rover P4 1949-1959
Rover 3 & 3.5 Litre Gold Portfolio 1958-1973
Rover 2000 & 2200 1963-1977
Rover 3500 & Vitesse 1976-1986
Saab Sonett Collection No.1 1966-1974
Saab Turbo 1976-1983
Studebaker Gold Portfolio 1947-1966
Studebaker Hawks & Larks 1956-1963
Avanti 1962-1990
Suzuki SJ Gold Portfolio 1971-1997
Vitara, Sidekick & Geo Tracker Perf. Port. 1988-1997
Sunbeam Tiger & Alpine Gold Portfolio 1959-1967
Toyota Land Cruiser Gold Portfolio 1956-1987
Toyota Land Cruiser 1988-1997
Toyota MR2 Gold Portfolio 1984-1997
Toyota MR2 Takes On The Competition
Triumph TR2 & TR3 Gold Portfolio 1952-1961
Triumph TR4, TR5, TR250 1961-1968
Triumph TR6 Gold Portfolio 1969-1976
Triumph TR7 & TR8 Gold Portfolio 1975-1982
Triumph Herald 1959-1971
Triumph Vitesse 1962-1971
Triumph Spitfire Gold Portfolio 1962-1980
Triumph 2000, 2.5, 2500 1963-1977
Triumph GT6 Gold Portfolio 1966-1974
Triumph Stag Gold Portfolio 1970-1977
Triumph Dolomite Sprint Limited Edition
TVR Gold Portfolio 1959-1986
TVR Performance Portfolio 1986-1994
VW Beetle Gold Portfolio 1935-1967
VW Beetle Gold Portfolio 1968-1991
VW Beetle Collection No.1 1970-1982
VW Karmann Ghia 1955-1982
VW Bus, Camper, Van 1954-1967
VW Bus, Camper, Van Perf. Portfolio 1968-1979
VW Bus, Camper, Van 1979-1989
VW Scirocco 1974-1981
Volvo PV444 & PV544 1945-1965
Volvo 120 Amazon Ultimate Portfolio
Volvo 1800 Gold Portfolio 1960-1973
Volvo 140 & 160 Series Gold Portfolio 1966-1975
Forty Years of Selling Volvo
Westfield Limited Edition

B.B. ROAD & TRACK SERIES
Road & Track on Alfa Romeo 1964-1970
Road & Track on Alfa Romeo 1971-1976
Road & Track on Aston Martin 1962-1990
R & T on Auburn Cord and Duesenburg 1952-84
Road & Track on Audi & Auto Union 1952-1980
Road & Track on Audi & Auto Union 1980-1986
Road & Track on Austin Healey 1953-1970
Road & Track on BMW Cars 1966-1974
Road & Track on BMW Cars 1975-1978
Road & Track on BMW Cars 1979-1983
R & T on Cobra, Shelby & Ford GT40 1962-1992
Road & Track on Corvette 1953-1967
Road & Track on Corvette 1968-1982
Road & Track on Corvette 1982-1986
Road & Track on Corvette 1986-1990
Road & Track on Ferrari 1975-1981
Road & Track on Ferrari 1981-1984
Road & Track on Ferrari 1984-1988
Road & Track on Fiat Sports Cars 1968-1987
Road & Track on Jaguar 1950-1960
Road & Track on Jaguar 1961-1968
Road & Track on Jaguar 1968-1974
Road & Track on Jaguar 1974-1982
Road & Track on Jaguar 1983-1989
Road & Track on Lamborghini 1964-1985
Road & Track on Lotus 1972-1983
R & T on Mazda RX-7 & MX-5 Miata 1986-1991
Road & Track on Mercedes 1952-1962
Road & Track on Mercedes 1963-1970
Road & Track on Mercedes 1971-1979
Road & Track on Mercedes 1980-1987
Road & Track on MG Sports Cars 1949-1961
Road & Track on MG Sports Cars 1962-1980
R & T on Nissan 300-ZX & Turbo 1984-1989
Road & Track on Pontiac 1960-1983
Road & Track on Porsche 1951-1967
Road & Track on Porsche 1968-1971
Road & Track on Porsche 1972-1975
Road & Track on Porsche 1975-1978
Road & Track on Porsche 1979-1982
Road & Track on Porsche 1985-1988
R & T on Rolls Royce & Bentley 1950-1965
R & T on Rolls Royce & Bentley 1966-1984
Road & Track on Saab 1972-1992
R & T on Toyota Sports & GT Cars 1966-1984
R & T on Triumph Sports Cars 1953-1967
R & T on Triumph Sports Cars 1967-1974
R & T on Triumph Sports Cars 1974-1982
Road & Track on Volkswagen 1951-1968
Road & Track on Volkswagen 1968-1978
Road & Track on Volkswagen 1978-1985
Road & Track on Volvo 1957-1974
Road & Track on Volvo 1977-1994
Road & Track - Henry Manney at Large & Abroad
Road & Track - Peter Egan "At Large"
Road & Track - Best of PS

B.B. CAR AND DRIVER SERIES
Car and Driver on BMW 1955-1977
Car and Driver on Corvette 1978-1982
Car and Driver on Corvette 1983-1988
C and D on Datsun Z 1600 & 2000 1966-1984
Car and Driver on Ferrari 1955-1962
Car and Driver on Ferrari 1963-1975
Car and Driver on Ferrari 1976-1983
Car and Driver on Mopar 1956-1967
Car and Driver on Mustang 1964-1972
Car and Driver on Pontiac 1961-1975
Car and Driver on Porsche 1955-1962
Car and Driver on Porsche 1963-1970
Car and Driver on Porsche 1970-1976
Car and Driver on Porsche 1977-1981
Car and Driver on Porsche 1982-1986
Car and Driver on Volvo 1955-1986

RACING & THE LAND SPEED RECORD
The Land Speed Record 1898-1919
The Land Speed Record 1920-1929
The Land Speed Record 1930-1939
The Land Speed Record 1940-1962
The Land Speed Record 1963-1999
The Land Speed Record 1898-1999
Can-Am Racing 1966-1969
Can-Am Racing 1970-1974
Can-Am Racing Cars 1966-1974
Can-Am Racing Portfolio 1966-1974
The Carrera Panamericana Mexico - 1950-1954
Le Mans - The Bentley & Alfa Years - 1923-1939
Le Mans - The Jaguar Years - 1949-1957
Le Mans - The Ferrari Years - 1958-1965
Le Mans - The Ford & Matra Years - 1966-1974
Le Mans - The Porsche Years - 1975-1982
Le Mans - The Porsche & Jaguar Years - 1983-91
Le Mans - The Porsche & Peugeot Years - 1992-99
Mille Miglia - The Alfa & Ferrari Years - 1927-1951
Mille Miglia - The Ferrari & Mercedes Years - 1952-57
Targa Florio - The Post War Years - 1948-1973
Targa Florio - The Porsche & Ferrari Years - 1955-1964
Targa Florio - The Porsche Years - 1965-1973

B.B. PRACTICAL CLASSICS SERIES
PC on Austin A40 Restoration
PC on Land Rover Restoration
PC on Midget/Sprite Restoration
PC on MGB Restoration
PC on Sunbeam Rapier Restoration
PC on Triumph Herald/Vitesse

B.B. HOT ROD 'ENGINE' SERIES
Chevy 265 & 283
Chevy 302 & 327
Chevy 348 & 409
Chevy 350 & 400
Chevy 396 & 427
Chevy 454 thru 512
Chrysler Hemi
Chrysler 273, 318, 340 & 360
Chrysler 361, 383, 400, 413, 426 & 440
Ford 289, 302, Boss 302 & 351W
Ford 351C & Boss 351
Ford Big Block

B.B. RESTORATION & GUIDE SERIES
BMW 2002 - A Comprehensive Guide
BMW '02 Restoration Guide
Classic Camaro Restoration
Chevrolet High Performance Tips & Techniques
Chevy Engine Swapping Tips & Techniques
Chevy-GMC Pickup Repair
Engine Swapping Tips & Techniques
Land Rover Restoration Tips & Techniques
MG 'T' Series Restoration Guide
MGA Restoration Guide
Mustang Restoration Tips & Techniques
The Great Classic Muscle Cars Compared

MOTORCYCLING
B.B. ROAD TEST SERIES
AJS & Matchless Gold Portfolio 1945-1966
BMW Motorcycles Gold Portfolio 1950-1971
BMW Motorcycles Gold Portfolio 1971-1976
BSA Singles Gold Portfolio 1945-1963
BSA Singles Gold Portfolio 1964-1974
BSA Twins A7 & A10 Gold Portfolio 1946-1962
BSA Twins A50 & A65 Gold Portfolio 1962-1973
BSA & Triumph Triples Gold Portfolio 1968-1976
Ducati Gold Portfolio 1960-1973
Ducati Gold Portfolio 1974-1978
Ducati Gold Portfolio 1978-1982
Harley-Davidson Sportsters Pref. Port. 1965-1976
Harley-Davidson Super Glide Perf. Port. 1971-1981
Harley-Davidson FXR Series Perf. Port. 1982-1992
Honda CB750 Gold Portfolio 1969-1978
Honda CB500 & 550 Fours Perf. Port. 1971-1977
Honda CB350 & 400 Fours Perf. Port. 1972-1978
Honda Gold Wing Gold Portfolio 1975-1995
Honda CBX 1000 Gold Portfolio 1978-1982
Honda RC30 Performance Portfolio 1988-1992
Kawasaki Z1 900 Performance Portfolio 1972-1977
Kawasaki 500/750 Triples Perf. Port. 1969-1976
Laverda Gold Portfolio 1967-1977
Laverda Performance Portfolio 1978-1988
Laverda Jota Performance Portfolio 1976-1985
Moto Guzzi Gold Portfolio 1949-1973
Moto Guzzi Le Mans Performance Portfoio 1976-89
Norton Commando Gold Portfolio 1968-1977
Suzuki GT750 Performance Portfolio 1971-1977
Suzuki GS1000 Performance Portfolio 1978-1981
Triumph Bonneville Gold Portfolio 1959-1983
Vincent Gold Portfolio 1945-1980
Yamaha RD350/400 Performance Portfolio 1972-79

B.B. CYCLE WORLD SERIES
Cycle World on BMW 1974-1980
Cycle World on BMW 1981-1986
Cycle World on Ducati 1982-1991
Cycle World on Harley-Davidson 1962-1968
Cycle World on Harley-Davidson 1978-1983
Cycle World on Harley-Davidson 1983-1987
Cycle World on Harley-Davidson 1987-1990
Cycle World on Harley-Davidson 1990-1992
Cycle World on Honda 1962-1967
Cycle World on Honda 1968-1971
Cycle World on Honda 1971-1974
Cycle World on Husqvarna 1966-1976
Cycle World on Husqvarna 1977-1984
Cycle World on Kawasaki 1966-1971
Cycle World on Kawasaki Off-Road Bikes 1972-1979
Cycle World on Kawasaki Street Bikes 1972-1976
Cycle World on Norton 1962-1971
Cycle World on Suzuki 1962-1970
Cycle World on Suzuki Off-Road Bikes 1971-1976
Cycle World on Suzuki Street Bikes 1971-1976
Cycle World on Triumph 1967-1972
Cycle World on Yamaha 1962-1969
Cycle World on Yamaha Off-Road Bikes 1970-1974
Cycle World on Yamaha Street Bikes 1970-1974

MILITARY
B.B. MILITARY VEHICLES SERIES
Allied Military Portfolio
Complete WW2 Military Jeep Manual
Dodge WW2 Military Portfolio 1940-1945
Hail To The Jeep
Military & Civilian Amphibians 1940-1990
US Military Vehicles 1941-1945
US Army Military Vehicles WW2-TM9-2800
VW Kubelwagen Military Portfolio 1940-1990
WW2 Jeep Military Portfolio 1941-1945

20/5Z0

CONTENTS

5	Buick Riviera	*Motor Trend*	Nov	1962
6	1963 Buick Riviera Road Test & Technical Review	*Car Life*	Oct	1962
12	Buick Riviera Road Test	*Car and Driver*	Oct	1962
15	Buick Riviera Road Test	*Motor Trend*	Apr	1963
20	The Car That Has Everything	*Auto Sports*	July	1963
22	Buick Riviera	*World Car Catalogue*		1963
23	Buick Riviera Road Research Report	*Car and Driver*	Dec	1963
30	Buick Riviera Gran Sport Drive Test	*Motor Trend*	Dec	1964
33	425 Gran Sport Riviera Road Test	*Cars*	Apr	1964
38	Buick Riviera Gran Sport Road Test	*Car and Driver*	June	1965
43	Buick Riviera Road Test	*Autocar*	July	1965
49	Grand Design by Buick Road Test	*Motor*	Sept 4	1965
55	'66 Models - Buick Riviera	*Autocar*	Sept 24	1965
56	Riviera Gran Sport Road Test	*Car Life*	Feb	1966
61	Toronado vs. Riviera	*Car Life*	Feb	1966
62	Buick Riviera GS Road Test	*Motor Trend*	Feb	1966
64	Buick Riviera Beauty only Skin Deep? Road Test	*Road Test*	July	1966
70	Toronado vs. Riviera Comparison Test	*Cars*	Sept	1966
77	Driving the Hot '67s	*Motor Trend*	Oct	1966
78	Five Luxury Specialty Cars - Riviera GS vs. Thunderbird vs. Grand Prix vs. Eldorado vs. Toronado Comparison Test	*Motor Trend*	Aug	1967
84	'68 Models - New Buicks & Pontiacs	*Autocar*	Sept 7	1967
85	Riviera - Two-Door Hardtop Road Test	*Car Life*	Nov	1967
90	Buick Riviera	*World Car Catalogue*		1968
91	Riviera for the Freeways Road Test	*Car Life*	Feb	1969
96	Buick Riviera	*World Automotive*		1968
97	Riviera GS - A Buick that Lives Up to its Slogan Road Test	*Road Test*	Nov	1970
103	Almost a Limousine - Riviera vs. Ford Thunderbird vs. Oldsmobile Toronado Comparison Test	*Motor Trend*	Dec	1970
109	One of a Kind Road Test	*Road Test*	Aug	1972
114	The Princely Pachyderm - Riviera GS 455 Stage I Road Test	*Cars*	Feb	1973
117	Buick Riviera	*Road Test*	Dec	1974
118	Four Luxury Cars - Riviera vs. Thunderbird vs. Grand Prix vs. Toronado Comparison Test	*Motor Trend*	June	1973
122	Buick Riviera Road Test	*Road Test*	July	1976
125	Buick Riviera Road Test	*Road Test*	July	1977
129	Buick Riviera	*Car and Driver Buyers Guide*	1977 &	1978
130	Buick Riviera 1963-1973	*Motor Trend*	Jan	1994
133	Spring Time on the Riviera	*Classic American*	Mar	1994
137	1963 Buick Riviera	*Automobile Magazine*	July	1988

ACKNOWLEDGEMENTS

When our original 100-page book on the 1963-1978 Rivieras went out of print, we decided to replace it with a new book which offered enthusiasts a little more. This Performance Portfolio is the result, and it includes more than 50 pages of new material on these cars which we were able to find in our archives.

Regular readers of our publications will know that Brooklands Books rely on the generosity and understanding of the world's leading magazine publishers to produce books like this one. So we are pleased to express our grateful thanks on this occasion to the proprietors of *Auto Sports, Autocar, Automobile Magazine, Car and Driver, Car Life, Cars, Classic American, Motor, Motor Trend, Road Test, World Automotive* and the *World Car Catalogue.*

R.M. Clarke

It is interesting to see how the products of car manufacturers go in cycles. The 1963 Buick Riviera was General Motors' response to the success of the four-seater Ford Thunderbird, which had grown out of the two-seater Thunderbird that had been Ford's response to GM's 1953 Chevrolet Corvette. In the early 1960s, Buick sales were going through a bad patch, and so the new personal-luxury coupé was assigned to that division to give it a boost.

The Riviera succeeded only too well. Always sold as a hardtop model with two doors, it played the performance card more effectively than Ford's Thunderbird. Power and performance gradually increased over the years and the Gran Sport model of 1965 could hit a genuine 125mph if there were no curves to hinder it's progress. Handling was also remarkably good for such a big car.

The first generation Riviera was a really striking looking car, but from '66 it succumbed to the growth trend of the times and became bigger and heavier. Buick kept to the traditional rear-wheel drive, but in other respects the two cars served similar ends. For 1970, the car took on a longer hood and was made available with the new 455ci V8, but from there on emissions regulations began to take their toll on performance, and the oil crisis in the early 1970s did much damage to sales.

Meanwhile, the '71 Riviera had become even bigger, and its new styling featured a dramatic 'boat-tail' rear which was too much for many buyers. Buick toned it down for the following year, but other factors were affecting sales by then, too. As the road tests in this book show, horsepower was disappearing in spadefuls in the mid-1970s, and from 1977 the only way to maintain credibility was to reduce weight by downsizing, in line with the rest of the industry.

Yet the Riviera name still has much of the magic which it enjoyed in the early days, and in the 21st century enthusiasts still enjoy running and restoring these classic Buicks. This book is for them.

James Taylor

NEW BUICK RIVIERA

BUICK'S BIG SURPRISE for 1963 is the introduction of the all-new Riviera. Built on a 117-inch wheelbase and with a styling treatment all its own, the Riviera will compete directly with Thunderbird for the personalized luxury car market.

The Riviera originally came off the drawing boards as a Cadillac styling study. When it was decided that a sports vehicle wasn't in keeping with the Cadillac image, the concept was let out for grabs. Pontiac wanted it, but Buick won out, and it became Buick's baby for a two-year development period.

Styling is both clean and functional, with a decided European look. The egg-crate grille is wide, massive, and has dual headlights set into each end. Parking and turn-signal lights are set into the vertical leading edges of the front fenders, and are covered by cast grilles. These light grilles are very similar in design to the radiator grille of the 1940 LaSalle. The roof line is thin and features an angular sculptured effect, accented by the almost completely flat backlight. Body sides have a long, lean look, with a sculptured line running their length. Rear-end treatment is in keeping with the rest of the car.

The chassis is basically the same as that on the big Buick. A "cruciform" frame is used, with independent coil-spring suspension at the front and rigid axle with coils, control arms, and track bar at the rear.

Originally slated to have a 425-cubic-inch version of Buick's famous V-8 as standard equipment, Riviera will reach the showrooms with the proven 401-incher. The bigger, more powerful engine will be optional. A Delcotron alternator-type generator is standard with both engines. There have been rumors that a four-speed manual transmission will soon be available, but at this writing only the super-smooth Turbine Drive automatic is offered.

/MT

MASSIVE FRONT END, ACCENTUATED BY LIGHT GRILLES, ANGULAR ROOF, AND "COKE BOTTLE" SIDE LINE, GIVES THE RIVIERA A EUROPEAN LOOK.

> *Prestige .. Power .. Performance ..*
> *Buick puts all the elements into a*
> *single package for a "GM T-Bird."*

Road Test & Technical Review
1963 BUICK RIVIERA

BY JOHN R. BOND

For more than three years there have been rumors of a new "personal" car from General Motors, designed particularly to compete with Ford's very successful 4-passenger Thunderbird. Most of the reports said Cadillac would build the new entry but a few more observing reporters noted that Cadillac's Michigan Ave. plant in Detroit had about all it could handle and had, in fact, not found it necessary or expedient to produce the LaSalle in postwar years.

Buick's factory in Flint has ample capacity—it has produced as many as a half-million cars in one year. It also has developed a reputation for quality that is second only to that of Cadillac. So it happens that one of the most conservative firms in the business is adding a "specialist" type vehicle to its car line.

The Buick Riviera is not just another "bucket seat with console" variation of a standard 2-door sedan. With a wheelbase of 117 in., it is 6 in. shorter than the big Buicks and 9 in. shorter than the Electra 225. It has its own frame, although it is the familiar X-type used in the large Buicks. Most of the mechanical components are the same as those used on the big cars but there are many detail changes, primarily because the Riviera track is 2 in. narrower than the LeSabre *et al.*

The Riviera body and, in fact, all sheet metal from nose to tail, are completely dissimilar, with no parts or sections taken from any other automobile. The front end treatment is reminiscent of the 1960 Cadillac but the front fenders are distinctly different. The cab or greenhouse area, along with the sweeping lines at the rear, provide a further extension of a theme long espoused by certain custom bodybuilders in England. Over there they call it "razor-edge styling." What the ad copy writers over here will call it, we don't know—and hesitate to guess. However, the new treatment comes off very well and in metropolitan areas where the Rolls-Royce is more or less common the rear view of this Riviera will seem vaguely familiar.

The Mechanical Features

For 1963 Buick has developed a modification of its 401-cu. in. V-8 engine. By suitable core changes the engineers have managed another increase in bore size: from 4.1875 to 4.3125 in. (The original bore size was 4.00 in.) This gives a piston displacement of 425 cu. in. and the new size will be standard equipment in the

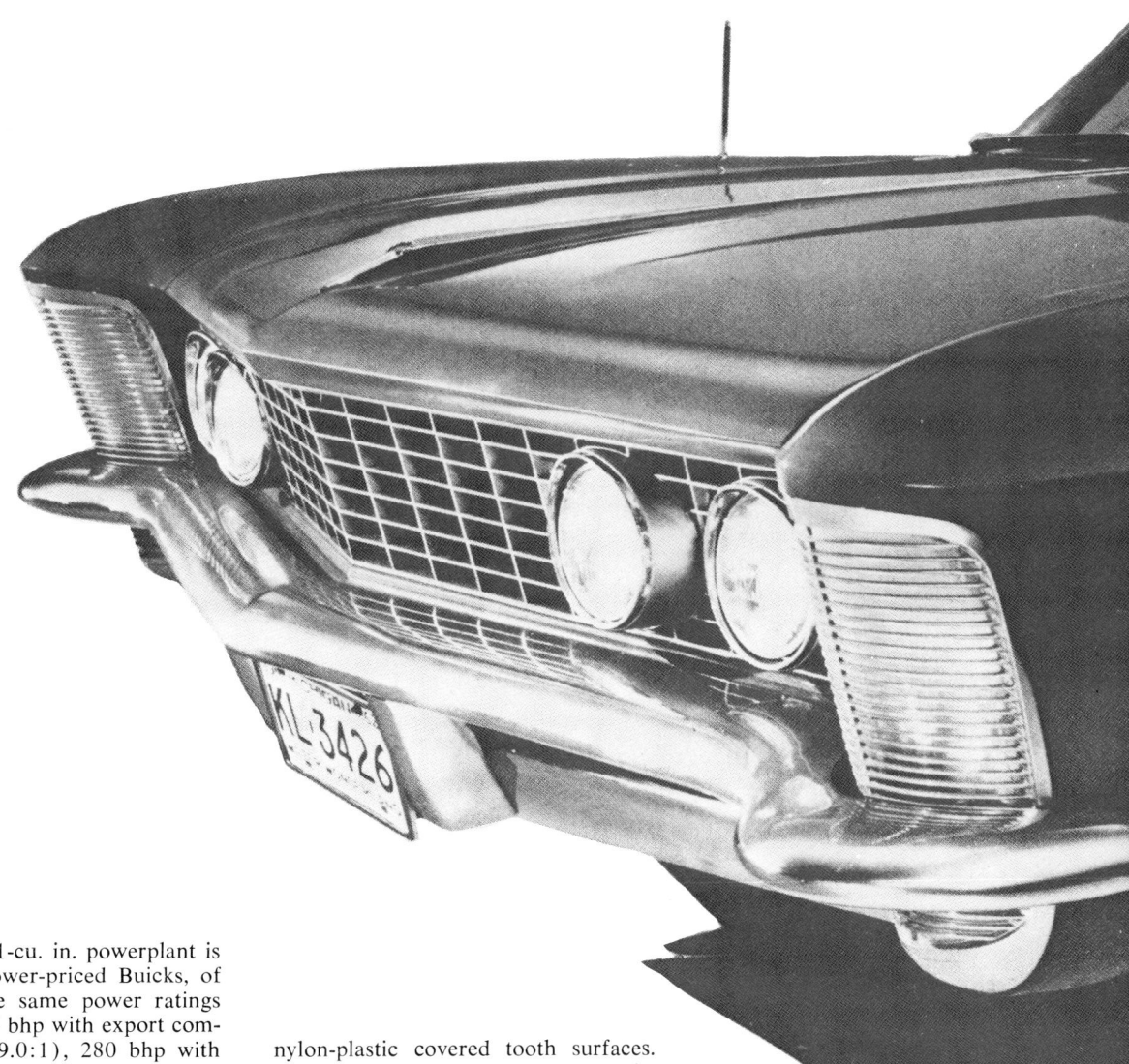

Riviera. The 401-cu. in. powerplant is continued for lower-priced Buicks, of course, with the same power ratings as last year: 265 bhp with export compression ratio (9.0:1), 280 bhp with 10.25:1 compression ratio and 325 bhp with 4-barrel carburetion.

The new 425 variation is available only with 10.25 compression ratio and 4-barrel carburetion. It is rated 340 bhp at 4400 rpm and the torque is a staggering 465 lb.-ft. at 2800 rpm. Incidentally, this larger engine also has a slightly more conservative valve timing than is used on the 401 engine, but otherwise all essential parts (except pistons) are interchangeable. For comparison purposes, here are the two valve timing sequences:

  401............28, 87—76, 46
  425............37, 79—73, 46

The above differences explain why the 425 develops fractionally less horsepower and slightly better torque per cu. in. than does the 401.

Externally, the two engines look the same but the Riviera installation has a special, lower, air cleaner and also a "dress-up kit" to improve the underhood appearance. An interesting internal change that applies to both the 401 and 425 engines is a cast aluminum camshaft sprocket which incorporates nylon-plastic covered tooth surfaces. The plastic is molded on, then the teeth are machined in the usual manner though very little material needs to be removed. Advantages are quieter running and longer life.

Although in 1963 Buick will offer the ubiquitous Warner-Gear model T-10 4-speed transmission in some models, the Riviera comes only with the justly popular twin-turbine automatic and a floor shift on the console similar to the one used last year in the Wildcat.

At this time there will be no options though the 4-speed may possibly be offered later. The standard axle ratio for the Riviera is 3.23:1. However, Buick makes other ratios: 2.78, 3.36, 3.58, 3.91 and 4.45:1.

The rear axle in the Riviera (and all the larger Buicks) has been redesigned and it is 10% lighter than before. This has been accomplished through slight changes in the differential carrier, smaller bearings, decreased housing thickness and smaller axle shafts. Torque capacity and fatigue life is as good or better than before; induction hardening of the axle shafts, for example, has increased their life by 50%. The Riviera axle is, of course, 2.0 in. narrower than the other models, in order to achieve a rear track of 59.0 in. instead of 61.0 in.

The drive line of the Riviera is rather interesting. As automobiles in general have gradually gotten lower and lower the problem of finding room for the propeller shaft has increased. Two years ago the situation became so acute that Buick was forced to drop its traditional torque tube drive and adopt a 2-piece open shaft with a fairly expensive constant-velocity universal joint in the center. This feature is continued in all models except the Riviera. The Riviera, being strictly a 4-seater with center console, doesn't need a low drive-line. Consequently this car uses a single conventional uni-

BUICK RIVIERA

versal in the middle of its 2-piece driveshaft because the drive is very nearly a straight line, from transmission to rear axle.

The front and rear suspension of the Riviera is virtually identical to that used on the 6-passenger cars. The Riviera has its own special frame and this accommodates the changes in mounting points which decrease the front track by 2 in. All models have minor changes at the front inner pivots for better sealing (to give permanent lubrication). The anti-dive and anti-squat features are also continued. At the rear, the Riviera uses lower rate springs (coil-type) than the other models because a 4-passenger car is not subject to as much load variation as is a 6-passenger sedan. Thus the rear ride rate is only 91 lb./in. as compared to 98 to 108 lb./in. in the big cars (dependent on model).

Buick will offer a unique option for 1963. "Superlift" shock absorbers are applied at the rear only and provide a uniform or constant trim height, regardless of vehicle load. While this option is not as necessary on the Riviera as on the others (per our remarks on ride rate), the Buick station-

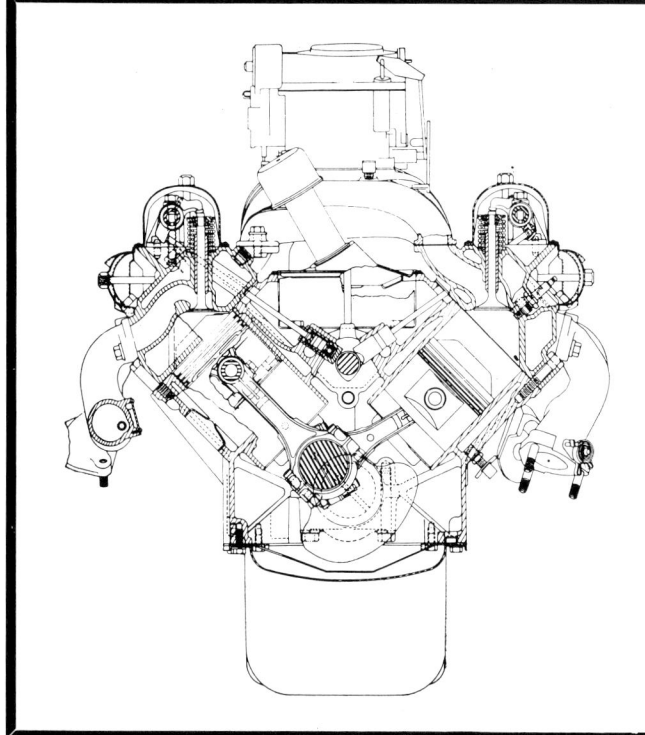

wagon buyer in particular will appreciate the advantages of Superlift. These Delco rear shocks incorporate an extra sealed chamber and conjunctive piston. To increase trim height, air is pumped into the chamber; to decrease height, air is allowed to escape. A special air-compressor to perform this function has been developed by Delco and it uses a pulsating diaphragm with manifold vacuum on one side as the power source, and air-pressure on the other side, of course. Control is by a hand lever just below the instrument panel.

As mentioned earlier, the Riviera has its own frame, though it is very similar to those used on the other models. Buick engineers describe this frame as a cruciform-type, too, (the smaller Special has unit construction). Changes for all models are minor, consisting principally of shortening the front rails by 2.4 in. to clear the new front bumper shape and to reduce weight. This shortening has also eliminated the bolted-on radiator support member used on last year's Buick. The cruciform design seems particularly well suited to the Riviera, where the massive tubular junction in the middle does not interfere with foot-room—since only 4 seats are provided.

Another Buick change for 1963, which includes the Riviera, is a new Delco alternator and a new double-contact voltage regulator designed to eliminate headlight flicker. The alternator has an output of 42 amps, maximum, and 17 amps at idle speed. It

INSIDE THE RIVIERA

Buick has enlarged its 401-cu. in. engine to a whopping 425 cu. in. to provide plenty of punch for Riviera buyers. The original 4.00-in. bores (see cross-section, far left) have been increased to 4.3125 in. while stroke remains the same at 3.64 in. Buick will continue the 401 engine for the more mundane models. The Riviera has a unique tilting wheel (left) to allow easier entrance and exit. This tilting mechanism also lets the driver select the most convenient of seven different positions for driving. A small lever locks it in the desired place (a shaft-mounted universal joint permits the movement). The Riviera frame (below) is not shared with other Buicks, although design is similar. Of cruciform type, it has a massive tubular section in the middle through which the driveline passes. The front track is 2 in. narrower, at 60.0 in., and wheelbase 6 in. less, at 117 in., than the full-sized LeSabre sedan. Suspension components are identical and utilize coil springs front and rear.

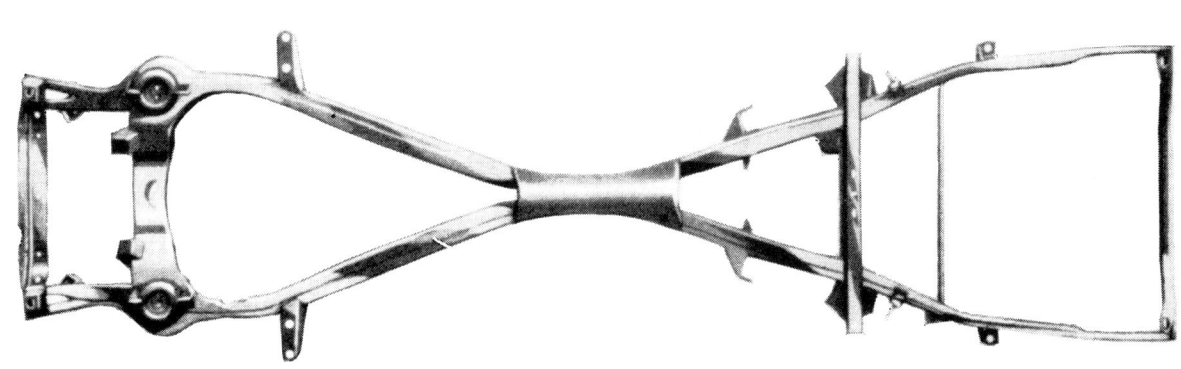

BUICK RIVIERA

runs at 2.51 times crankshaft speed and, with an aluminum housing, weighs 10 lb. less than the old generator. On air-conditioned cars the alternator runs 2.82 times crankshaft speed and develops 24 amps at idle.

A dual exhaust system is standard equipment on the Riviera and the mufflers use stainless steel for those portions which tend to corrode most rapidly. Aluminum-coated steel is used for the resonators and tail pipes.

Test Driving the Riviera

Late in June, the Buick people invited *Car Life*, along with other magazines, to a preview and trial of this new approach to personalized motoring. Our test crew spent the better part of a day at the GM Proving Grounds with the Riviera. Although this was in the busiest season, what with new model production only two months away, we were able to run off a complete set of performance checks using the 2-mile straightaway. This road allows 2-way traffic, has tight loops at each end and is calibrated with markers at each successive tenth of a mile.

The car used for testing was a prototype and you will notice in some of the pictures that certain die-cast trim pieces are missing. Other photos show the car as it will be produced. Note, however, that the car we drove was exactly to specifications in weight, engine power, axle ratio, etc. The engine, in fact, had come off the assembly line just a few days earlier and had had only 1400 miles of test running.

At 4190 lb. curb weight, the Riviera is roughly 200 lb. lighter than the big Buicks and with 340 bhp on tap, it packs a real wallop. By using the brakes on the starting line and holding the transmission in low range up to 65 mph we got an average of 25.0 sec. for the 0-100 mph tests—and this on a corrected speedometer. The larger engine develops no less than 465 lb.-ft. of torque, which is what really counts in normal driving, and the smooth twin-turbine transmission is still the best automatic made—in our opinion.

Our test car had some speedometer error, but Buick's experimental department has been told to develop ways and means of making the 1963 instruments as accurate as possible. We were shown the results of this work and it's not as simple a task as you might suppose. One device employed in test work is a magnetic recorder which counts the exact number of wheel revolutions per mile at steady speeds varying from 10 to 100 mph. The variation is considerable: over 30 revolutions per mile difference.

Buick tests on 7.10-15 size tires showed these results:

MPH	TIRE REVS/MILE
10	760
20	757
30	754
40	750
50	747
60	744
70	741
80	738
90	735
100	732

HOW BUICK'S NEW PERSONAL CAR MEASURES UP

	Special	Thunderbird	Riviera	LeSabre
Wheelbase, in.	112.1	113.2	**117.0**	123.0
Track, front	56.0	61.0	**60.0**	62.0
Overall length	192.1	205.0	**208.0**	215.7
width	70.2	76.0	**76.6**	78.0
height	54.0	52.5	**53.0**	56.4
Box volume, cu. ft.	421	473	**489**	546
Curb weight, lb.	2800	4292	**4190**	4350
Standard bhp rating	135	300	**340**	280
lb.-ft. torque	205	427	**465**	424
displacement, cu. in.	198	390	**425**	401
Top bhp available	200	340	**340**	325
lb.-ft. torque	240	430	**465**	445
displacement, cu. in.	215	390	**425**	401
Standard transmission	manual	auto.	**auto.**	manual
Axle ratio (automatic transmission)	3.08	3.00	**3.23**	2.78
Tire size	6.50-13	8.00-14	**7.10-15**	7.60-15
Brake swept area, sq. in.	223.8	234.0	**320.5**	320.5
Type of construction	unit	unit	**frame**	frame

As the tire grows in circumference at high speed, the speedometer tends to read slow. This can be corrected in the spacing of markings on the dial and, with some manufacturing tolerance, the Riviera speedometers will read somewhere between dead accurate at all speeds and no more than 3% fast at 70 mph, this speed being the worst point. In other words, a typical error curve may show no more than 1.0 mph "off" from 20 to 120 mph, and the worst error expected (in production cars) will be: accurate at 30 mph, 3 mph fast at 70, 1 mph fast at 100 and (perhaps) dead accurate again at 120 mph.

As a sidelight on speedometer accuracy, the Buick test people like to tell of their experiences with outsiders who drive the Riviera for the first time. A large number immediately comment that "the speedometer must be ridiculously fast—this feels more like an honest 65 than the indicated 80." The irony of it is that the car is so smooth and quiet at all speeds that the honest speedometer is hard to believe.

Aside from the overall appearance and performance of this unusual car, the most intriguing new feature is the swivel steering wheel. Being young and pliable, we seldom complain about entry and exit problems. Nevertheless, the swivel feature is an advantage everyone will appreciate. But what we particularly liked was the ability to get the wheel down very low and to be able to move it while driving. Just below the direction signal lever is a similar but shorter lever. By lifting the lever up against a concealed spring the wheel is free to swivel in an arc (up and down, not sideways). Any one of seven positions can be selected.

As might be expected, the Riviera ride is very soft indeed—in the manner preferred by most Buick customers. Heavy-duty springs and shock absorbers can be ordered at extra cost by drivers who anticipate long trips.

Al-Fin front drums, 12 in. in diameter, as featured on the bigger Buicks for the past three years, are used. These brakes are really up to the performance of the car and are just about the best in the business. Incidentally, speaking of performance, the honest top speed of the Riviera is 123-125 mph, timed under favorable conditions and averaged in opposite directions. The top speed is definitely limited by hydraulic lifter pump-up; this occurs at about 5200 rpm and a theoretical 130-131 mph. We had no opportunity to check fuel consumption, but from past experience with Buicks in several sizes we estimate that traffic operation should give 11.5–12.0 mpg while steady highway driving at 65 mph will provide up to 14 mpg. Remember, this car weighs more than 2 tons, has a huge engine and an automatic transmission.

The price of the Riviera hasn't been announced, but the out-the-door delivered price will certainly be over $5000. However, if you want prestige, power AND performance—this is it. ∎

CAR LIFE ROAD TEST

1963 BUICK RIVIERA

SPECIFICATIONS
List price	n.a.
Price, as tested	n.a.
Curb weight, lb	4190
Test weight	4500
distribution, %	55/45
Tire size	7.10-15
Tire capacity, lb	3960
Brake swept area	320.5
Engine type	V-8, ohv
Bore & stroke	4.31 x 3.64
Displacement, cu in.	425
Compression ratio	10.25
Bhp @ rpm	340 @ 4400
equivalent mph	110
Torque, lb-ft	465 @ 2800
equivalent mph	69.7

EXTRA-COST OPTIONS
Wsw tires, radio, air-conditioning and Cruise-control. (Twin-turbine automatic transmission and heater are standard equipment).

DIMENSIONS
Wheelbase, in	117.0
Tread, f and r	60.0/59.0
Over-all length, in	208.0
width	76.6
height	53.0
equivalent vol, cu ft	489
Frontal area, sq ft	22.6
Ground clearance, in	5.5
Steering ratio, o/a	20.5
turns, lock to lock	3.5
turning circle, ft	
Hip room, front	60.2
Hip room, rear	54.4
Pedal to seat back, max	40.9
Floor to ground	13
Luggage vol, cu ft	n.a.
Fuel tank capacity, gal	20

GEAR RATIOS
3rd ( ), overall	
2nd (1.00)	3.23
1st (1.82)	5.88
1st (1.82 x 3.4)	20.0

PERFORMANCE
Top speed (avg), mph	123
best timed run	125
3rd ( )	
2nd ( )	
1st (5100)	70

ACCELERATION
0-30 mph, sec	3.1
0-40	4.3
0-50	5.8
0-60	7.7
0-70	10.0
0-80	13.6
0-100	25.0
Standing ¼ mile	16.2
speed at end	86

FUEL CONSUMPTION
Normal range, mpg	11.5-14

SPEEDOMETER ERROR
30 mph, actual	29
60 mph	56
90 mph	83

CALCULATED DATA
Lb/hp (test wt)	13.2
Cu ft/ton mile	132
Mph/1000 rpm	24.9
Engine revs/mile	2410
Piston travel, ft/mile	1460
Car Life wear index	35.2

PULLING POWER
80 mph, lb/ton	385
60	520
40	565
Total drag at 60 mph, lb	140

ACCELERATION & COASTING

NEW CARS

Buick's newcomer begins a new breed of American auto

Road Test: BUICK RIVIERA

The Buick Riviera has a Cadillac-inspired frontal treatment with quad headlights.

Accessories such as an air-conditioning unit (left) crowd the engine compartment.

The trunk is very low and wide but relatively shallow as a concession to styling.

Never in Buick's history has the old-established Flint company brought out a car such as the Riviera. It is a big and fast touring car with restrained styling and luxurious equipment.

After some initial disappointment at its massive size, we were still so intrigued with the car that nothing less than a road test could satisfy us. Our sports-car-conscious testers warmed to the car on closer acquaintance. Clearly a completely new design and not just another body style on the big Buick chassis, it is much closer in concept and execution to the Bentley S-2 Continental than to the Ford Thunderbird, to which it will be a direct price competitor.

The 340-bhp cast-iron V-8 engine gives the car tremendous acceleration. Its performance puts it above many sports cars, and it is noteworthy that this large and very smooth-running power plant has a compression ratio as high as 10.25 to one.

The engine is a 425-cubic-inch V-8 based on the 401-cube unit used in the Le Sabre, Invicta and Electra series. It is coupled to the latest Dual Path Turbine Drive transmission. No transmission options are offered or possibly even contemplated—but with current Detroit interest in floor-mounted stick shifts and four-speed gearboxes, such components would be readily available if the decision should be taken to add a manual-control option.

The chassis is based on a true cruciform structure, with two crossmembers at the front and rear ends. Both front and rear springing is by coil springs, and the front wishbones are designed and anchored to give the lowest possible camber variations. The spring rates are fairly low, giving a soft ride over bumps at low speeds, and naturally, permit wheel deflections at speed also, but vertical wheel travel seems to be limited more strictly than in the regular Buick lines.

Much has been done to reduce body roll in the Riviera, with the result that the car offers little re-

Turn signals are behind fender grilles.

The abundance of space in the plush interior makes for comfortable long trips.

The instruments are large and legible, and the steering wheel of simple design. The wide seats are softly padded and give a reasonable amount of lateral support.

sistance to initial lean, but soon reaches its limit. In other words, the car will go through the whole corner at an almost constant roll angle, which is not excessive by any standards that can be set for a car of the size and weight of the Riviera.

The car is very well balanced, with increasing understeer as speeds rise. The power steering is geared for 3½ turns lock to lock, and steering response would be immediate but for a slight delay in overcoming basic understeer.

On winding roads, the car can be placed very accurately into the turns, and S-bends cause no undesirable reactions either in the suspension or the steering.

The brakes are in keeping with the performance. Buick power brakes have been working well for all the recent large Buicks, and seem to be able to cope effectively with the added speed potential of the Riviera. With low pressures and high potency, this brake system closely rivals existing disc-brake applications for all-round suitability.

BUICK RIVIERA CONTINUED

The Riviera comes as a two-door sedan and no other body styles are envisaged. Wind noise was found to be low and the effect of lateral wind gusts was negligible. This has of course not been achieved accidentally, but is a result of both laboratory tests with the body shape and high-speed tests with the actual car at the GM proving grounds near Phoenix, Arizona.

The driving position deserves the highest praise. The wide separate front seats are comfortable and give some sideways support, and the test car was fitted with seat belts. The backrest angle is not adjustable, but is set to provide an acceptable position for a majority of drivers, and we found it just right. Fore-and-aft seat adjustment is ample. The robustly hinged accelerator pedal is large enough for a truck, and the brake pedal is wide enough for either foot to be used with a minimum of sideways movement. The space between the brake pedal and the parking brake pedal (with a lift-up release under the dash) is wide enough to provide the driver with floor space to brace himself.

The steering wheel in its normal position is at the right height and a convenient angle. The Riviera offers a seven-position adjustment as an option, a nice idea which has not, in this instance, been carried to its logical conclusion. The column remains fixed while the boss can be tilted, with the result that when the wheel is nearest a horizontal position, it is also at the maximum height from the seat, while it ought to be at the minimum. Conversely, when nearest to vertical, it is at minimum height, when space is essential for the wheel to go clear of the driver's thighs.

The controls are, on the whole, conveniently laid out. The transmission selector lever is floor-mounted in the wide console which separates the front seats, and moves in the familiar P-N-D-L-R pattern. Sideways pressure on the lever is necessary to enter reverse and park; the other positions are in line.

Top speed in low range is about 65 mph, and above 85 mph the car stays in direct drive with the torque converter acting as a plain hydraulic coupling. Below 85 mph, kickdown will actuate the converter and, if the speed is low enough, will engage low ratio. Thanks to the continuous variation in the angle of the stator blades, the shift from low to drive is undetectable, even on full-throttle acceleration, regardless of gradient.

The air-conditioning unit is completely separate from the heater and defroster, which offers improved temperature control by elimination of the water-control valve. Now the water circulates through the heater core at all times, regardless of heater-control settings.

The air conditioner is mounted in the dash with its accessories as near as possible. The compressor is mounted over the right cylinder head, and the condenser is located in front of the radiator. A fan clutch is used, engaging the fan when required by the air conditioning.

Following the current trend, the Riviera has a Delcotron alternator in place of a generator. It is rated at 42 amperes, turning at 2.51 times crankshaft speed.

Summing up, the Buick Riviera is an unusual car. It is rapid and safe, heavy yet nimble, comfortable and elegant. The engine works in such silence and freedom from vibration that one is almost unaware of its presence, yet its performance is almost taken for granted. The Riviera proved perfectly at home under all conditions encountered during the test, and we feel that this is a car which will not look out of place on any road or street in the world.

BUICK RIVIERA

Price as tested: To be announced
Manufacturer:
Buick Motor Division,
General Motors Corporation,
Flint, Michigan

ENGINE:
- Displacement............425 cu in, 6,966 cc
- Dimensions. V-8 cyl, 4.31-in bore, 3.64 in stroke
- Valve gear: Pushrod-operated overhead valves with hydraulic lifters
- Compression ratio............10.25 to one
- Power (SAE)............340 bhp @ 4,400 rpm
- Torque............465 lb-ft @ 2,800 rpm
- Usable range of engine speeds....750-4,600 rpm
- Carburetion..Single four-barrel Carter AFB carburetor
- Fuel recommended............Premium
- Mileage............8-18 mpg
- Range on 20-gallon tank............160-360 miles

CHASSIS:
- Wheelbase............117 in
- Track............F 60 in, R 59 in
- Length............208 in
- Ground clearance............8.8 in
- Suspension: F: Ind., wishbones and coil springs, telescopic shock absorbers, anti-roll bar.
  R: Rigid axle, radius arms and one upper torque arm and vertical coil springs, telescopic shock absorbers.
- Steering............Recirculating ball
- Turns, lock to lock............3½
- Turning circle diameter between curbs............41 ft
- Tire size............7.10 x 15
- Pressures recommended............F 24, R 24 psi
- Brakes; type, swept area: 12-inch drums, 320½ sq in
- Curb weight (full tank)............4,200 lbs
- Percentage on the driving wheels............47

DRIVE TRAIN:
Clutch: Dual Path Turbine Drive five-element torque converter.

Gear	Ratio	Overall	Mph per 1,000 rpm
Rev	1.82-6.19	5.90-19.90	Max 16.8
Low	1.82-6.19	5.90-19.90	Max 16.8
Drive	1.00-3.40	3.23-10.96	Max 32.8

Final drive ratio: 3.23 to one

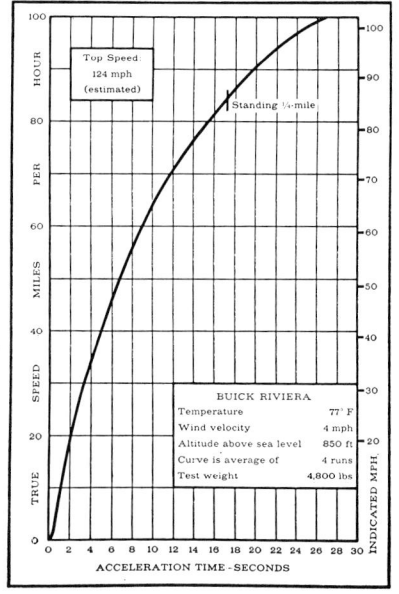

Buick Riviera MT Road Test

A BOLD MOVE IN A NEW DIRECTION FOR BUICK COULD PAY OFF IN SALES

by Jim Wright, *Technical Editor*

WHEN ANY CAR THAT'S NEW and different in concept is offered for the first time, it's met with a barrage of questions from the public. What about its purpose and practicability, degree of class or quality, construction details, cost and economy, comfort and roadability — how does it stack up against its competition?

Here at MOTOR TREND, we're no different from our readers. A new car like the Riviera creates just as much interest and raises just as many questions with us. After logging over 2500 miles in a Riviera, we've managed to answer just about every question but one — just how big a slice of the personalized luxury car market is the Riviera going to be able to carve off in its first year?

We think the Riviera has a lot going for it from a sales standpoint. First of all, the 80-some-odd-thousand sales that Thunderbird racked up last year show there's a large market for a car of this type. Second, the Riviera's all new, while its only competitor offers a body style that's in its third (and probably last) year without any definite styling changes... meaning that if Buick had waited until next year when the T-Bird will be greatly changed, they wouldn't have nearly so good a chance to cut into Ford's market. This is probably the best single point in the Riviera's favor. Also to be considered is that the Riviera comes from a

maker who has an excellent image for building quality vehicles, and the price of the Riviera compares very favorably with the Thunderbird's.

A big 425-cubic-inch engine was originally scheduled as standard equipment for the Riviera, but at the last minute it was decided to drop this idea in favor of the 401-cubic-inch V-8 that's standard in all other Buicks. The "425" is offered as an option, but the average owner will probably be more than satisfied with the performance of his Riviera with the standard 325-hp engine.

Our test car was equipped with the standard engine driving through the standard Turbine Drive automatic transmission and 3.23 rear axle. As extras go, this one was rather sparsely equipped: power seat and windows, adjustable steering wheel, plus the usual radio, wheel covers, remote-control side-view mirror, and other small items. Both power steering and power brakes are standard on the Riviera. This kept down both weight (4192 pounds curb) and price ($5158.61).

With two men aboard, plus our test equipment and a full tank of gas, the Riviera weighed about 4500 pounds. But even at 2¼ tons, this one's still plenty lively. The standing quarter-mile runs were made at San Gabriel drag strip and were electronically clocked by the strip's Chrondek timing gear. We made several runs, and all were in the low 16-second-ET, 85- to 86-mph bracket. Best was a 16.01-second ET, 85.71-mph trip. The 0-30, 0-45, and 0-60-mph fractions were recorded in our usual manner with stopwatches and the fifth-wheel-operated Weston electric speedometer and came up in 3.2, 5.5, and 8.1 seconds respectively.

It's interesting to note that without the added weight of test equipment and passenger, the Riviera's capable of cutting 0-60 mph in *less* than eight seconds. The engine is so smooth around town that you never get a hint of just how exceptional the acceleration really is in this car.

If 0-60 mph in under eight seconds isn't fast enough for some prospective buyers, we suggest they choose the 425-

RAZOR-EDGE STYLING AND A TASTEFUL USE OF CHROME TRIM ADD A TOUCH OF ELEGANCE TO AMERICA'S NEWEST PERSONAL LUXURY CAR.

Buick Riviera

cubic-inch, 340-hp engine option and combine it with the 3.36, 3.58, 3.91, or 4.45-to-1 optional rear axles.

With a little set-up work, this car could even be a real sleeper at the drags. The standard 325-hp engine would run in F/Stock Automatic, while the 340-hp powerplant would put the car in E/Stock Automatic (under the NHRA classification system). At present, the record in E/SA is held by a '62 Pontiac at 98.10 mph and 14.18 seconds ET. No national record in F/SA is listed in the NHRA books at this writing. You can almost bet that someone will show up at the Winternationals with a Riviera.

There've been some rumors that Buick will be offering a four-speed manual transmission for the Riviera, but so far they haven't announced anything official one way or the other. For a *pure* automatic transmission, the Dual-Range Turbine Drive is hard to beat, either in smoothness or performance. Starting in DRIVE, there's no discernible shift of gears as the engine winds out — this is all done by torque multiplication through the variable-pitch turbine blades. Starting LOW engages a lower-ratio gearset and is good up to approximately 75 mph before the driver has to shift into DRIVE. This shift is quick and positive, and there's very little slip apparent. Several top-speed runs gave an average of 115.5 mph, with our electric tachometer reading near 4400 rpm. Given more room than Riverside Raceway's backstretch, top speed would easily reach 120 mph with the 3.23 rear axle.

During the 2500 miles we had the Riviera, it averaged between 11 and 15 mpg on premium gasoline. Overall average was 13.2 mpg for all road and traffic conditions. Around-town traffic, such as one would normally encounter between home and office or home and supermarket, gave a low average of 11.2 mpg, while extended highway trips pushed the figure up to a high of 14.9 mpg. The factory offers one "economy" rear axle with a 2.78-to-1 ratio, which could put the fuel consumption figures in the 12- to 16-mpg range.

The excellent Al-Fin aluminum front brake drums (standard equipment on big Buicks for the past several years) are used on the Riviera, too. Rear drums are finned cast iron and look as if they came from the same mold as the fronts. In terms of effective lining area, Buick brakes are small compared with several cars that weigh a lot less than the Riviera, but the quick cooling afforded by the big, finned drums makes them more effective than those with more lining area. These brakes will survive at least two more panic stops than other cars with cast-iron drums all around that we've tested. When they do fade completely, they require only about half the cool-down time before they're ready to go again.

We've never been too happy with the power brake system

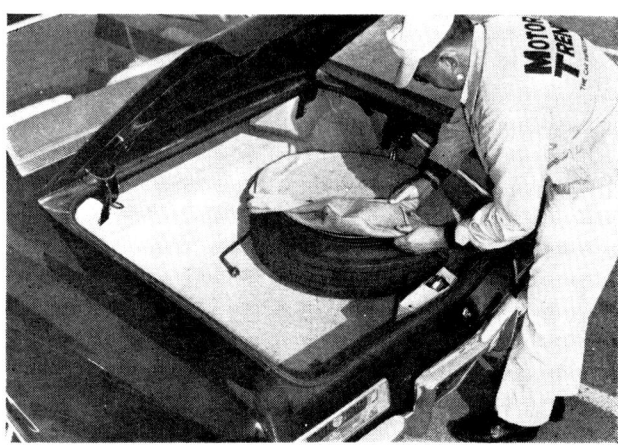

Spare is covered with foam-rubber-padded boot to keep luggage from scuffing against it. Area is plentiful enough for needs of average motorist.

(LEFT) *There are bigger drums, but none more efficient than Buick's finned aluminum units.*

PHOTOS BY BOB D'OLIVO

(RIGHT) *Standard 401-cubic-inch engine supplies the power, with an optional 425-incher also available. Delcotron alternating generator is standard equipment, as are power brakes and steering.*

HANDLING QUALITIES ARE SURPRISINGLY GOOD, MAKE THE RIVIERA A PLEASANT CAR TO DRIVE.

BUICK RIVIERA

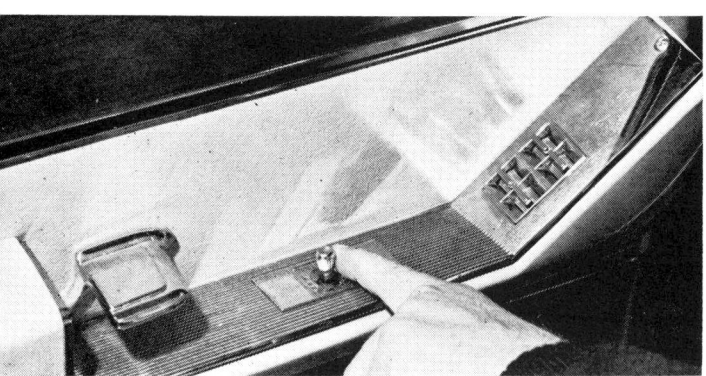

Interiors are in good taste, with a minimum of flash. Still, we'd like to see more instruments in a dashboard like this.

Controls for windows and driver's seat are carried on door panel. Seat and adjustable steering wheel are good extras.

Doors are wide enough to allow easy entry and exit. Riviera is designed to carry four large adults in complete comfort.

used by Buick — it's just too touchy and takes a long time to get used to. About the time we *could* make smooth stops without applying too much pedal pressure, the rainy season started, and we had to learn how to use them all over again.

While the Riviera uses the same X-type frame used on bigger Buicks (only shorter), the rear axle's been modified to the point where it's lighter but just as strong as the others. Where the larger Buicks have a rear track of 61 inches, the Riviera has a track of 59 inches. The front's been narrowed from 62 to 60 inches. Different spring rates, combined with the lighter weight of the Riviera, give a firmer ride than the big Buicks, although it's still quite soft by anyone's standard. At high cruising speeds, the Riviera floats too much, but we think this could be cured with slightly stiffer shocks. Directional stability is excellent, due mainly to suspension geometry and the Panhard-type track bar incorporated in the rear suspension. It completely eliminates side sway. This means the Riviera's little affected by all but the highest crosswinds.

Cornering in the Buick causes a bit of surprise at first because it does it so well. A stiff anti-roll bar at the front keeps the Riviera very flat even in short, sharp corners. With the low recommended pressures in the two-ply tires, there's quite a lot of noticeable scrub when cornering hard, but this is easily cured by boosting the pressures up to around 30 psi. With harder tires, the ride's still comfortable and the Riviera has much-improved handling characteristics. The tendency for the front end to plow is eliminated completely. Once the driver gets firmly acquainted with the light, quick (3.5 turns lock to lock) power steering, the Riviera can be whipped over twisty mountain roads with the best of them.

Around town, the Riviera's as completely at home as it is out on the road. It handles easily in traffic and can be parked by anyone. All-around visibility is good, but tall drivers will find that the low rear window limits their line of sight to about a half-block back.

Our test car had the seven-position adjustable steering wheel. Used in conjunction with the four-way-tilt driver's seat, it allowed us to find a driving position that was comfortable and well suited to our particular frame. We've tried this wheel before in a car that didn't have the power seat and weren't too impressed with the practicability of the different positions. Still, together with the seat, it becomes very effective.

The semi-bucket seats allow comfortable seating for four passengers, with plenty of hip, head, and leg room available both front and rear. Standard upholstery is all vinyl, but the test car had optional vinyl and nylon materials. Genuine leather isn't available this year.

Buick craftsmanship was evident on the exterior, where all panels were perfectly fit — and on the inside, where detailing is top-notch. We were a bit disappointed in the instrument panel. A speedometer, odometer, trip odometer, and fuel gauge are all housed in the two large dials; lights do the job (?) for oil pressure, temperature, and ammeter. A car of this sort should really have a full complement of gauges to accentuate its character.

Most engine accessories are out in the open for easy servicing, and the trunk's large enough to accommodate several large suitcases plus a few smaller ones for weekenders or longer trips.

In our opinion, the Riviera would be a very satisfying car to own. It offers plenty of performance and roadability plus traditional Buick quality, a combination that could make it a leader in the personalized luxury car field. /MT

BUICK RIVIERA
2-door, 4-passenger hardtop

OPTIONS ON CAR TESTED: Power seats, power windows, adjustable steering wheel, radio, cornering lights, deluxe wheel covers, special upholstery, tinted glass, trunk release

BASIC PRICE: $4333
PRICE AS TESTED: $5158.61 (plus tax and license)
ODOMETER READING AT START OF TEST: 5614 miles
RECOMMENDED ENGINE RED LINE: 5500 rpm

PERFORMANCE
ACCELERATION (2 aboard)
- 0-30 mph....................................3.2 secs
- 0-45 mph....................................5.5
- 0-60 mph....................................8.1

Standing start ¼-mile 16.01 secs. and 85.71 mph
Speeds in gears
- Low...76 mph @ 5500 rpm
- Drive.......................115.5 @ 4400 rpm (observed top speed)

Speedometer Error on Test Car
Car's speedometer reading	32	46	51	62	72	83
Weston electric speedometer	30	45	50	60	70	80

Observed miles per hour per 1000 rpm in top gear..............24.5 mph
Stopping Distances — from 30 mph, 35 ft.; from 60 mph, 151 ft.

SPECIFICATIONS FROM MANUFACTURER

Engine
Ohv V-8
Bore: 4.1875 ins.
Stroke: 3.64 ins.
Displacement: 401 cu. ins.
Compression ratio: 10.25:1
Horsepower: 325 @ 4400 rpm
Torque: 445 lbs.-ft. @ 2800 rpm
Horsepower per cubic inch: 0.81
Ignition: 12-volt coil

Gearbox
Dual-Range Turbine Drive; console-mounted shift lever

Driveshaft
Two-piece — open tube

Differential
Hypoid — semi-floating
Standard ratio: 3.23:1

Suspension
Front: Coil spring with upper and lower control arms, direct-acting tubular shocks, and anti-roll bar
Rear: Rigid axle, with coil springs, leading control arms, track bar, and direct-acting tubular shocks

Steering
Recirculating ball and nut, with integral power
Turning diameter: 43.6 ft.
Turns: 3.5 lock to lock

Wheels and Tires
5-lug, steel disc wheels
7.10 x 15 2-ply (4-ply rating) tubeless rayon tires

Brakes
Hydraulic, duo-servo
Front: 12-in. dia. x 2.25-ins.-wide finned aluminum drums
Rear: 12-in. dia. x 2.0-ins.-wide finned cast-iron drums
Effective lining area: 156.9 sq. ins.

Body and Frame
Cruciform (X-type) frame with separate body
Wheelbase: 117.0 ins.
Track: front, 60.0 ins.; rear, 59.0 ins.
Overall length: 208.0 ins.
Curb weight: 4192 lbs.

OPTIONAL DELUXE WHEEL COVERS ARE BOLTED TO WHEEL. 'KNOCK-OFF' CAPS GIVE ACCESS TO LUGS.

QUARTER-MILE PERFORMANCE WITH THE STANDARD ENGINE IS DEFINITELY ABOVE AVERAGE.

We Spell RIVIERA With An E For
THE CAR THAT HAS EVERYTHING

Photos by Sports Car Photo Service

A sleek sports car silhouette gives the Buick Riviera a look of classic beauty. It's high-fashion lines have been referred to as "international" and have appeal for the lady of the house as well as the sports-enthusiast-masculine driver.

REGAL is the Riviera, Buick's new international classic car designed to appeal to the most discriminating lady driver, as well as the power-loving males. As a queen is taught to walk above her mortality, subduing the human side of her being for the nobility of her post, so the Riviera walks head high, almost convincing one that it's not a car with a motor, but some immortal dream boat.

When we test drove the Riviera through city and suburban traffic, as well as on tollways, we found ourselves forgetting that we were driving, we so enjoyed the comfort of her accoutrements.

IMAGINATIVE is one way to describe them. The console which divides the bucket seats in the front of the two-door hardtop we had at our command, put every control in stylish, well-designed order. Before us at the wheel, in unusual clusters were, from left to right, the clock-face-design speedometer, in the center of which both trip miles and the odometer readings are recorded. In a companion circle at the right are such data as fuel quantity, engine temperature, and oil pressure interestingly designed in a circular arrangement with flashing lights revealing the information you need.

Over the Turbine Drive Selector, at the right between the seats, is a V-shaped console including from bottom to top in decks, ash tray, knobs for lights and windshield wiper, the AM/FM radio and then a series of levers for controlling heat, vents, defrost, and antenna—all within easy reach of the driver, yet many which concern the passenger can be operated by him or her.

VELVET smooth is another phrase descriptive of this powerful automobile. The Riviera's finned aluminum front brakes come to velvet smooth stops. And starts of the 90° V-8 Wildcat engine are equally as smooth. Because the Riviera is so regal, you don't realize you have a powerful Wildcat under the hood, yet when you need it for quick get-aways, the power is there—325 h.p. at 4,400 r.p.m. with torque of 465 pounds-feet at 2,800 r.p.m. Compression ratio is 10.25 to 1. The four-barrel carburetor and dual exhaust, which are standard, keep the engine from going flat or choking up. And we're told the car has a totally efficient, long-lasting muffler. Velvet smoothness is also apparent with the power steering system, which gives you the feel of the road, while it does 90 per cent of the work for you.

INTELLIGENT—you'd almost think this classic car had a mind of its own—yet one that will obey your commands instantly. It's the Cruise feature that makes you feel most like a pilot instead of a driver. Dial the speed you'd like to maintain, from 30 m.p.h. on up to 90, press the Cruise control at your left, and this thinking car takes over for you on the gas pedal. You still handle the wheel and the brakes, and a touch of the wide brake pedal puts you back on the job, requiring a reset of the Cruise device to go back to Easy street driving.

The fact that the driver's seat is electrically adjustable, and the steering wheel movable in seven positions, assures you this car is really **thinking** of your comfort!

EUROPEAN you might call this car which is destined to be considered the classic style in international circles. As it's name implies, the Riviera is meant for superhighways from Maine to California, as well as the tricky mountain roads of the Riviera itself. It would be at home in any situation. The understated, uncluttered tailoring of this car with a new body construction technique makes it look like a custom coach. Chrome is at a minimum, and windscreen and rear window are sealed tight to the body, rather than encased in metal or rubber. This, too, gives the car the European look of high fashion.

RACY—yes, we'd say the Riviera is racy, but of course in a most dignified way! That's because of its sports-car type of ride. You'd think you were driving on plush carpeting, because the Riviera never lets you know there are bumps in the road. Coil springs and hydraulic shock absorbers at all four wheels assure that the secret of the roadway is kept. Sharp turns aren't sharep at all with the control this car expresses. Its back wheels track perfectly with the front, and the whole body stays level throughout your ride.

ALLURING is everything about the Riviera from its low center of gravity and body-tailored elegance to its four passenger bucket seats and inside styling. Standard on the $5,158.61 car are all-vinyl trim seats; carpeting on floor, cowl, and door panels; and electrically operated windows. The sheer glass side windows have no metal frames at all, again part of the understatement of the Riviera's beauty.

No matter how you spell R-I-V-I-E-R-A, you'll have to say it's an elegant, international classic. For the driver who **wants** everything, the car is here!

Cornering lights, direction signals, and parking lights all come from behind the smartly styled grille at the outer edge of the car front. Headlights offer regular beam and brights in neat pairs on either side of the front.

Only touches of chrome are the rim on the body line which follows the contour of the wheels and the tailored "fake" vents.

The windscreen and rear window and rear window are sealed tight to the body, adding to the sleek look of the sports car.

Handsome spoke wheel covers contribute to the distinctive design of this international sports car.

Individual bucket seats for everyone are another feature of the Riviera. The trim console is another styling detail. Glove compartment at the right lifts up, rather than away from the dash board. Windows of the car have no metal frames, adding to the feeling that this is a custom import, yet it's all American made.

Buick Riviera

ENGINE CAPACITY: 401 cu in, 6556.35 cu cm;
FUEL CONSUMPTION: 14.1 m/imp gal, 11.8 m/US gal, 20 l x 100 km;
SEATS: 4; MAX SPEED: 124.9 mph, 201 km/h;
PRICE: $ 3,955.

ENGINE: front, 4 stroke; cylinders: 8, Vee-slanted at 90°; bore and stroke: 4.18 x 3.64 in, 106.2 x 92.5 mm; engine capacity: 401 cu in, 6556.35 cu cm; compression ratio: 10.25 : 1; max power (SAE): 325 hp at 4400 rpm; max torque (SAE): 445 lb ft, 61.4 kgm at 2800 rpm; specific power: 49.6 hp/l; cylinder block: cast iron; cylinder head: cast iron; crankshaft bearings: 5; valves: 2 per cylinder, overhead, in line, with push rods and rockers, hydraulic tappets; camshaft: 1, at centre of Vee; lubrication: gear pump, full flow filter; lubricating system capacity: 4.1 imp qt, 5 US qt, 4.7 l; carburation: 1 Carter AFB downdraft 4-barrel carburettor; fuel feed: mechanical pump; cooling system: water; cooling system capacity: 15.4 imp qt, 18.5 US qt, 17.5 l.

TRANSMISSION: driving wheels: rear; gear box: Turbine Drive automatic, 4-stage hydraulic torque convertor with variable pitch stator and planetary gears with 2 ratios + reverse, max ratio of convertor at stall 3.4, possible manual selection; gear box ratios: (I) 1.82, (II) 1, (Rev) 1.82; gear lever: central; final drive: hypoid bevel; ratio. 3.23 : 1.

CHASSIS: box-type, X cross members; front suspension: independent, wishbones, coil springs, anti-roll bar, telescopic dampers; rear suspension: rigid axle, trailing arms, coil springs, transverse linkage bar, telescopic dampers.

STEERING: recirculating ball, servo; turns of steering wheel lock to lock: 3.5.

BRAKES: drum, servo; braking surface: total 197.32 sq in, 1272.71 sq cm.

ELECTRICAL EQUIPMENT: voltage: 12 V; battery: 70 Ah; ignition distributor: Delco-Remy; headlights: 4 front.

DIMENSIONS AND WEIGHT: wheel base: 117.00 in, 2972 mm; front track: 60.00 in, 1524 mm; rear track: 59.00 in, 1499 mm; overall length: 208.00 in, 5283 mm; overall width: 74.60 in, 1895 mm; overall height: 53.20 in, 1351 mm; ground clearance: 5.50 in, 140 mm; dry weight: 4190 lb, 1900 kg; distribution of weight: 55 % front axle, 45 % rear axle; turning radius (between walls): 22.2 ft, 6.8 m; width of rims: 5.5''; tyres: 7.10 - 15; fuel tank capacity: 16.72 imp gal, 20.00 US gal, 76 l.

BODY: coupé; doors: 2; seats: 4; front seat: double.

PERFORMANCE: max speed in 1st gear: 75 mph, 121 km/h; max speed in 2nd gear: 124.9 mph, 201 km/h; power-weight ratio: 12.8 lb/hp, 5.8 kg/hp; useful load: 706 lb, 320 kg; acceleration: standing 1/4 mile 16.2 sec, 0 — 50 mph (0 — 80 km/h) 5.8 sec; speed in direct drive at 1000 rpm: 24.9 mph, 40.1 km/h.

PRACTICAL INSTRUCTIONS: fuel: petrol, 100-105 oct; engine sump oil: 3.3 imp qt, 4.0 US qt, 3.8 l, SAE 5W-20 (winter) 10W-30 (summer), change every 6000 miles, 9600 km; gearbox oil: 10.0 imp qt, 12.0 US qt, 11.3 l; final drive oil: 1.0 imp qt, 1.2 US qt, 1.2 l; steering box oil: 0.9 imp qt, 1.1 US qt, 1.1 l; greasing: every 6000 miles, 9600 km, 9 points; valve timing: (inlet) opens 28° before tdc and closes 87° after bdc, (exhaust) opens 76° before bdc and closes 46° after tdc; tyre pressure (medium load): front 24 psi, 1.7 atm, rear 24 psi, 1.7 atm.

VARIATIONS AND OPTIONAL ACCESSORIES: limited slip final drive.

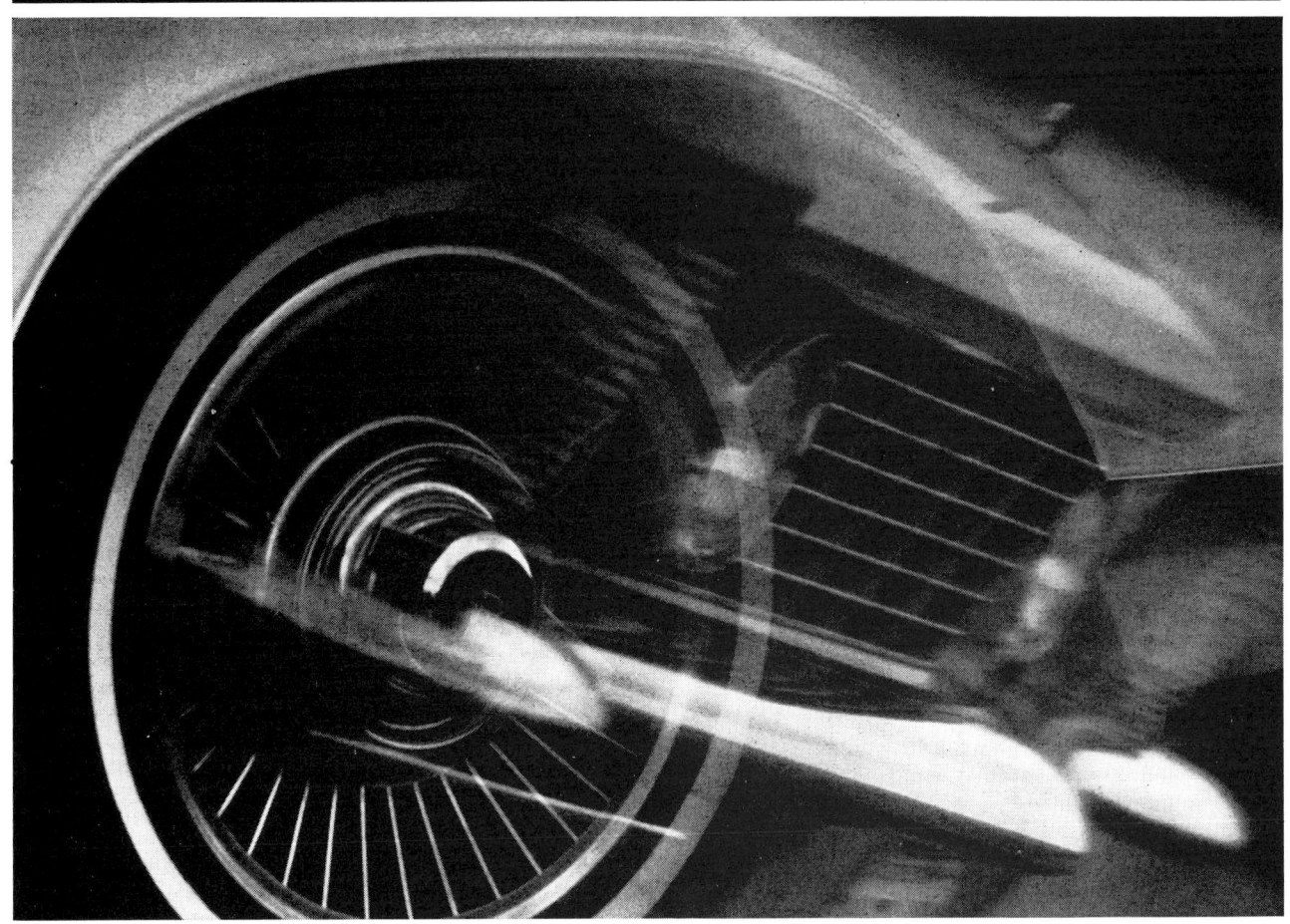

CAR and DRIVER
ROAD
RESEARCH
REPORT

BUICK RIVIERA

The 1964 model of the car that most impressed us in '63 survives an acid test

Our editorial experience with the Buick Riviera has led us into many an argument about the qualities of this car. We like it so much that the editorial staff has run up an aggregate total in excess of 5000 miles on assorted Rivieras, and we often extoll its virtues at the lunch table or at cocktail parties. Our opponents assert that the car is a big heavy Buick and therefore completely undesirable for people who have enjoyed Jaguars, 300 SLs, or even Corvettes. Actually the Riviera is different from the other big Buicks, and it stands alone among American cars in providing a combination of luxury, performance and general roadworthiness that approaches Bentley Continental standards at less than half the price.

Buick's design objectives make it clear that the Riviera is not a sports car. The engineers wanted the ride to be firm and well-controlled with precise handling and a good feel of the road but without compromising the riding comfort which is expected in a luxury car. An acceptable compromise is what they aimed at, but we felt a little too isolated from the road, without precise information about what's really going on. The wheel travel seemed excessive while the shock absorbers were just inadequate.

Its overall behavior is still so good that we were often tempted into using sports car driving methods with the Riviera. We sometimes amused ourselves catching TR-4s and big Healeys on fast bends—this is not only well within the realms of possibility but completely safe. The car is well balanced, although a firm understeerer, which means that at the point where the sports cars begin to hang their tails out, the Riviera is plowing a bit. It's only on rough roads that the Riviera loses something of its composure. On small bumps the direction of the car will be affected (although the steering wheel remains in splendid isolation from road shocks) and steering corrections will be necessary, sometimes even for traveling in a straight line. The absolute worst was experienced when negotiating a winding road with a succession of dips and rises at a fast clip, when the car moved forward in a series of enormous lurches, the springs being fully compressed one moment and fully extended a few seconds later. Fortunately we were comfortably seated and strapped in and never got really worried. One can forgive a lot when correctly seated.

As Buick well knows, the design factors which produce sports car handling are not normally compatible with those that produce a luxury car ride. In the early design analysis of the Riviera, Buick's engineers evaluated numerous combinations of parameters affecting ride and handling. They considered variations of wheelbase, front and rear track, spring stiffness and roll steer geometry. From this analysis, and from subsequent development work on early test cars, they arrived at a combination which was built into the final pre-production prototypes. There may be, says Buick, harder-riding cars with handling characteristics more to the liking of sports car enthusiasts, but the Riviera is an excellent overall blend of riding comfort and handling qualities. We agree that the design objectives have been achieved, but we also wish that the objectives had been more in line with the needs of a rally driver. Yet, in view of what can be done in major rallies by a car such as the Rover 3-liter, with its lower power, inadequately clamped down rear axle and relatively soft springs, it is logical that the Riviera should be at least equally suitable for competition.

But the British car that the Riviera can perhaps best be compared to is the Jaguar Mark X, which, with a similar forward accent in weight distribution, has nearly neutral steering characteristics. This is mainly because the roll axis of the Riviera is sloping forward while that of the Mark X is almost horizontal. It is interesting also to bring the Corvette into this comparison:

	Roll center height (in)	
	Front	Rear
Buick Riviera	1.63	12.60
Corvette 1962	0.00	9.00
Corvette 1963	3.40	8.13
Jaguar Mark X	4.38	4.72

Basically, a high roll center gives reduced lateral weight transfer, lower roll couple rates, and, with independent suspension, permits the retention of negative camber on deflection. It's clear that the Riviera has far greater weight transfer at the front than at the rear, inducing understeer, while the Mark X has just slightly higher weight transfer at the front.

While the spring rates of the Riviera are higher at the front and lower at the rear than on the Wildcat and Electra models, they are somewhat out of line with European practice, as even much lighter cars of old-world origin prefer higher front spring rates:

	Spring rates lbs/in (at the wheel)			
	Front		Rear	
	Load	Rate	Load	Rate
Buick Riviera	1114	99	986	91
Corvette 1963	757	93	750	125
Jaguar Mark X	1115	175	1013	116.5
Volvo P-1800	672	107	545	95

The directional stability of the Riviera is superior to almost any normal road car. It is not greatly affected, with its very high polar moment of inertia, by changing road camber and is markedly insensitive to crosswinds. In view of these characteristics and the considerable weight of the car (although about 500 pounds lighter than an Electra 225), power steering was considered a necessity. It is geared to give 3½ turns of the wheel lock to lock, which is a bit slow—the turning circle is 43.2 feet. The steering unit is made by Saginaw, and as Saginaw also produces the excellent power steering for the Corvette, it is a pity, and almost puzzling, that Buick did not try to adapt it for the Riviera. While the muscular effort required to turn the car is very low, even at low speeds, the amount of twirling that has to be done with the wheel feels excessive. But the gearing, strangely, is quick enough to make it possible to beat the power assist. If you try to throw the Riviera into a turn, you may find yourself halfway into it, with a sudden, if momentary, loss of power assist, and lacking the physical strength to turn the wheel enough to get through in clean style. Fortunately the power mechanism catches up with you in time to complete the maneuver without disgrace. The car responds best to a smooth, almost gentle, style of driving. By such methods it is, in fact, possible to get around sharp corners with great agility. But the Riviera likes to be held back before the turn, then accelerated through it. The same applies on winding roads, but with increased familiarity with the Riviera, the driver will find that the bends and turns he has to brake for get fewer and farther between. We found that on hilly and winding but fast roads we got the best results by putting on plenty of lock on the way into the curve, finding the correct throttle opening, and just holding the wheel beautifully still until it could be eased back to a straight position, while drivers of cars of other makes were sawing wildly at the wheel trying to keep up.

The Riviera leans very little and never looks out of shape on a fast bend. The low center of gravity (at 19.7 inches) is a major factor here; so is the 0.844-inch anti-roll bar. Reduced roll almost invariably provides higher ultimate cornering capacity and more precise maneuverability at speed. The front roll couple for the Riviera is slightly greater than for the Electra, with the front wheels taking over 57%, as against 56% in the other big Buick. P.C. Bowser and S.C. Richey, the Buick engineers mainly in charge of developing the Riviera, say quite frankly that they do not believe the Riviera has just exactly the right combination of roll couple, front and rear understeer and camber geometry, but if they had to do it over again, they would be hard pressed to find a better starting point. This way of looking at the Riviera indicates that the manufacturer regards it in the same perspective that we

It's all done with mirrors—and Dave Gittens' camera. Clean and functional design puts cranks and handles unobtrusively where they are needed. Ashtray and lighter are hidden under panel in front of shift lever. Exterior is unchanged except for trim and cosmetic items. Nobody ever said it wasn't luxurious.

Road Research Report: Buick Riviera

Manufacturer: Buick Motor Division of General Motors Corporation
East Hamilton Avenue, Flint, Michigan.

PRICES:
Basic price		$3,995.00
Options fitted	Air conditioner	430.00
	Tilting wheel	43.00
	Power seat and windows	178.45
	AC Cruise Control	56.97
	Radio	90.30
	Seat belts (front)	17.00
Price as tested		$4,810.72

ENGINE:
Water-cooled 90° V-8, cast iron block, 5 main bearings.
Bore x stroke .... 4.31 x 3.64 in, 109.5 x 92.5 mm
Displacement .... 425 cu in, 6918 cc
Compression ratio .... 10.25 to one
Carburetion ..... Single four-barrel Carter AFB (1.56-in primary, 1.69-in secondary).
Valve gear .... Pushrod-operated overhead valves, hydraulic lifters
Valve diameter .... Intake 1.875 in, exhaust 1.50 in
Valve timing:
Intake opens .... 29° BTC
Intake closes .... 81° ABC
Exhaust opens .... 71° BBC
Exhaust closes .... 48° ATC
Valve lift .... 0.44 in
Power (SAE) .... 340 bhp @ 4400 rpm
Torque .... 465 lb-ft @ 2800 rpm
Specific power output .... 0.80 bhp per cu in, 49 bhp per liter
Usable range of engine speeds .... 500-5000 rpm
Electrical system .... 12-Volt, 70-Amp-hr battery, Delcotron alternator
Fuel recommended .... Premium
Mileage .... 12-18 mpg
Average throughout test .... 15.21 mpg
Range on 20-gallon tank .... 240-360 miles

DRIVE TRAIN:
Transmission: Super Turbine 400 hydraulic torque converter and three-speed planetary transmission.

Gear	Ratio	Overall	Max mph
Rev	2.08	6.78	−55
1st	2.48	7.61	48
2nd	1.48	4.54	82
3rd	1.00	3.07	125

Maximum torque multiplication (at stall) .... 2.15 to one
Final drive ratio .... 3.07 to one

CHASSIS:
Cruciform channel-section frame, all-steel closed body.
Wheelbase .... 117 in
Track .... F 60, R 59 in
Length .... 208 in
Width .... 75.5 in
Height .... 53.2 in
Ground clearance .... 5.70 in
Curb weight .... 4200 lbs
Test weight .... 4460 lbs
Weight distribution % front/rear 53/47
Pounds per bhp (test weight) 13.9
Suspension: F: Ind., wishbones and coil springs, anti-roll bar.
R: Rigid axle, trailing arms and torque member, panhard rod, coil springs.
Brakes .... 12-in drums F and R, 320.5 sq in swept area
Steering .... Recirculating ball
Turns lock to lock 3.5
Turning circle .... 43.2 ft
Tires .... 7.10 x 15
Revs per mile 744

MAINTENANCE:
Crankcase capacity .... 4 qts (without filter)
Oil change interval .... 5000 miles
Number of grease fittings 9

ACCELERATION:
Zero to	Seconds
30 mph	3.1
40 mph	4.4
50 mph	6.0
60 mph	8.3
70 mph	11.1
80 mph	14.6
90 mph	19.0
100 mph	25.5
Standing quarter-mile	16.6 sec @ 83 mph

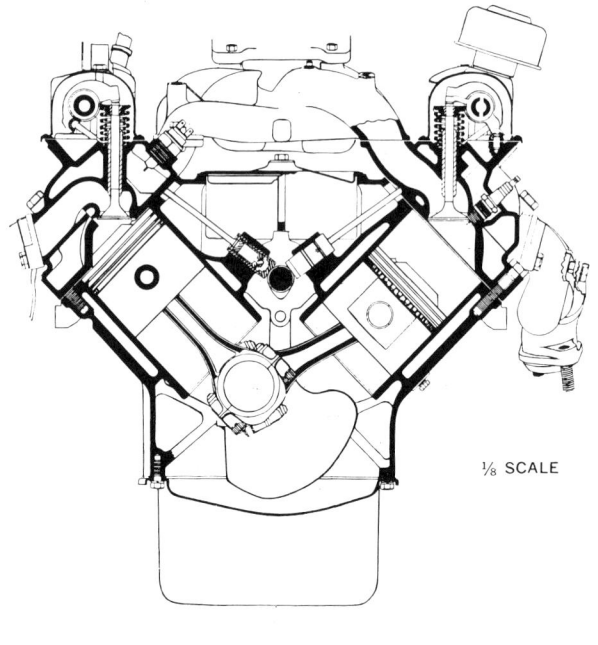

⅛ SCALE

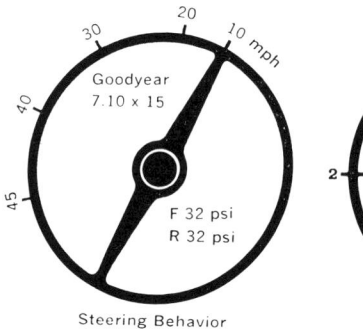

Steering Behavior
Wheel position to maintain 400-foot circle at speeds indicated.

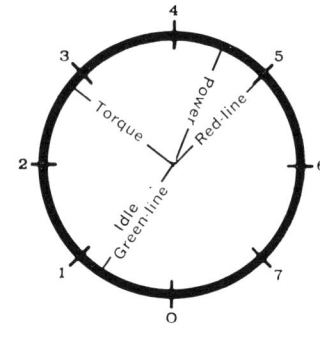

Engine Flexibility
RPM in thousands

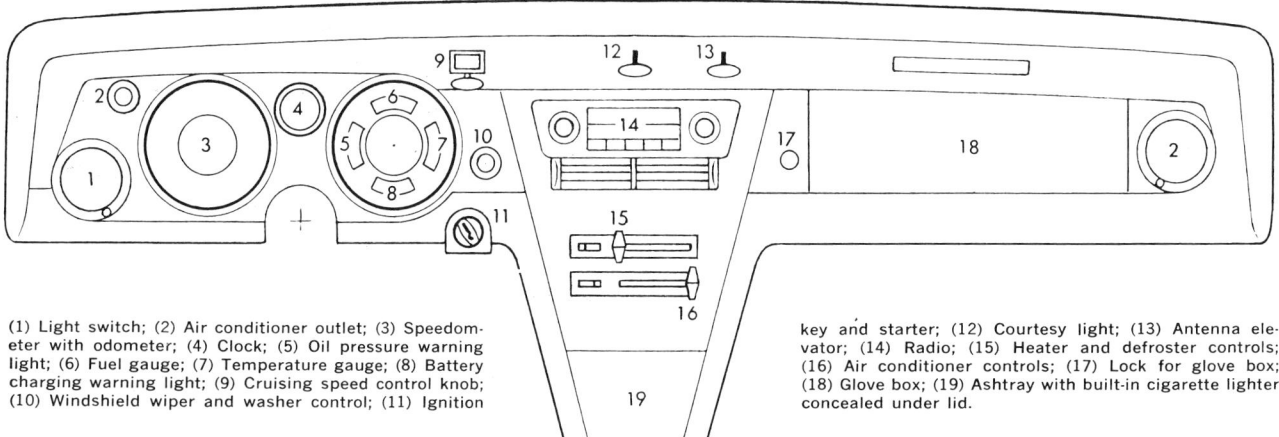

(1) Light switch; (2) Air conditioner outlet; (3) Speedometer with odometer; (4) Clock; (5) Oil pressure warning light; (6) Fuel gauge; (7) Temperature gauge; (8) Battery charging warning light; (9) Cruising speed control knob; (10) Windshield wiper and washer control; (11) Ignition key and starter; (12) Courtesy light; (13) Antenna elevator; (14) Radio; (15) Heater and defroster controls; (16) Air conditioner controls; (17) Lock for glove box; (18) Glove box; (19) Ashtray with built-in cigarette lighter concealed under lid.

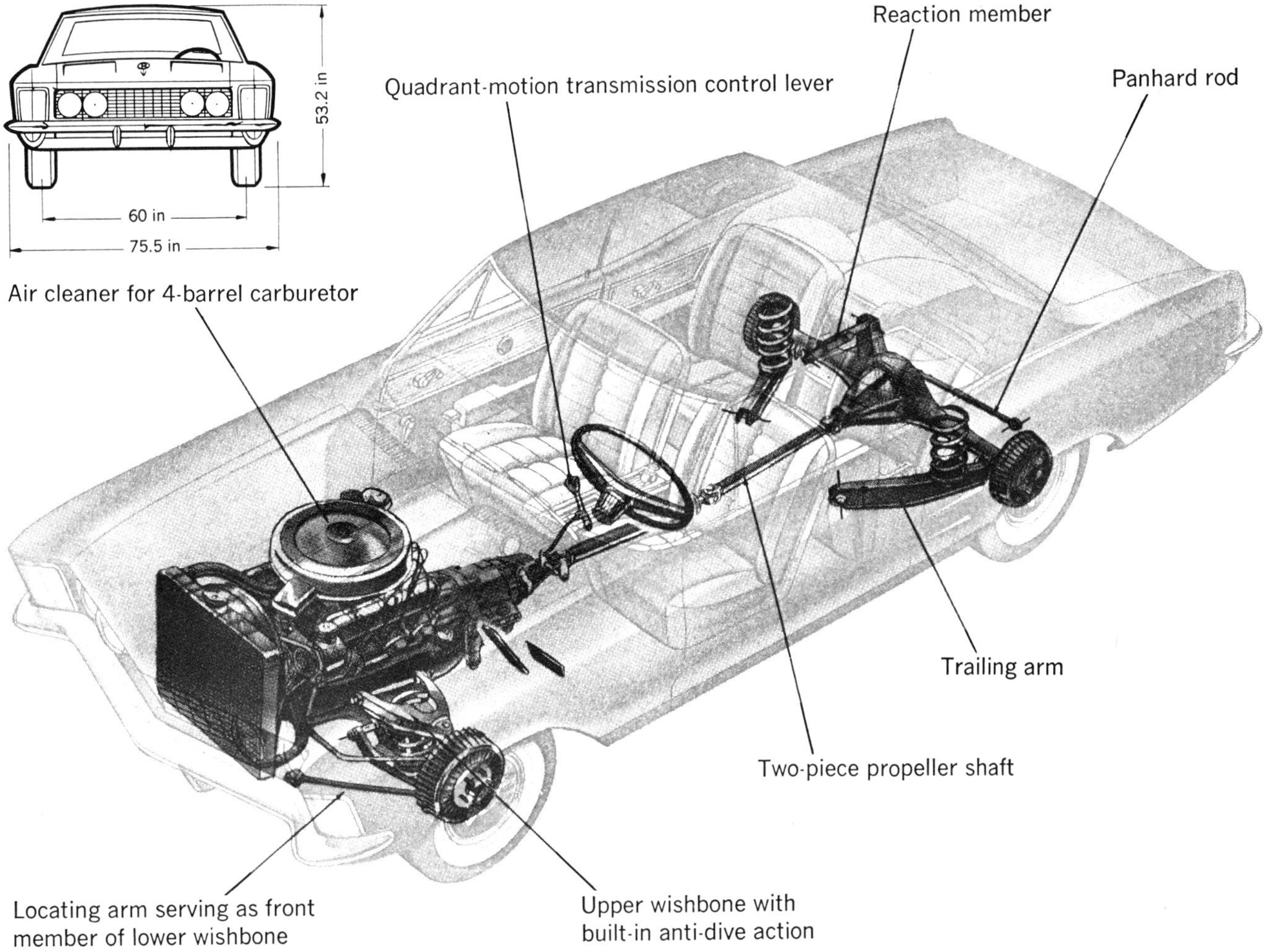
53.2 in
60 in
75.5 in
Reaction member
Quadrant-motion transmission control lever
Panhard rod
Air cleaner for 4-barrel carburetor
Trailing arm
Two-piece propeller shaft
Locating arm serving as front member of lower wishbone
Upper wishbone with built-in anti-dive action

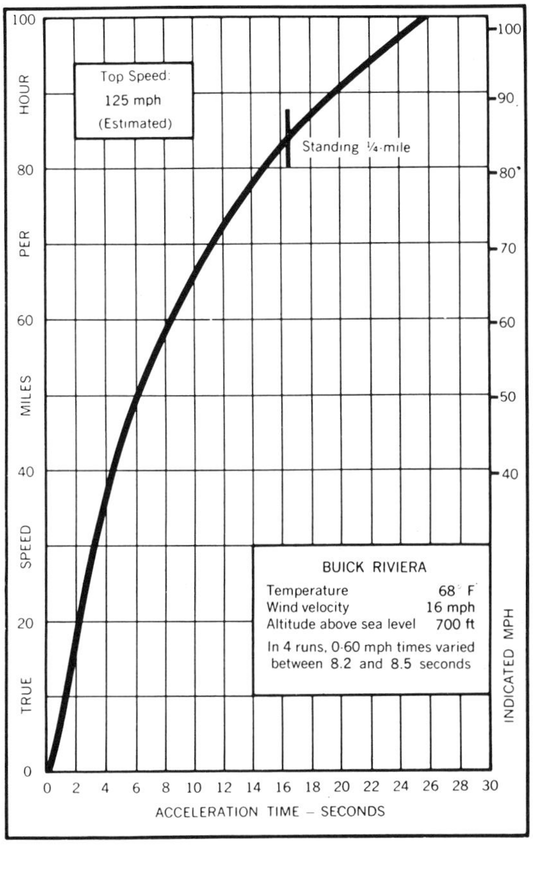
TRUE SPEED MILES PER HOUR
INDICATED MPH
ACCELERATION TIME – SECONDS
Top Speed: 125 mph (Estimated)
Standing ¼-mile
BUICK RIVIERA
Temperature 68° F
Wind velocity 16 mph
Altitude above sea level 700 ft
In 4 runs, 0-60 mph times varied between 8.2 and 8.5 seconds

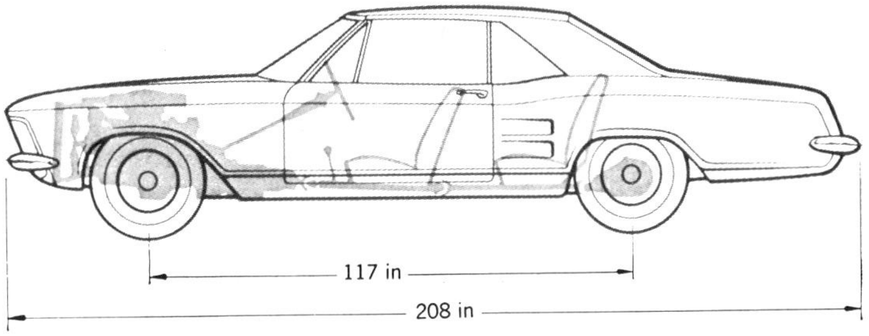
117 in
208 in

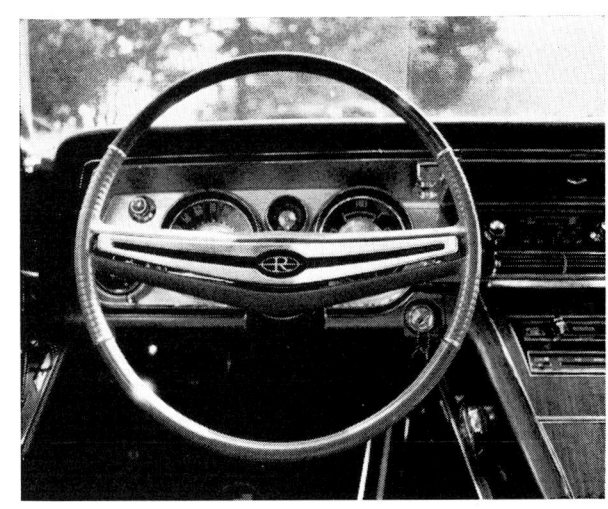

The Riviera copies nothing—it has a true American style and an indefinable personality that is bound to find many followers— within General Motors as well as outside.

have come to look on it. It's the first of a new breed of American automobile, with a chassis design that has been liberated of all superstitions and prejudices while constituting nothing so radical as to shock the vehicle operator who is totally unaccustomed to sports cars.

Our readers will remember that Buick seemed wedded to the torque tube from pre-war days through 1960. At that time the open drive line was introduced in conjunction with the new rear suspension, and this is the system the Riviera has. Using two lower trailing control arms, a panhard rod for lateral location, plus a reaction member on the right-hand side of the axle housing (in the manner of the C-type Jaguar) this system prevents rotation about the attachment points of the two trailing arms during braking and acceleration. It effectively prevents axle wind-up, but the torque of the Riviera engine is so great that the right rear wheel does lose grip on full-throttle acceleration, although there is no axle tramp and the wheel is in visible ground contact all the time. The torque forces on the axle housing are so great as to overcome the individual wheel loading.

The intended boulevard ride of the Riviera is good for any speeds the car is capable of attaining, so long as the surface is smooth. It's on the turnpike that the car is at its luxurious best, with low wind noise, no mechanical noise, and tire noise depending entirely on the road surface. It will cruise all day at any speed between 0 and 120 mph, and when we say cruise, this means a steady speed with a maximum momentary deviation of 2.5 mph from the desired average, regardless of gradient, thanks to the AC Electro-Cruise Speed Control System.

Its operation couldn't be simpler. You set a special second needle on the speedometer at the desired speed, press the "cruise" knob, and accelerate until the standard needle reaches or passes it. Then a green light comes on and the accelerator can be released, while the car travels at the set speed. To disengage the speed control system, either pull the knob back or touch the brake pedal. Exceeding the set cruising speed, for passing, for instance, is possible by merely depressing the accelerator, and this maneuver does not disengage the cruise control. When the accelerator is again released, the car resumes the set speed. We were hesitant about accepting the speed control system purely as a means of reducing driver fatigue on modern superhighways, but have become quite convinced of its value.

How does it really work? The desired cruising speed is fed into a speed-sensing transducer, which is an integral part of the speedometer. The set speed is then compared to the prevailing road speed as measured by the speedometer. The difference between the desired speed and the indicated speed represents a speed error. This speed error, in the form of a pulse-modulated electrical signal, is sent through a transistorized current amplifier to a vacuum diaphragm power unit, which is coupled to the throttle linkage. In response to the signal, the power unit adjusts the throttle linkage to cancel the speed error, speeding up or slowing down the engine as directed.

The choice of an engine for the Riviera was a simple one. Buick's first V-8 from 1953 has been modernized over the years, and a special big-bore version (425 cu. in. instead of 401) was produced to reach the performance goal intended for this car. With a single four-throat carburetor it develops 340 bhp; a twin four-throat setup is optional and boosts power output to 360 bhp. Both block and head are cast iron, and the steel crankshaft runs in five main bearings of 2½ in. diameter. The block extends well below the crankshaft center line. Some other automotive divisions of GM have more modern engines than Buick, both in basic concept and in detail design. But the Riviera has a well-tried and reliable high-performance unit, and what a major redesign would achieve would chiefly be a weight reduction.

Ever since the introduction of the Dynaflow in 1948 Buick has led the development of torque-converter transmissions (although Packard's Ultramatic was a close second in the early 50s). The latest Buick development is the Super Turbine 400, a water-cooled unit which has an electrical-impulse kickdown control, contains an aneroid bellows in the shift mechanism to compensate for changes in altitude, and carries counter-phased (for quiet running) planetary gears in sets of four (instead of the normal three) pinions for increased durability. The Super Turbine 400 eloquently confirms Buick's position of leadership.

Getaway from standstill, while never really a weak point with the Turbine Drive of the 1963 Riviera, has been much improved in the Super Turbine 400 transmission of the 1964 model. The limiting factor in acceleration now is wheelspin, while it used to be transmission flexibility.

The transmission is controlled by a lever moving in a quadrant on the console between the front seats, its pattern being the P-R-N-D-L currently favored by most manufacturers. The Super Turbine 400 is based on the Turbine Drive, and consists of a three-element torque converter (incorporating the Buick-developed variable-pitch stator) coupled to a planetary transmission with two gear trains, one for Low range, the other for Drive range. The new transmission starts in first, giving a 50% increase in starting thrust over the Turbine Drive, and intermediate and direct are later engaged according to speed and throttle opening. In direct drive, the planetary transmission is locked up and rotates as a unit, while all needs for gearing changes are taken care of by the torque converter. The changes in the planetary transmission are carried out by overrunning (one-way) clutches and multiple-disc clutches in combination. One gear is released by the instantly-effective over-running clutches while the next is engaged by smoothly acting multiple-disc clutches.

With a minimum throttle opening, the car gets into intermediate range at 10 mph and direct at 20 mph. Opening the throttle to the halfway point (where an extra return spring gives added resistance to the accelerator) moves the change points up to 35 mph and 55 mph. On full throttle, first gear is held to 48 mph and intermediate to 82 mph. If the driver wishes to use Low in the speed range between 35 and 50 mph *without fully opening the throttle,* as for instance on a winding road with both up and down gradients, this can be done by moving the shift lever into Low position. For extra acceleration in Drive range, below 70 mph, simple kickdown is enough to get Intermediate, which then carries the car up to 82 mph, at which point the planetary transmission locks up and the torque converter alone provides a down-gearing. Its maximum torque multiplication is 2.15.

Using the engine as a brake is possible in the new Riviera. Moving the lever into Low position between 60 and 30 mph engages Intermediate, and the torque converter is sufficiently reversible to provide a moderate braking force in this condition. When the speed falls to 25 mph, 1st gear is automatically engaged and the car is again ready for maximum acceleration. If full engine braking is still needed, after speeding up, merely leaving the lever in Low position will keep 1st gear engaged. But if only moderate braking is desired, this can be achieved by changing from Low to Drive and right back again.

Of course, all the efficiency and versatility of the new transmission have not been achieved without introducing some disadvantage. The new Riviera has a rather strong creep, although without the accompanying vibration usually associated with automatic transmissions when held back on the brake.

With such performance as the Riviera offers, it's obvious that above-average brakes are needed. Buick found that the Electra brakes with specially developed organic linings gave satisfactory results. Since Buick introduced the finned aluminum brake drum with bonded cast iron liners on the front wheels of the 1958 models we have held them to be the best in the industry —probably about twice as good as any other drum brakes fitted to American cars. Most of our complaints about American drum brakes lie in their poor heat dissipation. Buick's aluminum alloy drum conducts heat faster through the drum (heat conductivity of aluminum is three times that of cast iron) to the peripheral cooling fins. These fins swirl air into contact with the hottest surface areas of the drum. Aluminum also dissipates heat to the air quicker than iron. Because more heat can be carried off, more heat can safely be generated, and the brakes can be made to operate at high loads for long periods while keeping the temperature of the brake linings below the point of beginning brake fade.

Rear wheel drums on the Riviera are cast iron, but also carry fins for improved heat dissipation. The Moraine servo unit is tremendously powerful and almost too sensitive. A mere 30 pounds of pedal pressure gives a 400-pound line pressure, and the car can be brought to an abrupt stop almost inadvertently by a driver unaccustomed to hyper-sensitive power brakes. In an emergency, even a conditioned Riviera driver might react by pushing too hard on the pedal, and we feel that a more conventionally balanced power assist would be an improvement. But this is the only improvement we can think of. The hardest driving we could put the car through failed to produce any fade or smell of burned brake lining, the car invariably pulled up in a straight line; and, again a tribute to the suspension, there is no nose dive and the rear wheels do not lose their grip. Even a rough surface could not upset braking effect.

For the 117-inch wheelbase Riviera, Buick decided to use a separate frame rather than integral construction because, in Buick's experience, a frame allows more flexibility of design. The cruciform frame is based on that of the large Buicks (introduced in 1961). The absence of side rails alone means a weight saving of some 70 pounds, and passenger com-

A sectional view of the Super Turbine 400 shows the very compact mechanical parts.

fort is better because the underbody sections can be lowered and the entrance and exit dimensions of the door sill stepover can be reduced. Buick also claims improved lateral stiffness with less shake and vibration from their method of spreading the rails in the rear.

The Riviera is a passenger's car as much as the driver's. It's spacious and extremely well finished, with deep, soft seats and plenty of legroom, hiproom and headroom. But the driver is the privileged one, having a four-way power-operated seat,

Continued on page 55

BUICK RIVIERA
GRAN SPORT *Drive test*

Luxury gets helping hand from hotter engine, new handling package

CAPABLE OF FIERCE ACCELERATION, GRAN SPORT LIFTS NOSE AS IT CHARGES OFF THE LINE. BLACK STRIP CAME FROM A PREVIOUS RUN.

by Bob McVay, *Assistant Technical Editor*

MAKING AN ALREADY fine car better is a big job, but that's just what Buick Division's done with the Riviera for 1965. A special, high-performance version of the Riviera, called the Gran Sport, will be introduced later in the model year. Believe us, it's worth waiting for.

Although we had this car for only two days, it was enough to whet our appetite for a full-scale road test in the near future. What Buick's done with the Gran Sport Riviera is this: They've kept the excellent ride and luxurious comfort, but vastly improved performance and handling. It's still as smooth and quiet as before, but it goes and handles much better than its 1964 counterpart.

Buick's 425-cubic-inch V-8 block has been reinforced wherever any distortion might occur. Main bearing webbing and cylinder walls are stronger, and new piston rings give better sealing. Mounting two big Carter AFB carbs, which open simultaneously, the Gran Sport gives its driver 360 willing horses at the tip of his right toe. With 465 pounds-feet of torque available, there's always instant acceleration.

In addition to the engine, suspension modifications include stiffer springs and shocks and a thicker anti-roll bar up front. The Super Turbine 400, Buick's three-speed automatic, has been modified to give different speed range changes from the standard Riviera. Positraction and a 3.42 rear axle are also part of the Gran Sport package. Yet, that's not all. A higher-capacity exhaust system gives less back pressure and is laminated to eliminate some of the noise.

From the driver's seat, the changes are subtle during normal driving, but as speed increases, they make themselves more noticeable. For a car of its size and weight, the Riviera Gran Sport makes short work of long distances. The faster steering ratio saves some arm movement and gives more precise control. And that tremendous reservoir of power is always ready to be tapped.

Acceleration, though fierce by big-car standards, is also smooth, quiet, and without flat spots, right up to our top observed speed of 123 mph. A longer run should carry the needle well past the 125-mph mark. Even at very high speeds, control was good, with the front end feeling lighter as speed increased. Since our acceleration runs [*see spec chart*] were made at Willow Springs Raceway, they're a bit misleading. Climate and track surface at Riverside Raceway would better the times slightly.

Not too many exterior changes have been made in the Riviera, and we're glad of it. But the changes underneath, the ones that spell out Gran Sport, have made this already outstanding car even more so. It goes and handles better than before, and that's quite an improvement. /MT

Quiet and stable at top speed, Gran Sport managed an honest 123 mph, should be capable of well over 125 with longer run.

Carter AFB carbs open simultaneously, give excellent response at any speed, with no flooding or starving through hard turns.

Winding roads showed off car's fine handling and moderate body lean. Quicker power steering plus 360 hp gave very good control.

PHOTOS BY DARRYL NORENBERG

Gran Sport package uses heavier front anti-roll bar, stiffer springs and shocks, and a higher-capacity dual exhaust system.

RIVIERA GRAN SPORT
2-door, 5-passenger hardtop

OPTIONS ON CAR TESTED: Gran Sport package, air conditioning, 4-way power seat, power windows, Guide-matic, Cruise Control, radio, whitewalls, rear-window defroster, misc. access.

PERFORMANCE

ACCELERATION (2 aboard)
- 0-30 mph...3.2 secs.
- 0-45 mph...5.0
- 0-60 mph...8.4

PASSING TIMES AND DISTANCES
- 40-60 mph...3.4 secs.
  243.9 ft.
- 50-70 mph...4.3 secs.
  258.0 ft.

Standing start ¼-mile 16.2 secs. and 87 mph

Speeds in gears @ 5300 rpm
- 1st............43 mph   3rd............123 mph
- 2nd............75   (observed) @ 5900 rpm

Speedometer Error on Test Car
Car's speedometer reading...	33	48	54	64	73	85
Weston electric speedometer..	30	45	50	60	70	80

Observed miles per hour per 1000 rpm in top gear...............21.0 mph
Stopping Distances – from 30 mph, 35.5 ft.; from 60 mph, 155.5 ft.

BUICK MOTOR DIVISION

The new Riviera Gran Sport or, How we put muscles on the Riviera's muscles

If you start messing around with a fairly normal looking Riviera someday and it suddenly commences making loud noises and leaves you fast sinking astern, that we're happy to say, was no normal Riviera.

What we've gone and put together is a land version of the wartime Q boat, i.e., a merchantman with hidden guns.

What's this? you say. Buick rattling its sabre and uttering warlike cries? They're supposed to be in the business of making nice, big, reliable, well-engineered, soft-riding automobiles.

We still are. But we've opened a new branch office.

Which brings us back to the Riviera Gran Sport. It packs what might be termed pretty heavy artillery: 2-4BBL, 425 cubic inches, 360 horsepower and 465 lb-ft of torque. And it plasters all this down on the road via a limited-slip differential with 3.42:1 gearing.

The steering is power assisted, with an extra-quick 15:1 gear ratio available for it. The brakes, also power assisted, are massive 12-inch finned aluminum drums up front, 12-inch finned cast iron on the back. Specify the heavy-duty set of springs, shocks, and stabilizer bar and you have the complete Q boat.

Next month we're doing something loud and strong with the Skylark. Keep watching this space.

More Riviera Gran Sport Standard Equipment: *Automatic transmission—3-speed torque convertor; 2¼" low-restriction dual exhausts; 8.45 x 15 tires on 6JK rims; bucket seats; console; padded dash; tilting steering wheel; full carpeting; 2-speed wipers; washers; map light; back-up lights; trunk light; smoking sets, front and rear; electric clock; speed warning buzzer; trip mileage indicator; things like that.*

ROAD TEST
425 GRAN SPORT RIVIERA
BY GORDON CHITTENDEN

GRAN SPORT

CARS MAGAZINE has just completed its comprehensive road test of the '65 Buick Riviera Gran Sport over Los Angeles freeways, city streets, desert roads, GM's tough Mesa, Arizona proving grounds and topping it off on the tortuous Apache Trail in Arizona. The final impression: The Buick Riviera Gran Sport is for those who demand the best in luxury and performance.

The luxury is apparent in around-the-town and highway driving; the performance shows up when you're on a twisting mountain road watching a sports car driver sweat trying to outcorner you, and on the first straight strip of road you blast through and leave him choking in the dust.

Few American cars can turn the trick against a sports job. Following are the whys and wherefores of why the Riviera is capable of doing so.

The Riviera's chassis, not radical in design, is basically the parent Electra 225 chassis with cruciform frame. However, the Riviera's has a high degree of stiffness to provide a solid feel, reduced dimensions to accommodate a shorter wheelbase and revised front and rear tracks.

Front and rear suspension geometry are tailored to the Riviera's specific needs. The frame is a separate frame rather than a body frame. To achieve flexibility of design, the front suspension is parallel arm, independent type with rubber cushioned fore and aft strut rod as a portion of the lower control arm, for optimum isolation of noise and impact.

A feature of this suspension is the very low kingpin-to-wheel offset, due to the lower ball joint being nestled into a pocket formed in the brake backing plate. This results in excellent directional stability even when driving over parallel ridges in the road surface.

The steering system is 17.5 to 1 ratio power steering gear combined with a conventional parallelogram type steering linkage with a 1.18 to 1 ratio. This gives an overall steering ratio of about 18.5 to 1, and provides 3.5 turns lock to lock. A ratio that many smaller and less well-behaved cars could well adapt.

The rear suspension is a highly successful three-link and track bar type. This design is very flexible and makes possible correction for power squat and brake lift with less compromising of roll steer and swing arm length than in any other suspension. Coil springs are used front and rear.

Handling on the Riviera takes the driver by surprise. It is probably the best handling of any large, full-sized American luxury car and is far above the handling of any comparable European car. And even those statements don't do it complete justice.

The Riviera takes about 57 percent of the roll couple on the front wheels so that there is less than 9 percent understeer in the front suspension. The rear suspension has just less than 9.5 percent understeer along with a rate of camber change of about 0.4 of a degree per inch of wheel movement at the one-inch jounce position.

The selection of tires for the Riviera could not be dictated merely by the requirements for a car of the GS's weight. This was discovered when standard 7.10 x 15's were mounted. They lacked the sure-footed grip that the Riviera's designers had worked for, so tire consultants were

Remove the air cleaner, right, and there sit two AFB's, which operate in tandem. Below, on Arizona's Apache Trail.

The complete, but *complete*, instrument panel is an enthusiast's dream. Steering wheel is adjustable, wood-grained.

The bucket seats are probably the most comfortable to come out of Detroit. Door panels and console are wood-grained.

called in to develop tires specifically for this car. They have a widened tread, reduced cord angles and a contoured shoulder. (Note to Riviera owners: when ordering new tires, order only those specified in the owner manual.)

The Riviera uses variable spring rate track bar bushings. These provide a built-in sweet spot, or soft cushioning when going over minor pavement flaws, yet assure firm lateral control during handling and transition maneuvers.

Body mounts use a special dual compound hardness in the rubber which has both a soft and hard compound for shake control and noise isolation. Ride considerations have been worked out so that there is approximately a 1.25 to 1 suspension deflection. This provides excellent high-speed control, yet a pleasant boulevard ride.

Brakes on the Riviera are especially good. They are not the disc type which are so much in the news this year, but a perfected combination of finned aluminum front drums and finned cast iron rear drums using a specially developed organic lining. The combination is such that one could actually set the brakes on fire before they would fade!

The result is almost unmatched

The tight mountain roads of the Apache Trail were no match for the Riviera GS.

GRAN SPORT

braking for drum type brakes. And it is doubtful that existing disc brakes could match the Riviera's in a car of equal weight. While not racing type brakes, they compare very well with competition sports car brakes. A test on braking in pedal pounds shows that after the 12th panic stop, the average luxury car requires almost 150 pounds of pedal pressure to stop, where a sports car will require but 20 to 30 pounds of pedal pressure after the 12th panic stop. The Riviera required, on its 12th panic stop, only 30 pounds of pedal pressure to stop! On the first of the stop tests, all cars required but 10 to 15 pounds pedal pressure, yet by the 12th stop, only the Riviera and sports cars with disc type brakes needed less than 30 pounds of pedal pressure.

The power train for the Riviera Gran Sport is the well developed 425 cubic inch V-8 OHV engine, coupled with the excellent Super 400 Turbine transmission. Bore and stroke is 4.31 x 3.64 inches. Compression ratio is 10.25:1 and the intake system uses two four-barrel Carter AFB carburetors operating in tandem for instant response. Cam timing for the 360 HP Gran Sport engine is as follows: int.O 29°, int.C.81°, exh.O. 71°, exh.C. 48°, intake duration is 290°, and exhaust duration is 299°, valve overlap is 77 degrees.

Intake valve head diam. is 1.875 inches, exhaust valve head diameter is 1.500 inches. At zero lash, intake valve lift is .439 inches, and exhaust valve lift is .441 inches.

The Carter carbs, both AFB series,

Without holding back any rough stuff, the Riviera Gran Sport was put through its paces at GM's Mesa, Ariz., test track. It was a case of track and driver vs. car. Riviera GS won in thoroughbred style.

use primary barrels 1.5625 inches and secondary venturis 1.6875 inches in diameter.

The Riviera Gran Sport uses a large diameter, dual exhaust system which is the high capacity, low back-pressure type, laminated to reduce noise.

Transmission consists of a Super Turbine 400, three-speed automatic with higher than normal shift points, a Positraction rear axle with a 3.42 to 1 final drive gear and modified shock and roll suspension settings.

The engine specifications—360 hp @ 4,440 rpm, and 465 ft/lbs. of torque @ 2,800 rpm—and shipping weight of the Riviera add up to unimpressive performance—but only on paper. The road test demolishes all the figures. Acceleration of the Riviera is far better than that of any luxury car on the market—including, surprisingly, the Mustang.

The Riviera Gran Sport will shock a lot of so-called hot-car owners just the way it's delivered. In testing the car with four people aboard, a full load of fuel, luggage in the trunk and using only the DRIVE range of the transmission with no attempt at power-shifting, standing quarter-mile speeds were in the 90's, with E.T.'s as low as 15.4 for the quarter!

Try to match that with an absolutely stock 289 Mustang with four aboard.

The shift points in the Super Turbine transmission have a reserve of power at almost any speed up to its top of just over 130 mph!

Both carburetors, working in tandem, show up with a total lack of flat-spots in acceleration.

Overall performance is what one might call phenomenal, since the 0-60 jumps up in 7 seconds, the 60 to 80 in 4.4 seconds; and 0 to 100 comes in at 19.5 to 20 seconds.

Passing speeds in the 50 to 70 mph bracket will turn out at 4.1 seconds. These times were with four aboard!

Acceleration is quiet, with no excessive wheel spin, no indication of power—suddenly, you're gone, without effort. And for a car whose weight with all aboard was just over 4,700 pounds, the ride and noise level are fantastic.

At a glance, the interior of the Riviera explains why anyone who can afford to buy one will not be able to pass it by. Consider: the most comfortable bucket seats in any American car, both front and back, adjustable steering wheel, six-way adjustable power-operated seats, plush carpeting, AM/FM radio, cruise control, remote controlled outside mirrors and, for the ladies, a purse holder.

And after all the surprises, the clock on the test car kept good time!

SPECIFICATIONS

TYPE: Four passenger luxury Coupe
Length Overall: 209.0 inches
Wheelbase: 117.0 inches
Width: 76.6 inches
Weight (dry): 4080 pounds
Engine: V-8 OHV
Displacement: 425 cubic inches
Horsepower: 360 @ 4400 RPM
Compression Ratio: 10.25:1
Carburetion: dual Carter AFB quads.
Transmission: three-speed auto.
Final Drive: 3.42 to 1
Tire Size: 8.45 x 15
Performance;
SS ¼ mile: 15.4 sec.ET
SS ¼ mile: 92 mph
Top Speed: 130 mph plus.

BUICK RIVIERA GRAN SPORT

CAR and DRIVER ROAD TEST

Inside, it's luxurious,
Buick-bred silence.
Outside, it's Daddy Warbucks'
high-powered runabout

We're going to drive to the Chicago Auto Show from Detroit, so we're going to need wheels, right? There are four of us, we're not small, and we want to make good time. Who do we call for a car? You guessed it—Buick. We borrow a Buick Riviera Gran Sport, because on form, it figures to be a pretty good vehicle. Why not? Every Riviera we ever drove was a swinger—from the very beginning—and the Gran Sport has better suspension than the standard Rivieras, more power, and it looks like a winner.

As it turned out, it *is* a winner. It did all the right things and we loved it.

We walked out of the Detroit Metropolitan Airport into a blizzard, to find our Gran Sport sitting at the curb, driven there by our blue-eyed midwestern space cadet, Trant Jarman. 1965 is the first time that Jarman has missed driving the Monte Carlo rally in three years, and it was abundantly clear that he intended to make up for it on the road to Chicago.

Our test car was painted a rich shade of British Racing Green, which ought to tear up the purists, and it had the greatest-looking wheels that ever went round and round, with ultra-skinny whitewall tires. The interior was black, trimmed with simulated oiled-walnut, and it was handsome. The instruments, the seats, the controls, the materials and finishes chosen, all said *AUTOMOBILE (EXPENSIVE)*.

We popped the trunk lid open to find that Buick's designers have devised a fiendishly clever test of the traveler's luggage-stowing ingenuity, in the form of a shallow trunk filled mostly with a center-mounted spare tire. The Riviera's luggage space is probably no more restricted than on many imported cars, but one of the expected advantages of big American cars is big luggage space, right? We reorganized our cargo three or four times, finally got it all in, and slammed the trunk lid on the sleeve of the publisher's topcoat—which resulted in a couple of small punctures from the lid's latching mechanism and a lot of colorful language from the publisher. *Important Note: Never slam the trunk lid on the sleeve of your boss's topcoat!*

Cargo aboard, everyone climbed in, and the journey commenced. The first clue that the Gran Sport was anything special was the exhaust note, which had that stumbling, sort of Chris-Craft V-8 rumble, much beloved of small boys—and ex-small boys—all over these United States. Inside, all was luxurious, Buick-bred silence. Outside, it was Daddy Warbucks' sleek, high-powered runabout, waiting at the dock for Punjab and the Asp, who are setting the explosive charges that will forever obliterate Little Orphan Annie's latest group of tormentors, carousing in their secret hideout.

So onto Interstate 94 and Chicago. The big superhighway is broad and open enough that the blowing snow hasn't yet started to collect—buckle the seat belts, scan the area for Fuzz, and open the throttle. HOT DAMN! Nobody puts a watch on it, but it hauls off down the road pretty well, considering its great burden of people and baggage. Reach down, grasp the setting knob for the Cruise Control and move the yellow needle to 77 mph. Push the button on the dash that engages the device, and feel the car surge up to the desired speed and level off independently. Indecent luxury, but nice.

Cruising this way is absolutely effortless in the Riviera. It's quiet and smooth and the driver is free to shift his position, or stretch, or whatever he wants to do—short of taking a walk, or turning around in his seat—to relieve fatigue. We find that the Cruise Control is not only a worthwhile way toward easing the stress of long-distance driving, but it's also lots of fun to play with when you don't like what's on the radio.

It didn't take long for the rear seat occupants to begin grumbling about the leg room back there, but with the front seats pushed about halfway forward the gripes subsided. The front seats are really first class. They give good lateral support, and they seem to be set at just the right height for a good driving position. Although the backs aren't adjustable, Buick's six-way power seat adjustment is a pretty popular option on the Riviera, and it does offer a broad range of seating angles and positions. (The steering wheel was also adjustable for angle, but we found this feature to be of limited value—the opinion of many General Motors-types, who think it's the greatest thing since canned beer, notwithstanding.)

All of the controls are easily found and used, except that a few, toward the center of the panel, are a bit hard to reach. The instruments look just like instruments, a fact for which we are eternally grateful. The automatic transmission selector is a little annoying, because one must really *look* at the lever to insure proper selection of a gear. The standard 17.5:1 power steering lacks feel in most driving situations, and that's too bad, but the steering is accurate and quite fast enough for the non-enthusiastic driver—the Gran Sport offers a quicker 15:1 power steering ratio that's great with us.

The Gran Sport's handling surprised us—twice. We negotiated an eighty-five mph bend at about eighty, and found that the car was rock-steady, with minimal roll. The handling seemed to be gradually and predictably changing from understeer to oversteer, and we liked it. Then we charged a thirty-mph bend just about as hard, and the Riviera plowed like something you'd find in an Iowa corn field. Like it was virtually out of control, LOST, and heading for the ditch. Lots of steering and gently, gently, with the brakes and we regained equilibrium (that is, the car did—we didn't) and missed the Indescribable Awful at the side of the road. Whew!

The other thing that we found fault with in the area of handling, was very bad crosswind behavior. The weather was such that we were in some kind of crosswind all the time—which is to say that we were getting blown off course more or less continually. This is not unique to this year's Riviera; in fact, it's the case with every one of the GM senior series cars we've driven—Olds, Pontiac, and Buick. The big GM cars have all altered their front suspension for 1965, and it looks like somebody fed some of the wrong stuff into the old computer. It is not a subject that anybody there wants to be very informative about, but it is nonetheless a real, nasty, who-the-hell-is-responsible-for-this, kind of a foul-up.

The chassis situation on this version of the Riviera is more-or-less traditional for a General Motors high performance V-8. The standard Riviera's stabilizer bar

"Every Riviera we ever drove was a swinger... and the Gran Sport has better suspension... more power and it looks like a winner"

is retained at the front, but stiffer shock absorbers and springs are used at all four wheels, along with stiffer bushings in the rear suspension. All this results in a ride that is a bit more sporty (spelled harsh) and more inclined to pitch, though not unpleasantly. Apart from the reservations mentioned earlier, we found that the Riviera "GS" went where it was pointed, and was a very stable platform for the enthusiastic driver.

The Riviera Gran Sport is available with only one engine and one transmission, unlike the Wildcat which offers all of the dozens of engine/transmission permutations that we've come to expect from Detroit. The Gran Sport's engine is a 425 cu. in. V-8 that produces 360 bhp at 4400 rpm, and 465 lbs. ft. of torque at 2800. Color it strong. The transmission is the latest 3-speed automatic from GM's Hydramatic Division, and it is, without question, the best automatic transmission in the world. Nobody, but maybe Chrysler, is even close in this very critical area of automotive development.

The 425 engine, the 3-speed automatic, the limited slip differential with its 3.42:1 ratio, and the taut compactness and balance of the Riviera make it a very nice, American-style car. It has the important added advantage of being built on a 117-in. wheelbase, compared to the Wildcat's longer-than-longish 126. As we drive more and more cars like the F-85, the GTO, the Plymouth Belvedere, and the Dodge Coronet, we *know* that there's no excuse for the giants—and the Riviera proves it. When a car in the so-called intermediate size bracket is manufactured with the same tender loving care as its bigger, more expensive brothers, it is just as comfortable, just as useful, and a LOT nicer to drive.

We had a feeling that we were going to like this newest edition of the Riviera, and we were right. It goes well, rides smoothly, corners better than most, and—thanks to Buick's long-time concern with brakes —stops with great authority. What's more, it isn't too big. It makes us think about another car that we really love, the Rover 2000. If the Rover people wanted to replace their big 3-liter, they could take the best features of their lovely little 2000, combine them with all the best features of the Buick Riviera, and the result would be the best car in the world. As it is, the Riviera, either in standard trim or in the Gran Sport version, is one of this country's best offerings to the automotive world. It isn't tiny, and it won't get to a hundred in ten seconds, and it'll never be what you might call one of the low-priced three, but then neither is Sophia Loren.

BUICK RIVIERA GRAN SPORT

Manufacturer: Buick Motor Division
General Motors Corporation
Flint, Michigan

Price as tested: $4,714.38

ACCELERATION

Zero to	Seconds
30 mph	2.4
40 mph	4.1
50 mph	5.8
60 mph	7.2
70 mph	8.9
80 mph	11.0
90 mph	13.2
100 mph	16.1
Standing ¼-mile	95 mph in 15.5

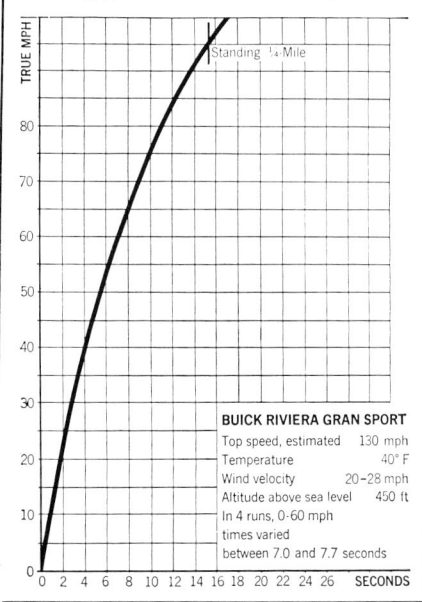

BUICK RIVIERA GRAN SPORT
Top speed, estimated 130 mph
Temperature 40° F
Wind velocity 20–28 mph
Altitude above sea level 450 ft
In 4 runs, 0–60 mph times varied between 7.0 and 7.7 seconds

ENGINE

Water-cooled 90° V-8, cast-iron block, 5 main bearings
Bore x stroke.4.31 x 3.64 in. 109.5 x 92.5 mm
Displacement............425 cu in 6918 cc
Compression ratio..............10.25 to one
Carburetion...Single 4-bbl Carter AFB (1.56-in primary, 1.69-in secondary)
Valve gear........Pushrod-operated overhead valves, hydraulic lifters
Power (SAE)............360 bhp @ 4400 rpm
Torque............465 lbs-ft @ 2800 rpm
Specific power output!........84 bhp per cu in, 53 bhp per liter
Usable range of engine speeds.500–5000 rpm
Electrical system...12-volt, 70 amp-hr battery, Delcotron alternator
Fuel recommended..............Premium
Mileage..............12–18 mpg
Range on 20-gallon tank........240–360 miles

DRIVE TRAIN

Transmission.....Super Turbine 400 (hydraulic torque converter and three-speed planetary transmission)

Gear	Ratio	Over-all	mph/1000 rpm	Max mph
Rev	2.08	7.11	11.4	—57
1st	2.48	8.48	9.6	48
2nd	1.48	5.06	16.0	80
3rd	1.00	3.42	23.7	118.5

Final drive ratio..............3.42 to one

CHASSIS

Cruciform channel-section frame, all-steel body
Wheelbase..............117 in
Track..............F 60.2, R 59.0 in
Length..............209 in
Width..............77 in
Height..............52.1 in
Ground clearance..............5.70 in
Curb weight..............4166 lbs
Test weight..............4480 lbs
Weight distribution front/rear..........53/47%
Pounds per bhp (test weight)..............12.4
Suspension F: Ind., unequal-length wishbones and coil springs, anti-roll bar.
R: Rigid axle, trailing arms and torque member, panhard rod, coil springs.
Brakes..............12-in drums, F and R, 320.5 sq in swept area
Steering..............Recirculating ball
Turns, lock to lock..............3.4
Turning circle..............43.2 ft
Tires..............8.45 x 15
Revs per mile..............739

CHECK LIST

ENGINE
Starting..............Good
Response..............Good
Noise..............Excellent
Vibration..............Excellent

DRIVE TRAIN
Clutch action
Transmission linkage
Synchromesh action
Power-to-ground transmission......Good

BRAKES
Response..............Excellent
Pedal pressure..............Excellent
Fade resistance..............Fair
Smoothness..............Good
Directional stability..............Good

STEERING
Response..............Good
Accuracy..............Good
Feedback..............Excellent
Road feel..............Poor

SUSPENSION
Harshness control..............Fair
Roll stiffness..............Good
Tracking..............Good
Pitch control..............Fair
Shock damping..............Good

CONTROLS
Location..............Excellent
Relationship..............Excellent
Small controls..............Fair

INTERIOR
Visibility..............Excellent
Instrumentation..............Excellent
Lighting..............Good
Entry/exit..............Fair
Front seating comfort..............Excellent
Front seating room..............Excellent
Rear seating comfort..............Fair
Rear seating room..............Poor
Storage space..............Fair
Wind noise..............Good
Road noise..............Good

WEATHER PROTECTION
Heater..............Excellent
Defroster..............Good
Ventilation..............Good
Weather sealing..............Good
Windshield wiper action..............Excellent

QUALITY CONTROL
Materials, exterior..............Good
Materials, interior..............Good
Exterior finish..............Good
Interior finish..............Good
Hardware and trim..............Good

GENERAL
Service accessibility..............Good
Luggage space..............Poor
Bumper protection..............Good
Exterior lighting..............Good
Resistance to crosswinds..............Poor

Buick Riviera 6,949 c.c.

Autocar Road Test
NUMBER 2036

MANUFACTURER:
Buick Motor Division, General Motors Corporation, Flint, Michigan, U.S.A.

BRITISH CONCESSIONAIRES:
Lendrum and Hartman Ltd., Flood Street, London, S.W.13.

PRICES:
Basic	.. .. ..	£3,010 0s 0d
Purchase Tax	.. ..	£628 12s 11d
Total (in G.B.)	.. ..	£3,638 12s 11d

EXTRAS
Radio with power aerial (Standard
Seat belts, lap straps only on cars
Rear window demister for British
Power-operated driving seat. market)

PERFORMANCE SUMMARY
Mean maximum speed	..	122 m.p.h.
Standing start ¼-mile	..	15·5 sec
0-60 m.p.h.	.. ..	7·4 sec
30-70 m.p.h. in Intermediate		7·3 sec
Overall fuel consumption		10·8 m.p.g.
Miles per tankful	.. ..	179

AT A GLANCE: Handsome American coupé; four seats, and superb standard of detail finish; high performance engine; exceptionally smooth automatic transmission; power brakes fade after extended use; power steering very light, high-geared and positive.

To the European motorist the ways of the American seem strange. Climbing into one of the typically large and rather flamboyant sedans, we sometimes feel ill-at-ease with so much free space and no clear indication of where the extremities lie. To launch forth into London's traffic and congested side streets is a test of confidence, particularly if the machine in question is an exclusive luxury car—like the Buick Riviera—with a price tag bordering on £4,000 and left-hand drive.

Judged in its home environment, of course, such a car would give a very different impression; yet after less than a week to familiarize ourselves it became second nature to thread this 17ft 5in. by 6ft 5in. monster through almost any gap with impunity and to enjoy every minute behind the wheel.

The 1965 car we have been testing is distinguished from last year's by its concealed headlamps, which appear automatically as "stacked quads" when the switch is pulled and small electric motors divide and retract pairs of eyelid shutters in the front of each wing. Body styling of this car, first of the General Motors range to feature the kicked-up "coke bottle" line above the rear wheel arches, is unchanged.

In essence, the Riviera is a close-coupled four-seater—a kind of gentleman's 2-door coupé version of the long-wheelbase Cadillac limousine, enjoying a somewhat parallel position to the Bentley Continental in relation to a standard Rolls-Royce

Until switched on the headlamps are hidden behind metal covers, with the sidelamps and winkers below the bumper

Autocar Road Test 2036

MAKE: Buick

TYPE: Riviera

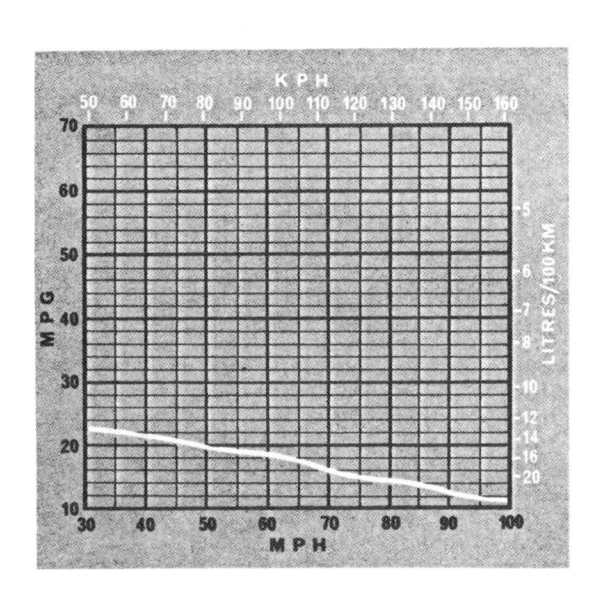

Maximum speeds and acceleration times
Speed range, gear ratios and time in seconds

m.p.h.	Top (3·42–7·58)	Inter (5·06–11·21)	Low (8·48–18·80)
10—30	—	—	1·8
20—40	3·8	2·9	2·1
30—50	4·1	3·2	2·8
40—60	4·6	3·7	—
50—70	5·0	4·3	—
60—80	6·4	5·0	—
70—90	7·7	6·5	—
80—100	8·4	—	—
90—110	11·5	—	—

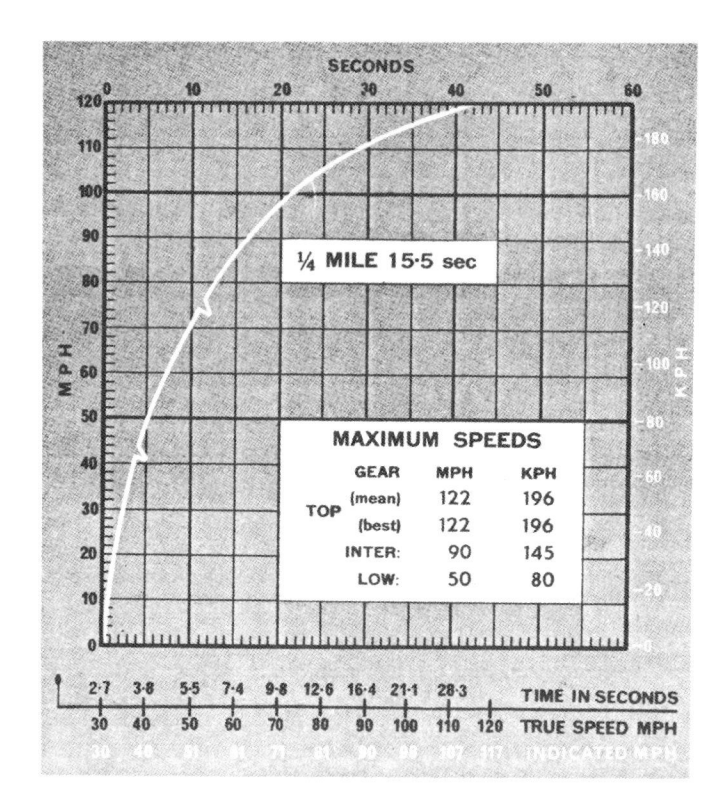

TEST CONDITIONS
Weather	Dry and sunny with no wind
Temperature	18 deg. C. (64 deg.F.)
Barometer	29·90in. Hg.
Surfaces	Dry concrete and tarmac

WEIGHT
Kerb weight (with oil, water and half-full fuel tank): 39·0 cwt (4,369lb-1,983kg)
Front-rear distribution, per cent F, 57.3, R, 42.7
Laden as tested   42·0 cwt (4,705lb-2,138kg)

TURNING CIRCLES
Between kerbs	L, 42ft 8in.; R, 44ft 3in.
Between walls	L, 45ft 3in.; R, 46ft 9in.
Steering wheel turns lock to lock	3·3

PERFORMANCE DATA
Top gear m.p.h. per 1,000 r.p.m.	23·8
Mean piston speed at max. power	2,665ft/min
Engine revs at mean max. speed	5,125 r.p.m.
B.h.p. (gross) per ton laden	172

OIL CONSUMPTION
SAE 10W/30 .. .. .. 3,000 m.p.g.

FUEL CONSUMPTION
At constant speeds
30 m.p.h.	22·1 m.p.g.	70 m.p.h.	15·8 m.p.g.
40 ,,	21·0 ,,	80 ,,	14·2 ,,
50 ,,	19·8 ,,	90 ,,	12·6 ,,
60 ,,	18·4 ,,	100 ,,	11·4 ,,

Overall m.p.g.   10·8 (26·2 litres/100km)
Normal range m.p.g. 10-15 (28·3-18·8 litres/100km)
Test distance .. .. .. 1,340 miles
Estimated (DIN) m.p.g. 14·4 (19·6 litres/100km)
Grade .. .. .. Super (100·3-101·8RM)

¼ MILE 15·5 sec

MAXIMUM SPEEDS
GEAR		MPH	KPH
TOP	(mean)	122	196
	(best)	122	196
INTER:		90	145
LOW:		50	80

BRAKES	Pedal load	Retardation	Equiv. distance
(from 30 m.p.h.	25lb	0·45g	67ft
in neutral)	40lb	0·75g	40ft
	50lb	0·85g	35·4ft
Handbrake		0·30g	100ft

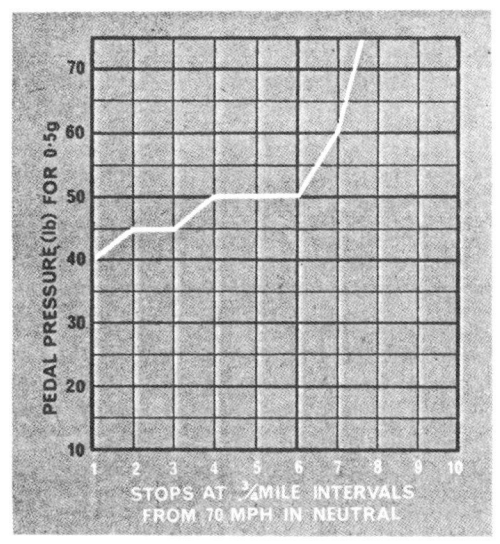

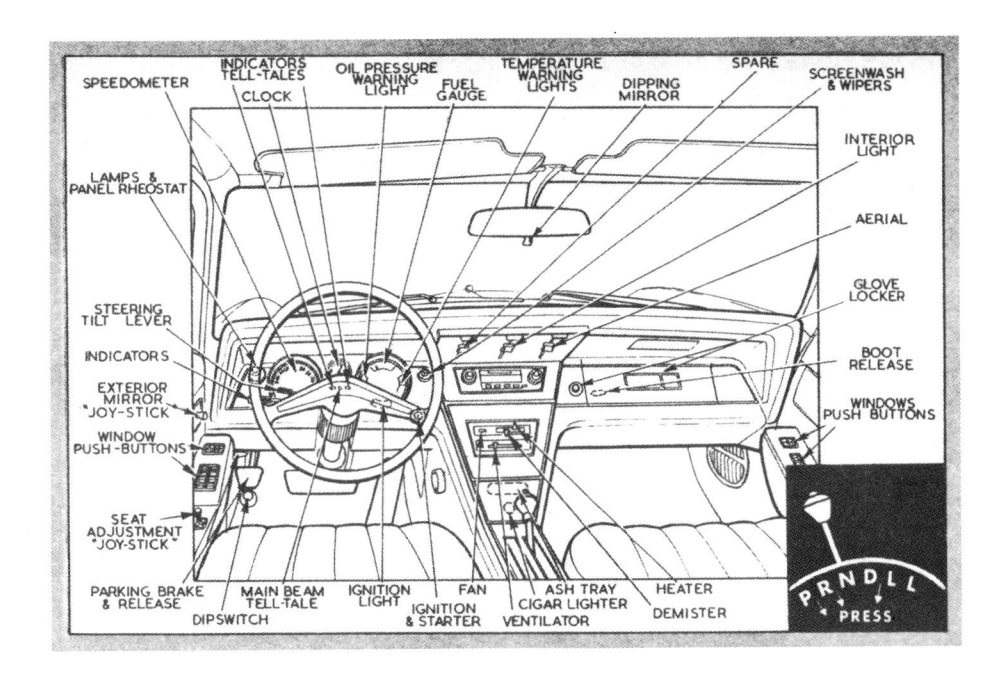

Silver Cloud. With seven litres, 360 b.h.p. gross at 4,400 r.p.m., and—best of all—465lb. ft. torque at 2,800 r.p.m., it is very fast on the road, with acceleration to match most high-performance GT and sports cars. For this year a third, low ratio has been added to the Super Turbine automatic transmission (which has variable stator blades in its torque convertor) and the step-off from rest is extremely fast, leaving twin black marks on dry surfaces at full throttle despite 8.45-15in. tyres.

Smooth Transmission

This transmission has been carefully "tuned" to the engine characteristics, and even by overriding the automatic changes we could not improve the time from rest to 100 m.p.h. by more than half a second, our mean being a very exhilarating 21·1sec with a spread of only 1sec for four runs in opposite directions. The consistent way the performance could be repeated also shows up in the maximum speed—122 m.p.h. in either direction time after time. Over the standing quarter-mile, the Riviera is nearly as quick as the Jaguar E-type.

With the big central selector stick against the D of its quadrant and the accelerator "floored" low gear catapults the car up to 42 m.p.h. in about 4sec, when intermediate takes over and surges on to 74 m.p.h. before the change to top. Low can be held to about 50 m.p.h. by selecting L1 below 40 m.p.h., and intermediate (L2) runs up to about 90, but nothing is gained as the engine is then well over the peak of its power curve. For maximum engine braking from high speeds one presses the release button on the stick and knocks it back into either L2 or L1, since a governor protects the engine by preventing L1 coming in until the speed has dropped to 40 m.p.h. The button is only needed to change down out of D, the lever being free to move between L1 and L2 or back to D without it.

In addition there is the usual kick-down working-off the accelerator, the maximum speeds for using this being 64 m.p.h. for L2 and no more than 15 m.p.h. for L1. This moderate speed for L1, with the fact that the pedal must be pushed hard to the floor for the kick-down to operate, is a help on slippery surfaces as it prevents any unwanted—and embarrassing—surges into low. A limited-slip differential is standard, and although traction on dry roads is generally good, one has to guard against wheel-spin in the wet.

Except at full throttle it is virtually impossible to detect the gear changes, which are not only smooth but fast. Kick-down selection is also completely jerk-free and our staff were unanimous in praising this automatic as the best yet made by anyone and eminently suited to the car and its big vee-8.

With strong power assistance, the steering is extremely light but not insensitive once one is used to its feel. There are only 3·3 turns from lock to lock on a mean turning circle of about 43ft, so it is quite high geared for this sort of car. Initially in corners one tends to turn the wheel too much and too suddenly, causing the soft front suspension to dip at the outside and the car to wallow untidily. With a bit of practice, however, a more delicate touch becomes natural and the car then corners on a surprisingly flat and even keel. In fact, grip and cornering power are much greater than one expects and there is stable understeer all the way to the limit, with no rear-wheel lifting even under full power in tight turns.

When it rains, or even on dry dusty surfaces, the whole picture changes and one needs to slow right down and be ready for tail slides and snaking all the time. Even so, this big car responds quickly and predictably to corrective action.

Comfortable Ride

Although soft, the suspension is rather more firmly damped than is the case with most other American cars we have tried, and generally the ride on British roads is comfortable and free from floating. Big bumps displace the car considerably, but there is no recurrent pitching. As a

Under the large chromium air-cleaner there are two four-barrel carburettors. The alternator is on the left and the servo pump on the right.

Left: Mock wood panels are fitted to the doors, dashboard and centre console giving a very plush look to the well finished interior. Rubber mats protect the woven carpets and the upholstery is covered in metallised cloth. Right: In the back there are only two seats with a centre armrest which lifts up from between them. There is a reading lamp each side and a demister for the rear window

Buick Riviera...

result of the separate cruciform chassis frame, well insulated from the main body structure, we could drive on washboard at any speed from 30 to 70 m.p.h. very smoothly and with no vibration and little steering column shake. On *pavé* there was much thumping and bottoming of the suspension, and the back of the car was kicked about from side to side.

When driven fast the Riviera ran true, but we had a perfectly still day for the high-speed testing. However, there is no free play in the steering and on motorway curves one can hold the car accurately on line, even at 100 m.p.h. and over.

With large self-wrapping shoes and a vacuum servo the drum brakes are somewhat fierce at town speeds. The weight of one's foot is usually sufficient for quite a rapid stop, and one must then lift off to prevent the nose diving and passengers' heads jerking forwards. It is easy to lock the wheels, the back ones first at only 40lb load on the pedal from 30 m.p.h. Another 10lb locked the front ones, too, so we could not better 0·85g retardation. At high speed the pedal feels more "dead," although there was none of the usual harshness and judder of American drum brakes when they become overheated.

When tested for fade from 70 m.p.h. at 0·5g, the brakes became in-creasingly ineffective until after eight applications at ¾-mile intervals we could only just push hard enough (140 lb) to reach this retardation. After a few minutes' rest the system had fully recovered.

For the parking brake there is a foot pedal (where the clutch might have been) which held the car securely on 1-in-3 facing either way. It easily locked the back wheels at 30 m.p.h., recording 0·3g. There is the usual transmission lock as a supplement, this position on the selector being guarded by the press-button—as is reverse.

Low Noise Level

On the test car the offside passenger door did not seal effectively round its top window frame, and there was a good deal of wind noise from about 70 m.p.h. upwards. There was also a fair amount of induction roar from the two 4-barrel carburettors fitted on the Super Wildcat engine when accelerating hard, which spoilt an otherwise near-silent car. Exhaust, transmission and mechanical engine noises are all practically unheard, and one normally wafts along making easy conversation with those in the back or listening to the crystal-clear tones of the AM-FM radio—which, incidentally, can be fitted with a reverberator for the rear speaker to give a "concert hall" effect.

The Buick has several other entertaining gimmicks, some with very practical purposes. Like the headlamp covers mentioned earlier, the radio aerial and the driving seat are also powered. This latter adjustment, controlled by a little joystick on a panel in the door, raises and lowers the back edge of the seat in one plane and slides the whole seat back and forth in the other. The other front seat is not powered and cannot be tilted, unless one pays extra. In addition to the simple and versatile seat adjustment, the driver can alter the angle of the steering-wheel

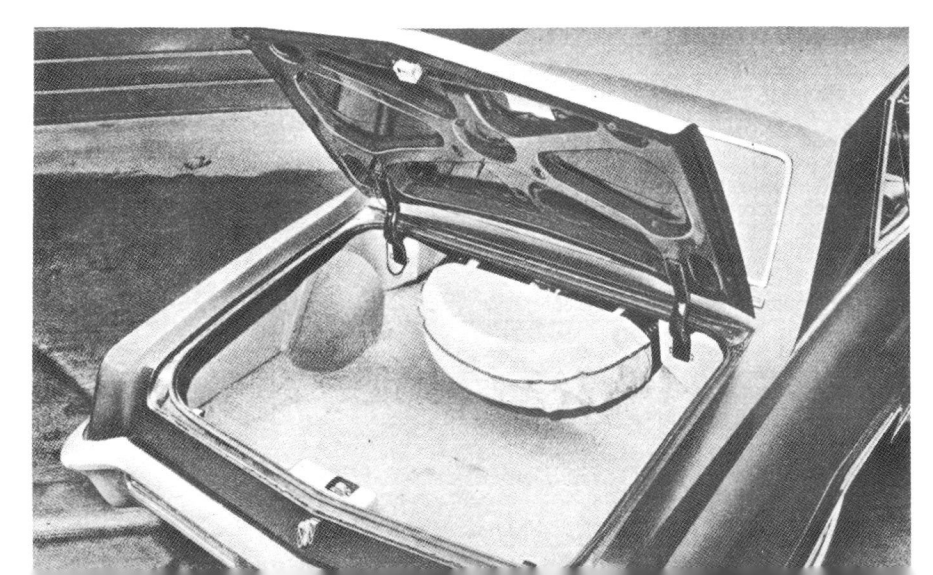

The large countersprung boot lid can be released with a key from outside or electrically by pulling a T-handle inside the glove locker. There is a lot of luggage space but it is a struggle to remove the spare wheel

One of the best examples of General Motors styling, the Riviera looks discreetly sleek without being ostentatious. The wire spokes of the wheels are dummies

through six positions, although all of us chose a half-way setting at right angles to the column.

Then again, on the driver's door there are another trigger for remotely setting the outside auxiliary mirror and a battery of six switches for opening all the side windows—front quarterlights each side, main side windows in the doors and rear quarter panes. With all windows lowered the sides are clear and free from pillars. There are individual switches (which can be overriden by the driver) by each window.

When either door is open no fewer than six interior lamps light automatically; there is an automatic one for the glove box, too, when its lid is opened. Turning the lighting master switch on the dashboard brings into operation two of these—one each side of the rear quarter panels for reading with the doors shut; when looking for things in the back the one on the tunnel between the seats can be switched on by a trigger in its frame.

The doors can be unlatched by a large lift-up lever at either end, so that a back-seat passenger need not stretch over the front seats to open the door. One can almost squeeze past the front seats into the back, so wide is each door, but the backrests tip to make it easier. For a car of such proportions the room in the rear is disappointing, and some extra inches might well have been allowed for legs—and less for luggage.

Individual Seating

All four seats—there is room for a third person in the back but no padding in the centre—are covered in a metallized cloth which is soft to touch and grips quite well. By tailoring the car for only four it has been possible to give the seats good shape, and one does not slide about even when cornering fast.

Facing the driver under the steering-wheel are a pair of matching circular dials. On the left is a very accurate speedometer (up to 90 m.p.h., at least) with clear white markings on a black background. A small knob on the dial sets a second, yellow hand to any speed between 30 and 100 m.p.h. and as soon as the chosen speed is reached a buzzer sounds to warn the driver. On its maximum setting it is switched off.

In the standard American positions of top left and right each side of the wheel rim, the lamps and wipers switches are both multiple units incorporating several functions. Pressing a small button in the middle of the wiper switch squirts the washers and starts the blades sweeping at the slower of their two speeds. These stayed on the glass when driving fast and cleared great wide arcs most efficiently. There is a dip-switch on the floor, but no headlamp flasher—an odd quirk of American legislation.

At night the headlamps gave a very poor showing, despite being in pairs each side and protected from road dirt by the shutters. The range is

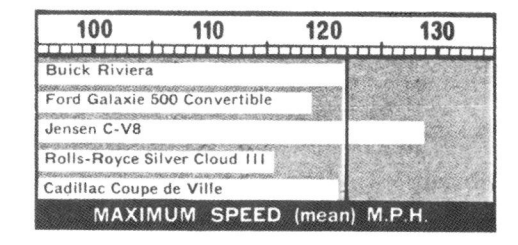

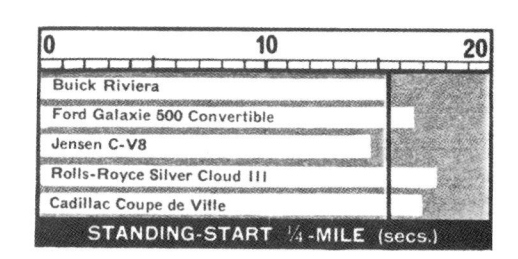

HOW THE BUICK RIVIERA COMPARES:

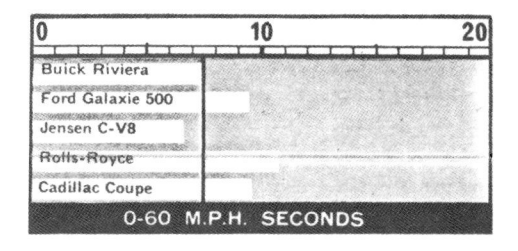

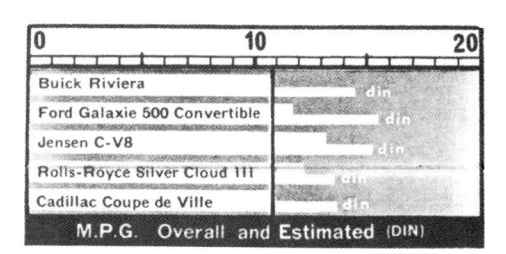

	100	110	120	130
Buick Riviera				
Ford Galaxie 500 Convertible				
Jensen C-V8				
Rolls-Royce Silver Cloud III				
Cadillac Coupe de Ville				
MAXIMUM SPEED (mean) M.P.H.				

	0	10	20
Buick Riviera			
Ford Galaxie 500 Convertible			
Jensen C-V8			
Rolls-Royce Silver Cloud III			
Cadillac Coupe de Ville			
STANDING-START ¼-MILE (secs.)			

	0	10	20
Buick Riviera			
Ford Galaxie 500			
Jensen C-V8			
Rolls-Royce			
Cadillac Coupe			
0-60 M.P.H. SECONDS			

	0	10	20
Buick Riviera			din
Ford Galaxie 500 Convertible			din
Jensen C-V8			din
Rolls-Royce Silver Cloud III			din
Cadillac Coupe de Ville			din
M.P.G. Overall and Estimated (DIN)			

limited even on main beams, and there seemed to be little spread across the road.

With such a big engine giving lots of horsepower and an all-up weight of over two tons it is inevitable that the Riviera should be heavy on fuel. We managed an overall consumption of only 10·8 m.p.g. and most owners would hardly do better than 12. For a car that needs to pull in at the filling station so often—the range with a 16·6-gallon tank is effectively only 150 miles—it is annoying that the filler should be both clumsy to open and restricted in the rate at which it can take fuel. The hinged number plate meanwhile must be held down against a spring, while the small diameter cap is unlocked with one of the three keys, removed, and the nozzle inserted; this is below bumper level, so it means kneeling or crouching.

At its total price in Great Britain of £3,639 the Buick can compete very favourably with the world's best limousines. The specification for export here, incidentally, includes several items counted as extras in America, such as the Super Wildcat engine, radio, seat belts, power seat and tilt wheel, and the rear window demister with two-speed blower. In fact, the car comes as fully equipped as anyone could want, and the only other expense worth considering is a right-hand-drive conversion to ease overtaking (Ruddspeed of Worthing do a very professional job for £375).

Like all big American cars the Riviera is an eye-catcher here. But it has a rare grace of line, too, and a superb standard of finish for a car made in such quantities (36,313 last year alone). The performance is even more startling than the looks, and this Buick is without doubt the best American car we have tested.

SPECIFICATION : BUICK RIVIERA FRONT ENGINE, REAR-WHEEL DRIVE

ENGINE
Cylinders	8 in 90 deg. vee
Cooling system	Water; pump, fan and thermostat
Bore	109·5mm (4·31in.)
Stroke	92·5 mm (3·64in.)
Displacement	6,949 c.c. (425 cu. in.)
Valve gear	Overhead, hydraulic tappets and rockers
Compression ratio	10·25-to-1
Carburettors	2 four-barrel Carter
Fuel pump	Mechanical
Oil filter	Full-flow, renewable unit.
Max. power	360 b.h.p. (gross) at 4,400 r.p.m.
Max torque	465 lb. ft. (gross) at 2,800 r.p.m.

TRANSMISSION
Gearbox	Automatic Super Turbine; 3-speed with torque converter
Gear ratios	Top 1·0-2·22; Inter 1·48-3·28; Low 2·48-5·50; Reverse 2·08-4·62
Final drive	Hypoid-bevel with limited-slip differential 3·42-1

CHASSIS AND BODY
Construction	Cruciform frame and separate steel body

SUSPENSION
Front	Independent coil springs and wishbones, telescopic dampers, anti-roll bar
Rear	Live axle, coil springs and radius arms, telescopic dampers
Steering	Saginaw power-assisted recirculating-ball
Wheel dia.	16in.

BRAKES
Make and type	Bendix self-adjusting, drums front and rear
Servo	Suspended vacuum type
Dimensions	F, 12in. dia.; 2·25in. wide shoes R, 12in. dia.; 2·25 in. wide shoes
Swept area	F, 160sq.in., R, 160sq. in. Total: 320sq.in. (152sq.in.) per ton laden

WHEELS
Type	Pressed steel disc, 5 studs 6in. wide rim
Tyres	Firestone 130 tubeless
Size	8·45—15 in.

EQUIPMENT
Battery	12-volt, 70-amp. hr.
Alternator	Delco-Remy diode rectified
Headlamps	Vertical pairs, 37·5-55-watt
Reversing lamp	Standard, two
Electric fuses	16
Screen wipers	2-speed, self-parking
Screen washer	Standard, electric
Interior heater	Standard, fresh air type
Safety belts	Lap strap standard
Interior trim	Cloth seats; p.v.c. headlining
Floor covering	Carpet with rubber mats
Starting handle	No provision
Jack	Screw pillar
Jacking points	4, under bumpers
Other bodies	None

MAINTENANCE
Fuel tank	16·6 Imp. gallons (no reserve) (75 litres)
Cooling system	31 pints (including heater) (14 litres)
Engine sump	6·7 pints (3 litres) SAE 10W/30 Change oil every 6,000 miles; Change filter every 6,000 miles
Gearbox	19 pints SAE AQ ATF. Change oil every 24,000 miles
Final drive	3·7 pints SAE 90. Change oil every 24,000 miles
Grease	None required
Tyre pressures	F and R, 24 p.s.i. (normal driving); F, 24; R, 28 p.s.i. (full load

Scale ¼in to 1ft cushions uncompressed

OVERALL LENGTH 17'6"
OVERALL WIDTH 6'4"
OVERALL HEIGHT 4'7"
GROUND CLEARANCE 6"
WHEELBASE 9'9"
FRONT TRACK 5'0"
REAR TRACK 4'11"

ROAD TEST No. 36/65 ● Buick Riviera

Grand design by Buick

". . . designed to carry four people in four armchairs swiftly and quietly . . ."

MOTOR TESTED

THERE is always something grand about a design that has little or no compromise in it and even by American standards the Buick Riviera is certainly grand. It is a high-class prestige car with sporting inclinations, designed to carry four people in four armchairs swiftly and quietly with the absolute minimum of fuss. This it does supremely well with its 7-litre V-8 engine (giving 360 b.h.p. gross in "Super Wildcat" tune as tested) and one of the best automatic gearboxes in the world. Its impressive top speed of 128 m.p.h. may be only of academic interest to Americans plagued by low speed limits, but everyone can enjoy its staggering acceleration and surprisingly good road manners—virtues that will appeal especially to British motorists despite the car's enormous size.

This singleness of purpose has produced a vehicle which is unmistakably American in every way but has a certain classic grace. The sheer, smooth power, mechanical quietness and luxury of the furnishings—even the driver's seat is power operated—justify the name Riviera. Its one great failing lies in the drum brakes which may be adequate for America but fade hopelessly with their standard "soft" linings under quick stops from 100 m.p.h. and more—speeds which can be quite commonplace in Europe.

The test car had been converted to right-hand drive by Rudds of Worthing who had done a thoroughly good job and left no scars: even the window operating switches had been transferred from one side to the other, something which General Motors fail to do on models such as the Pontiac Parisienne which they "convert" themselves.

A price of £4,039 (including £400 for the r.h.d. conversion) and very heavy petrol consumption (10.1 m.p.g. overall) make the Riviera a rich man's transport, yet it has a strong family resemblance to many cheaper cars from the States which tend to lack individuality. Its very light, feelingless steering, feather-light brakes (at low speeds), poor window sealing, inadequate seat adjustment, slight body flexing and very soft floating ride are typical characteristics. Even so, it is an interesting and stimulating car and one of the best "big Yanks" we have tried.

Performance and economy

The Riviera is one of the fastest 4-seater cars *Motor* has tested, with a top speed approaching 130 m.p.h. People expect large cars to have large acceleration but even so the Buick will raise anyone's eyebrows.

PRICE £3,010 plus £628 12s. 11d. purchase tax equals £3,638 12s. 11d. Right hand drive (converted by Rudds of Worthing) £400 extra.

49

Although the Buick is nearly 17½ ft. long, fairly clean styling helps camouflage its size. The "wire wheels" are dummies.

Buick Riviera

At full throttle from low speeds, people are snapped back into their seats as the car surges forward with uncanny ease. Traction from the big Firestone tyres is usually sufficient except on vicious standing starts in low gear which leave long black lines on the road. In the wet, the back wheels can be made to spin at quite high speeds so the throttle must be treated with great delicacy and respect. With two people and test equipment on board, the car weighed over two tons yet would accelerate to 100 m.p.h. in 22.4 seconds. Hill climbing is absurdly effortless and the Buick fairly bolted away from standstill on a 1-in-3 hill.

If the automatic choke is used properly—press down then release slowly—starting is immediate from cold. The engine idles lumpily (carburetter adjustment would probably cure this) and the tappets are noisy until hydraulic pressure takes up the clearance. Like most American V-8s, the engine is astonishingly smooth at speeds above tick over and the car could be driven off immediately from cold without hesitation or spluttering.

Nearly seven litres of fairly well tuned engine in a massive car are not likely to give very good petrol consumption but it was still a shock to find that a 16-mile trip through London gobbled up 1½ gallons of petrol. On the open road, the figures improve a little—14.1 m.p.g. at a steady 80 m.p.h. for example. To anyone who can afford to run such a car, miles per tankful are perhaps more important than miles per gallon. Neither figure is good: at 10.1 m.p.g. you will only go 168 miles on a 16.6-gallon petrol tank which had a wildly inaccurate gauge on our test car. Despite an unusually high compression ratio of 10.25:1, the engine did not seem to pink on premium (98 octane) petrol.

Transmission

So smooth is the "Super Turbine 400" three-speed automatic box that you can only suspect that it changes gear—seldom can you actually feel it. Even when a lower gear is engaged with the kick-down switch, only the sudden increase in acceleration and a rising distant hum from the engine indicate that anything has happened. No driver, however skilled, could make every change on a manual box as imperceptible as this.

A central selector lever, working in a fore-and-aft plane on the transmission tunnel, gives the driver complete over-riding control although the performance in D (drive) is so good that it is pointless to change up through the box manually. Middle-gear hold is very useful, however, for driving quickly along a tight twisting road; its fairly wide speed range allows vivid acceleration out of slow corners yet high speeds along short straights. An easy nudge on the lever—set rather too far back if the seat is forward—is all that is needed when changing up, but a button must be pressed to change down. There is no "stop" between second and first and, since the lever moves smoothly, it is easy to go from top to first by mistake.

Experience with a sister car last winter showed that the transmission and throttle control are potentially smooth enough to drive on black ice without provoking slides but the lumpy idling and a rather stiff accelerator pedal on the second car made smooth manoeuvring difficult (and sometimes embarrassing) and caused the car to creep erratically and uncomfortably at traffic lights unless the gears were disengaged.

Handling and brakes

As on most American cars, the steering wheel can be turned with one finger despite higher than usual gearing and the power assistance makes it almost completely devoid of feel. Even so, the car is stable and controllable once you are accustomed to this lightness which tends to mask fairly strong understeer and encourages under-correction when leaving a corner fast. Despite the enormous power, a limited-slip differential allows the use of full throttle out of sharp

Performance

Test Data: World copyright reserved: no unauthorized reproduction in whole or in part.

Conditions
Weather: Warm and mild.
Temperature: 56°-58°F. Barometer 29.2 in Hg.
Surface: Dry tarmacadam.
Fuel: Premium (98 octane R.M.).

Maximum speeds

	m.p.h.
Mean of two opposite runs	127.6
Best one way ¼-mile	128.5
2nd gear	90
1st gear	50
"Maximile" Speed: (Timed quarter mile after 1 mile accelerating from rest.)	
Mean	124.4
Best	124.6

Acceleration times

m.p.h.	sec.
0-30	2.5
0-40	3.6
0-50	5.1
0-60	7.2
0-70	9.4
0-80	12.1
0-90	16.0
0-100	21.7
0-110	28.6
Standing quarter mile	15.9

m.p.h.	kick down
20-40	2.1
30-50	2.6
40-60	3.6
50-70	4.3
60-80	4.9
70-90	6.6
80-100	9.6
90-110	12.6

Speedometer
m.p.h.

Indicated	30	40	50	60	70	80	90	100
True	29½	40	50	60	70½	81	91½	102

Distance recorder . . . . 1.9% slow

Brakes
Pedal pressure, deceleration and equivalent stopping distance from 30 m.p.h.

lb.	g	ft.
25	0.55	54.5
50	0.88	34
75	0.96	31
Parking brake	0.36	83

Automatics tested by Motor

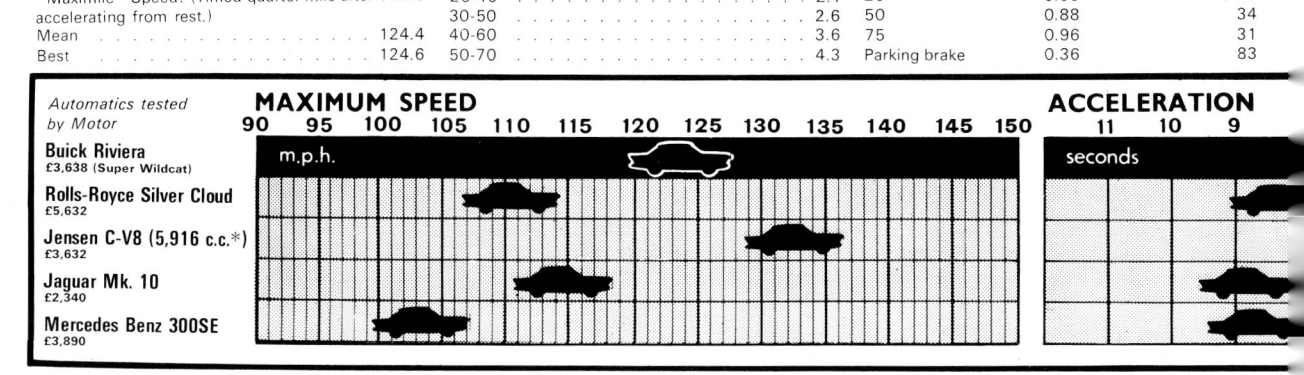

Buick Riviera £3,638 (Super Wildcat)
Rolls-Royce Silver Cloud £5,632
Jensen C-V8 (5,916 c.c.*) £3,632
Jaguar Mk. 10 £2,340
Mercedes Benz 300SE £3,890

* Latest car has more powerful 6,276 c.c. engine.

Despite the car's size, the Buick has been designed to carry only four people— hence the sumptuous armchairs (left) at the back instead of the usual bench seat. The armrest folds away to make room for a third person. Leg room is adequate. An ashtray and cigar lighter on the transmission tunnel serve rear-seat passengers.

Simple lap-strap safety belts (below) coil away automatically when not in use.

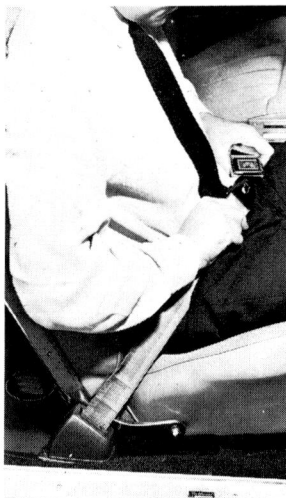

Fade

20 stops at ½g deceleration at 1 min. intervals from a speed midway between 30 m.p.h. and max. speed (= 79 m.p.h.)
                                lb.
Pedal force at beginning 35
Pedal force at 10th stop 40
Pedal force at 20th 55

Weight

Kerb weight (unladen with fuel for approximately 50 miles) . . . . 37¾ cwt.
Front/rear distribution 56/45
Weight laden as tested . . . . 41½ cwt.

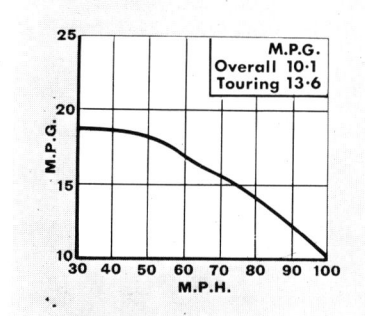

Fuel consumption
                                  m.p.g.
Touring (consumption midway between 30 m.p.h. and maximum less 5% allowance for acceleration) 13.6
Overall 10.1
                  = 28 litres/100km.

Total test distance . . . . 1,320 miles
Tank capacity (maker's figure) . . . 16.6 gal.

M.P.G. Overall 10.1 Touring 13.6

Steering

Turning circle between kerbs: ft.
Left 43
Right 41
Turns of steering wheel from lock to lock . . 2.9
Steering wheel deflection for 50 ft. diameter circle = 1.1 turns

Parkability

Gap needed to clear a 6 ft. wide obstruction parked in front

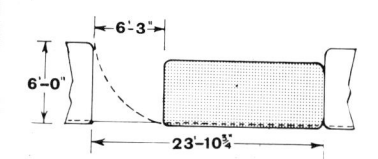

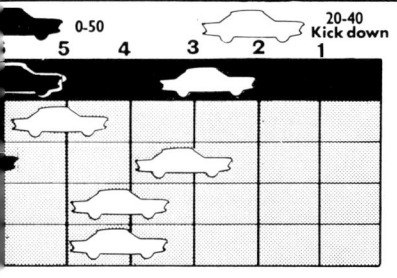

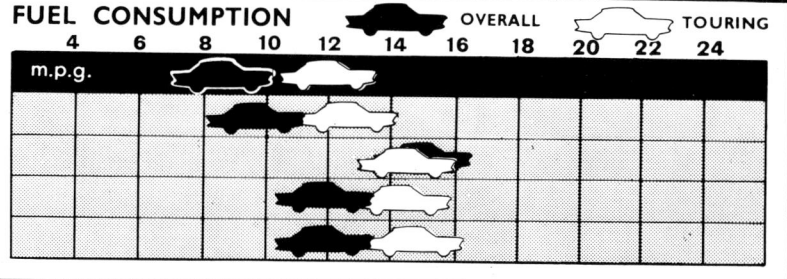

6'-3" 6'-0" 23'-10¾"

FUEL CONSUMPTION 0-50 20-40 Kick down OVERALL TOURING

Buick Riviera

(dry) bends without causing wheelspin or a slide, although the car will tighten its radius as more power is fed to the back wheels. Curiously, this predictable characteristic was far more pronounced when turning to the right.

Camber changes, even on a straight road, have a marked effect on the steering too and sometime call for quite large corrections. On a wet corner, an indelicate dab on the accelerator will send the tail flying outwards, a manoeuvre to be avoided since a sideways Riviera not only fills the road but demands some very rapid twirling of the steering wheel to recover. It is quite feasible, however, to balance engine against opposite lock and powerslide the monster if you are brave enough to try, though we found such a technique worried other motorists within a range of half a mile.

Despite this unsporting handling the Buick's roadholding is surprisingly good and it can be hammered round corners very fast indeed though not without a great deal of fuss from the tyres which deposit streaks of rubber on the road if you try too hard. An initial lurch as the car enters a corner suggests at first a lot of body roll but this is a false impression: in fact the body remains surprisingly level despite the car's very soft suspension.

For stopping from really high speeds the brakes are quite inadequate. Although we had the linings changed in the middle of our test, just one hard application from 100 m.p.h. was sufficient to fade them right out by the time the car had slowed to 40 m.p.h. In this one stop pedal pressure increased from around 40 lb initially to nearly 200 lb—or as hard as you can possibly push. The combination of duo-servo shoes, a powerful booster, and drum distortion from overheating (despite heavy finning) probably accounts for such rapid fade. Paradoxically, at lower speeds the brakes were good and they did not fade disastrously after 20 $\frac{1}{2}$g stops from 80 m.p.h., although they seemed to lose their balance and smoothness rather quickly. Never have we experienced such a Jekyll and Hyde character. No doubt the standard "soft" linings are adequate for American roads where speeds are generally limited to 75 m.p.h. at most, but in Europe much harder linings are needed if the car's performance is to be used safely.

Like many other American cars, the Riviera has a parking brake applied by foot and released by hand—a system that some drivers like and others do not. It works on the front drums and will just hold the car on a 1-in-3 hill yet is powerful enough to stall the engine if left on by mistake.

The paired headlights are normally concealed by clam-shell doors which keep the lenses clean but have no other useful function and prevent the driver from flashing the lights.

Comfort and controls

Luxury is the essence of the Riviera. The provision of only four seats in such a vast body creates the illusion of first-class travel in a transatlantic jet, and the driver does not have to exert himself in any way. All windows are electrically operated and so is the driver's seat movement: a small "joy stick" switch can be moved in four directions to bring hidden electric motors into action and so move the seat backwards or forwards, or alter its angle of tilt. By pulling on a stalk under the steering wheel, a ball joint at the top of the steering column is unlocked and the angle of the wheel can be changed through several positions.

All this effort to provide the ideal driving position is rather negatived by the fact that the only satisfactory driving position for most of our testers was with the seat fully back, and also fully tilted back, a situation governed largely by the length of the steering column. The accelerator pedal has a long travel and a 5 ft. 11 in. driver has to stretch right out to hit the kick-down position and there is little room to rest one's left foot beside the brake. The light steering calls for extended-arm use.

The seats themselves are very comfortable, if a trifle saggy, and hold the occupants fairly well, but the door and transmission tunnel can provide painfully hard knee rests when cornering hard. Electric operation is confined to the driver's seat and the front passenger has to resort to manual effort; no tilt is provided for the passenger.

Specification

1, facia locker. 2, rear window demister. 3, and 5, radio. 4, interior lights switch. 6, courtesy light. 7, side and head lights. 8, speedometer. 9, speed "buzzer" setting knob. 10, mileage recorder. 11, speed "buzzer" pointer. 12, clock. 13, direction indicators and main beam tell tales. 14, oil pressure. 15, petrol gauge. 16, temperature gauge. 17, washer/wiper. 18, gear selector. 19, heater fan. 20, heater controls. 21, parking brake release. 22, parking brake. 23, indicators. 24, steering wheel tilt control. 25, foot brake. 26, accelerator. 27, ignition/starter. 28, horn. Before Rudds' conversion, the steering wheel, pedals and instruments were on the other side.

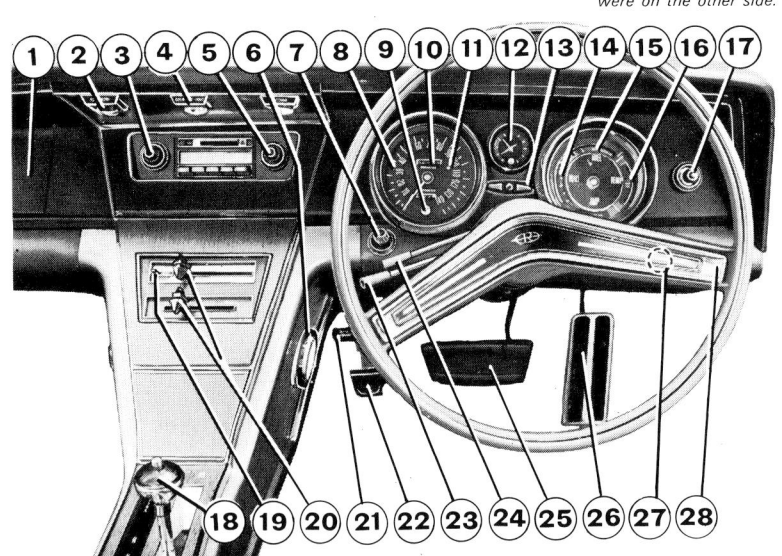

Engine

Cylinders	8
Bore and stroke	106.2 mm. × 92.5 mm.
Cubic capacity	6.965 c.c.
Valves	o.h.v. pushrod with hydraulic tappets
Compression ratio	10.25:1
Carburetters	2 4-barrel Carters with automatic choke
Fuel pump	A.C. mechanical
Oil filter	A.C. full flow
Max. power (gross)	360 b.h.p. at 4,400 r.p.m.
Max. torque (gross)	465 lb. ft. at 2,800 r.p.m.

Transmission

G.M. automatic transmission: torque converter and 3-speed epicyclic gear train.

Top gear	1.0–2.22:1
2nd gear	1.48–3.28:1
1st gear	2.48–5.50:1
Reverse	2.08–4.62:1
Final drive	Hypoid bevel, 3.07:1 with limited slip differential

Chassis

Construction	Cruciform frame with a separate steel body

Brakes

Type	Hydraulically operated drums, 12 in. × 2.25 in. front, 12 in × 2 in. rear. Servo assisted.
Total lining area	197 sq. in.

The ventilation system, though devoid of modern face-level outlets (unless air-conditioning is fitted) keeps the car nicely cool in hot weather with a strong blast from under the scuttle; in the left-hand-drive version tried last winter, it was found to produce furnace-like conditions in frosty weather. There is fine control of the temperature, but a fairly long lag before the new setting comes into effect.

Most of the dashboard switches are easy to reach but it is a pity that such over-ornate unlabelled knobs have been used. The centrally-mounted front ashtray is placed so as to be almost impossible to use without getting ash all round the outside. At speed, wind noise is high even with all windows shut and makes the mechanical quietness rather pointless, though we suspect that poor sealing of the driver's power window on our test car was largely to blame—even before the mechanism jammed an inch or two open.

The ride is soft and, if an undulating road is covered at speed, a certain amount of wallowing sets in but the seats do not bounce in sympathy and the driver is more aware of the condition than are the passengers. The rear seats, reached by tilting the front ones forward, are comfortable and a fifth person can be carried in the middle with the arm rest folded, but not in great luxury.

Forward and side visibility is good and the rear-view mirror shows all that is required, but bright sunlight can cause severe reflection of the facia in the front screen. Reversing into small spaces is very difficult; even when "sitting on tip-toe" the rear corners can not be seen at all. Otherwise it is an easy car to place, being slab-sided with high front corners.

The lights are not very good; they have ample spread but a poor range, even on full beam. They are concealed when switched off by electrically-operated clamshell doors, the relatively slow movement of which makes headlamp flashing out of the question. The only obviously useful function of this gimmick is to keep the lamp glasses clean.

Fittings and furniture

Four armchairs in a large space automatically give the Riviera a feeling of quality which is further augmented by deep carpets and subdued, tasteful colours. There is a massive central console which

A small "joy-stick" on the door controls movement of the seat—shown by the blurred operator. The cluster of window switches can be seen beneath the quarter light winder.

Although the boot is 65 in. wide, shallow depth makes it smaller than that of many comparable American cars. The test boxes total 9.4 cu ft.—less than the capacity of a Ford Corsair or Vauxhall Victor for instance. The ratchet-and-lever jack works very well.

Suspension and steering
Front	Independent by coil springs and unequal length wishbones
Rear	Live rear axle located by radius arms and coil springs
Shock absorbers:	
Front and rear	Telescopic
Steering gear	Saginaw, power assisted
Tyres	Firestone tubeless, 8.45 x 15

Coachwork and equipment
Starting handle	None
Jack	Pillar type with lever and ratchet
Jacking points	Under front and rear bumpers
Battery	12-volt, 70 amp-hour
Number of electrical fuses	14 plus 2 circuit breakers
Indicators	Self-cancelling flashers
Screen wipers	2-speed electric, self-parking
Screen washers	Push-button electric
Sun visors	2
Locks:	
With ignition key	Both doors
With other keys	Glove box and boot
Interior heater	Fresh air unit fitted as standard
Upholstery	Lurex cloth or p.v.c. according to colour
Floor covering	Carpet and rubber mats
Alternative body types	None

Maintenance
Sump	8.4 pints S.A.E. 10W/30
Gearbox	19 pints A.T.S.
Rear axle	3.7 pints
Steering gear	S.A.E. 90
Cooling system	31 pints (2 drain taps)
Chassis lubrication	Every 6,000 miles (see maintenance chart)
Ignition timing	12° b.t.d.c.
Contact breaker gap	0.016 in.
Sparking plug type	AC 445
Sparking plug gap	0.035 in.
Tappet clearances	Self-adjusting hydraulic
Front wheel toe-in	$\frac{7}{32} - \frac{5}{16}$ in.
Castor angle	$1° \pm \frac{1}{2}°$
Tyre pressures	24 p.s.i. front, 24-28 p.s.i. rear (according to speed and load)

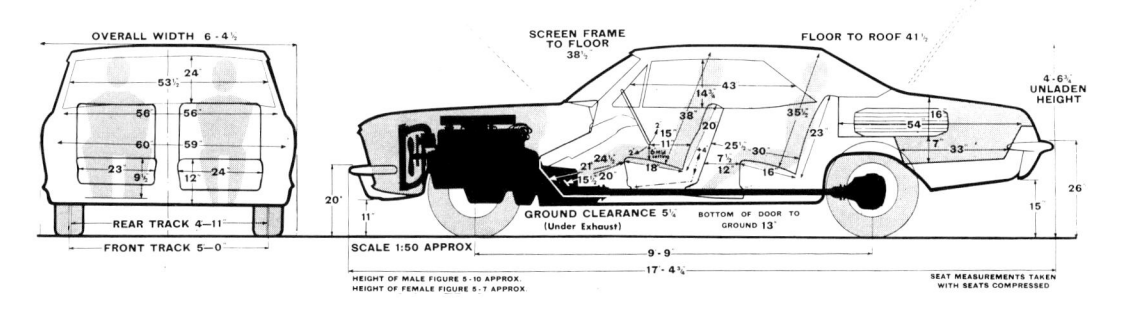

Buick Riviera

keeps the passengers well away from each other yet the flamboyant styling normally associated with American cars is conspicuously lacking.

Roof lining and door trim seem durable, practical and washable and wood inserts panel the facia and transmission tunnel. The instruments, housed in round dials, are clear and readable. Equipment includes six interior lights, a dipping mirror, rear window demister, coat hooks, front quarter lights opened by turning handles, two cigar lighters, lap straps, numerous Riviera emblems, a two-speed wiper and a screen washer that fires liquid like a machine gun.

There is not a lot of provision for odds and ends inside the car, although a great number of chattels could be laid on the floor without getting in anyone's way. Neither is the boot enormous by American standards: shallow depth and a large spare wheel make it more suitable for lots of small cases rather than a few big ones. Even so, it is fairly cavernous and its lid can be opened pneumatically by pulling a lever in the facia glove box.

The radio fitted (an extra) was an exceptionally good one with an electrically-operated aerial, and covered a very wide range of stations—Irish commercial radio and the B.B.C. Scottish Home Service, for example, coming through loud and clear in London E.C.1. The five push-buttons are lettered B-U-I-C-K, which is not very helpful.

No doubt strict speed limits in America make the "speed buzzer" (brought into operation when you exceed the speed set by a pointer on the speedometer) a useful extra but we found it very irritating. Fortunately, it can be permanently cancelled by setting at 100 m.p.h.

Servicing

Lifting the Riviera's bonnet, which is counterbalanced by springs, reveals an array of machinery which delights the heart of the engineer and strikes terror in the novice. Nevertheless, closer study reveals that everything is accessible although continuous stretching over the unit can be back-breaking. A large chromed air-filter of the pancake type completely conceals the carburetters and must be removed to reach them.

Routine maintenance is summarized below—not that an owner-driver of a Riviera is likely to do his own servicing. Not so clever is the fuel filler, concealed by the small low-mounted rear number plate which is spring-loaded shut with no catch to keep it open. Moreover, it is impossible to tip petrol in from a can without a length of tubing and a funnel.

Maintenance chart *left-hand drive model*

A   Power steering reservoir: check oil level (6,000 miles)
B   Petrol filter: replace (6,000 miles)
C   Oil filter: replace (6,000 miles or every 6 months—whichever comes first)
D   Crankcase ventilator: replace valve (12,000 miles)
E   Lower steering knuckle joints (2) and steering linkage (4): lubricate (6,000 miles or 6 months)
F   Upper steering knuckle joints (2): lubricate (6,000 miles or 6 months)
G   Engine sump oil: check periodically and replenish every 6,000 miles or six months
H   Upper control arm shafts (4): lubricate (6,000 miles or 6 months)
I   Automatic transmission: check oil level (6,000 miles); clean pan and refill (24,000 miles)
J   Manifold valve shaft: lubricate (6,000 miles)
K   Air cleaner: replace (12,000 miles)
L   Brake mechanism: lubricate (18,000 miles)
M   Limited slip differential: check oil level (6,000 miles). Flushing and seasonal changes not recommended
N   Universal joints on prop shaft: lubricate (6,000 miles)
O   Prop shaft slip spline: lubricate (12,000 miles)
P   Brake master cylinder: check and top up level (6,000 miles)
Q   Oil filler cap: wash and re-oil element (6,000 miles)

1, air cleaner. 2, brake servo. 3, windscreen washer bottle. 4, oil filler cap. 5, power steering pump. 6, fuse box. 7, battery. 8, gearbox dipstick. 9, engine dipstick. 10, alternator 11, petrol pump. 12, radiator filler cap.

MAKE Buick: MODEL Riviera: MAKERS Buick Division of General Motors Corporation, Flint, Michigan, U.S.A.: CONCESSIONAIRES Lendrum and Hartman Ltd., Flood St., London, S.W.13. Test car loaned by K. N. Rudd (Engineers) Ltd., 41, High St., Worthing 7773/4.

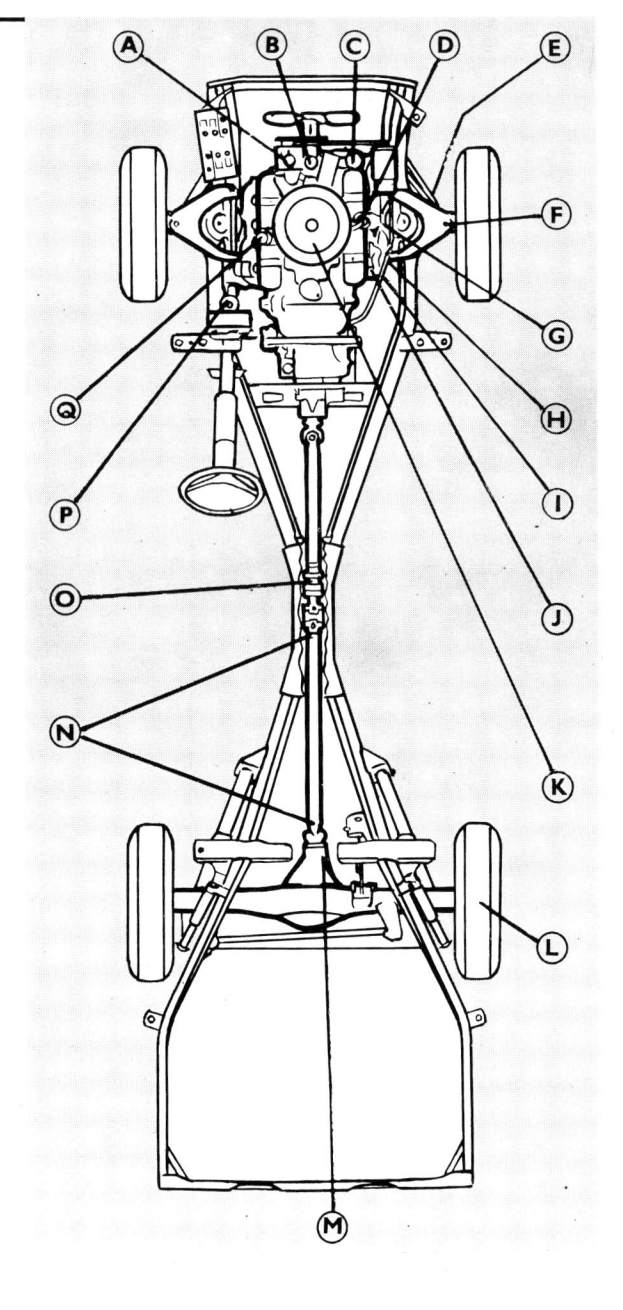

'66 Models

BUICK RIVIERA

ONE of the sleekest to look at, and best on the road, the Buick Riviera has been restyled for 1966. It is lower and longer with a wider look and many detail improvements. Standard power from the 6·5-litre vee-8 engine is 340 b.h.p., and the three-speed Super Turbine automatic transmission is practically unchanged.

At the front the grille has been revised to make the car look wider, and the headlamps have been moved back from the wings to behind the grille bars (where they used to be in 1963) with a drop-down mechanism that swings them forward when the switch is operated. Side lamps and turn indicators are now in the wings instead of under the bumpers.

Room for Six

Ventilation has been improved by positive extractors below the back window and the deletion of the front quarterlights. In addition to air outlets at foot level there are now three extra nozzles on the facia for face-level air flow.

The centre console is no longer fitted and there is room for three people in the front on a new bench seat with individual shaping. The panel on the passenger's side is farther forward than previously and incorporates a storage locker with a large drop-down lid. Instruments are all new with a rotating drum speedometer and dials instead of warning lamps. There is now the option of a floor shift lever and bucket seats, plus a woodrimmed steering wheel and refrigeration plant.

There are seven exterior colours and 15 interior ones, five more than before. Prices will not be available until the London Motor Show, 20-30 October.

Above: Headlamps are now behind the main grille, and the whole car looks longer, wider and lower for 1966. Below: Air now comes out of slots below the rear window and quarter-lights in the front windows are no longer needed. The body has much in common with the new Oldsmobile Toronado f.w.d.

Continued from page 29

and a seven-position steering wheel. These refinements however are of restricted utility. The seat has no variation of angle between the backrest and the seat cushion, and the wheel positions tend to the unnatural because the jointed boss is pivoted at a point on the steering column eight inches from the rim of the steering wheel. This means that when the wheel is nearest to a truck- or Indy-style position it is also at its maximum height from the seat while it ought to be at the minimum height. Conversely, when the wheel is nearest to a vertical position, it is at its lowest height, while it ought to be higher. Most of our driving was consequently done with the wheel in a perfectly normal position.

No matter what the road conditions or how many hours we stayed at the wheel, we never got tired. It's possible to spread the legs about as much as on a 300 SLR, and the arms can be held as straight as in a Grand Prix Maserati. The seat permits minute changes in position, so as to limit physical fatigue in any particular part of the driver's body without forcing him to sit differently. It's really very very nice, and our test drivers all agreed that they enjoyed getting back into the car every time.

The worst that can possibly be said about the Riviera from the passenger's point of view is that the air conditioner blows the ashes off his cigarette before he reaches the console-mounted ashtray. The air conditioner, of course, is a Frigidaire unit. It has three outlets; one wide grille in the center of the dashboard and two holes at the extremes, all with some adjustment for air flow direction. The fan has four speeds. During the 1963 model year, this air conditioner was fitted to 60% of the Riviera production. The air conditioning unit is completely separate from the heater and defroster, which offers particularly good temperature control by elimination of the water-control valve; the water circulates through the heater core at all times, regardless of heater control settings.

We can think of few more satisfying ways of travel than to ride behind the slim-rimmed wheel of a Buick Riviera, looking out over the wide and gently sloping hood and watching the fender tips and the oval Riviera emblem eat up the road ahead in majestic silence. The visual enjoyment is backed up by a degree of physical well-being which may well be unsurpassed. Like the Buick engineers, we might not make the Riviera exactly what it is if we were to start with a clean sheet, but we would be sorely tempted to use the existing model as a basis. **c/D**

CAR LIFE ROAD TEST

RIVIERA GRAN SPORT

SOME CARS are just plain harmonious—everything about them works together to form an impressive, eye- and ego-pleasing entity. Such is the 1966 Riviera, Buick's prestigious style-setter. It is far and away the most handsome car of the current crop, it has reasonably fine manners on the roadway and has good, strong performance; handsome is as handsome does!

Buick Motor Division of General Motors has considerably revamped its Riviera for the new model year and, while the mechanical package has been left virtually untouched, the car abounds in detail and styling improvements. Of course, the version tested here is the Gran Sport option, which puts on stiffer springs and things to make the car more appealing to the knowledgeable motorist. However, most of the improvements apply to all Rivieras, *Gran* or *limite*.

Most immediately apparent is the Riviera's new sleekness. Where before it had a rather chamfered crispness to its tailored looks, it now is frankly sensuous in its swooping lines. The broad, blunt front is still broad, but is more definitive in shape. Headlights now tuck up under the overhanging hood when not in use. The mid-section has a leaner look, yet swells into hip-like suggestions of rear fenders. Gone are the front corner vent windows, giving both the inside a better view outward and the outside a cleaner, neater window shape. The roofline flows rearward from the windshield header in true fastback fashion, truncating in a bobbed-off tail just like all the fast racing coupes of the sports car circuits. If the overall effect is reminiscent of certain European styled sports cars, at least the purity of their lines has been propagated and U. S. automotive styling is the better for it. Seldom does a single car emerge as visually exciting as this new Riviera.

Less apparent, because of the more careful styling, is that the '66 Riviera is a larger car than its predecessors. Where it previously had a 117-in.

an additional item of comfort for the long-distance driver, and which CL feels is a better arrangement than the buckets-and-console option. When the console is ordered, the automatic transmission (standard equipment for all Rivieras) shift lever is transferred from the normal steering column position and changed into an inverted U-shaped control atop the center divider.

Particularly appreciated by the CL testers were the slope-away fascia and the bin-type glove compartment. The instrument section is an inlay in the slope of the fascia, to present a well-ordered, black-backgrounded set of four dials, plus clock. The new digital-reading drum-type speedometer is extremely easy to read and a worthwhile innovation by GM.

The inside-out view has greatly improved with the elimination of the quarter panes. Upon entering the car, the driver feels he is in a greenhouse and immediately senses something missing. A few miles of driving and he wonders at all the visibility he'd missed before with that slim window-guide pillar in place. However, it's been replaced by a wind whistle—at least in the test car—at the front pillar.

Buick's new ventilation system utilizes the low-pressure area behind the fastback roof to draw out interior air. Pressurizing the passenger compartment by opening the front cowl vent also forces open a flap on the rear vent so fresh air can flow through. Unlike the Ford system, in which the rear vent is opened by a vacuum-powered valve, the Riviera's venting is automatic. On the test Riviera the fan-switch had to be "on" before the cowl vent would open. However, the outcome is the same, an abundant supply of noiseless fresh air without an annoying buffeting from opened side-windows. We expect this feature to be on all cars within a few years.

The Riviera chassis is probably the car's best selling feature outside of its handsome good looks. This chassis has the solidarity of a bridge truss and the integrity of a Federal Reserve Bank. In all driving conditions its performance is completely predictable and understood, fully without strange thumpings and bumping going on underneath. Particularly notable by its absence is that indefinite twisting, working "Flexible Flyer" feeling that seems to be part and parcel of all perimeter-frame type cars.

There's good reason for the absence:

wheelbase it now has 119 in.; where overall length and width were 209 and 76.6 in., they now are 211 and 78.8 in.; overall height has been increased 0.4 in. and curb weight has been increased by some 200 lb.

Most noticeable of all is the Riviera's high-styled interior. Here is where the car's elegance is manifested. Though leather-like fabrics are vinyl and the wood grain (GS models) is another form of plastic simulation, the overall effect is one of tastefully luxurious decor.

The bucket-type seats, of course, are optional, as is a bucket-shaped bench seat. The latter has a fold-down armrest between seatbacks, which provides

RIVIERA GS

The Riviera is one of the few U.S.-made passenger cars to retain the old self-supporting, rigid framework. Only Checker, Studebaker, Kaiser-Jeep Wagoneer, Chrysler Imperial and Cadillac Limousine continue this type of separate chassis and body construction. It is true that the perimeter frame cars also have separate bodies and frames, but their load-carrying assignments are completely different. On a perimeter frame car, the frame really serves only as a sub-frame, on which are attached engine, drive-line and suspension. The body is rigid and mounts atop the perimeter frame at the least number of points. The theory behind the perimeter car is to let the frame twist, and flex to damp out unwanted vibration while the body is isolated by soft rubber mounting pads. Noise, vibration and harshness are thus supposed to be prevented from reaching, and irritating, the passengers.

THE OLD RIGID, self-supporting frame which, for all intents and purposes, has been replaced by perimeters in the U.S. industry, harks back to Year One in automobile design. It is a direct descendant of the horse-drawn, and then horse-less, carriage. About 1929 Cord introduced a significant variation on the parallel-rail, ladder type of frame by putting an X-member in the middle, greatly increasing both beam strength and torsional rigidity. GM went a step farther in the late 1950s by removing the outer rails, leaving only a massive X-shaped chassis. But Buick, Cadillac and Chevrolet replaced their X or cruciform frames in '65, following the growing trend to perimeter frame/separate body construction started by Oldsmobile and Pontiac in 1961.

However, when the Riviera first appeared in the fall of '62, it was on a cruciform frame, despite the general trend of GM car design toward perimeters. And it has remained on the big X-frame since, even though the car was extensively redesigned for the '66 model and despite the fact that the sister-ship Toronado utilizes a perimeter type of understructure with its basically similar body.

Through its brute strength approach to the problem of structural rigidity, the cruciform frame achieves far more resistance to flexing and twisting than does the perimeter frame, which depends upon body rigidity to give the passengers and driver the feeling of vehicle strength. When a strong, semi-unit body such as the Riviera/Toronado structure is placed on top of an already strong chassis, the result is, as we've said, integrity and solidity. In this context, the Riviera knows no peer among General Motors passenger cars.

Operating from this sturdy bank vault of a frame/body construction are contemporary suspension systems, aided, in the case of the test car, by the Gran Sport option of stiffer springs and shock absorbers. The front suspension is a short- and long-arm independent system, incorporating ball-joints and link-type stabilizer. The lower arm incorporates a drag-strut front link. Integral power steering is standard equipment.

The rear suspension is pure GM live axle with four locating links and coil springs. Three links provide longitudinal location and stabilization, the fourth, a track bar, provides lateral location. One of the better systems now in use, it provides good axle location without incurring a penalty of extra stiff springing. With the two main links converging, that is pointing toward the center of the X-frame, some degree of

1966 BUICK RIVIERA GRAN SPORT HARDTOP COUPE

DIMENSIONS
Wheelbase, in.	119.0
Track, f/r, in.	63.5/63.0
Overall length, in.	211.2
width	78.8
height	53.4
Front seat hip room, in.	56.0
shoulder room	58.8
headroom	38.0
pedal-seatback, max.	47.0
Rear seat hip room, in.	55.0
shoulder room	57.4
leg room	35.2
head room	37.5
Door opening width, in.	49.5
Floor to ground height, in.	11.9
Ground clearance, in.	6.0

PRICES
List, fob factory	$4424
Equipped as tested	5940
Options included: GS package, chromed wheels, am/fm/stereo, speed control, air cond., power windows, bucket seats & console, power seat, tinted windshield, cornering lights, smog controls, 2x4 carburetion.	

CAPACITIES
No. of passengers	6
Luggage space, cu. ft.	10.3
Fuel tank, gal.	22
Crankcase, qt.	4
Transmission/diff., pt.	22/4.25
Radiator coolant, qt.	18.3

CHASSIS/SUSPENSION
Frame type.............cruciform
Front suspension type: Independent s.l.a., ball joints and coil springs; tubular shock absorbers within springs.
  ride rate at wheel, lb./in......180
  anti-roll bar dia., in.........0.781
Rear suspension type: Live axle, 4-link location; coil springs, tubular shock absorbers.
  ride rate at wheel, lb./in......160
Steering system: Power-assisted re-circulating ball nut; parallel links.
  gear ratio................15:1
  overall ratio.............16.6:1
  turns, lock to lock..........3.0
  turning circle, ft. curb-curb...44.0
Curb weight, lb................4375
Test weight...................4710
Weight distribution, % f/r....55/45

BRAKES
Type: Single-line hydraulic with self adjusting duo-servo shoes in composite drums.
Front drum, dia. x width, in..12 x 2.25
Rear drum, dia. x width....12 x 2.00
total swept area, sq. in......320.5
Power assist.........integral, vacuum, std. equipt.
  line psi @ 30 lb. pedal.......500

WHEELS/TIRES
Wheel size..............15 x 6.00L
bolt no./circle dia., in......5/5.00
Tire make, brand...Goodyear Power Cushion
  size..................8.45-15
  optional size available....8.85-15
  recommended inflation, psi.....24
  capacity rating, total lb......5120

ENGINE
Type, no. cyl..............ohv, V-8
Bore x stroke, in.........4.313 x 3.64
Displacement, cu. in...........425
Compression ratio............10.25
Rated bhp @ rpm........360 @ 4400
  equivalent mph..............104
Rated torque @ rpm.....465 @ 2800
  equivalent mph...............66
Carburetion..................2 x 4
  barrel dia., pri./sec..1.5625/1.6875
Valve operation: Hydraulic lifters, pushrods and rocker arms.
  valve dia., int./exh......1.875/1.50
  lift, int./exh.........0.439/0.441
  timing, deg.........29-81, 71-48
  duration, int./exh........290/299
  opening overlap...............77
Exhaust system: Dual, reverse-flow mufflers with separate resonators.
  pipe dia., exh./tail......2.25/2.00
Lubrication pump type.........gear
  normal press. @ rpm....40 @ 2400
Electrical supply..........alternator
  ampere rating min............15
Battery, plates/amp. rating....66/70

DRIVE-TRAIN
Transmission type: Torque converter with 2-position stator blades; planetary gearbox.
Gear ratio 4th ( ) overall....
  3rd (1.00)..............3.42
  2nd (1.48)..............5.06
  1st (2.48)..............8.48
  1st x t.c. stall (2.22).........18.7
  synchronous meshing....planetary
Shift lever location..........column
Differential type: Hypoid, pos. trac.
  axle ratio.................3.42

roll understeer is achieved. Earlier Rivieras had about 14% roll understeer, but the '66 model has about 20% — an increase of 50% which Buick engineers like to cite as "improving the handling." However, Gran Sport springing for the Riviera probably contributes more than the increased understeer to improved handling.

Changes in chassis and body for '66 have widened the Riviera's stance by 4 in. at the rear tread, 3 in. at the front. Rear springs are now mounted atop the Salisbury-type rear axle where they previously had been seated on the lower control arms. This allowed softer springs (105 vs. 160 lb./in. in '65 standard Rivieras) without unduly softening the ride—in fact, the '66s are a little firmer. Gran Sport springing is firmer still. Ride rates are 180/160 (front/rear) for the Gran Sport, as compared with 130/110 lb./in. for the standard Riviera.

Another change over the standard model is the Riviera's 15:1 steering gear ratio. This gives an overall ratio of 16.6:1 which is "faster" steering than any current U.S.-built car other than the Corvette. The steering wheel needs only three turns for lock-to-lock movement of the front wheels and this, along with the firm springing, imparts a feeling of nimbleness to the car. Instead of wallowing, it arrows along the highway and zips about town with the alacrity of a light-heavyweight boxer.

CL SAMPLED both engines available in the '66 Riviera, although it didn't collect acceleration data on the 425-cu. in./340-bhp standard version. The Riviera's only engine option is two 4-barrel carburetion which boosts horsepower to 360, but doesn't affect the torque rating. Buick says the 2x4 setup must be dealer installed, probably because of the lack of demand for it, and there are no other differences, other than carburetion, between the two engines. The single carburetor used is the new Rochester Quadrajet, which, as far as we could determine, delivered just as much performance as the optional, dual Carter AFB arrangement. As a point of comparison, the single Rochester has 10.92 sq. in. of throttle bore area at wide-open throttle, the dual AFBs have 16.62 sq. in.

The 425, of course, is Buick's standard big car engine of 401 cu. in. with an extra eighth of an inch bore. With the dual exhausts and low restriction air-cleaner fitted to the Riviera, the engine is a willing enough piece of machinery, although it seems to run out of revs too soon (at least by present HP and HO standards). During acceleration runs CL pulled over 5000 rpm in gears, but got better acceleration times by letting the transmission shift itself at 4200-4400 rpm. Though capability of only 16.7 sec. won't earn the Riviera any quarter-mile trophies, it at least is compatible with today's fast traffic-flow demands. The test car was equipped with the optional 3.42:1 axle ratio while the standard ratio is 3.23, which might reduce performance to a less than enthusiastic level.

One facet of the option list will interest those performance minded buyers of the Riviera GS. Standard tires are 8.45-15 Goodyear Power Cushion white-sidewalls. However, Firestone "Red-line" high performance nylon tires (low cord angle, but not radial ply) are available at no extra cost. Note that Riviera, along with all large Buicks, remains on 15-in. wheels. This gives Buick cars a better tire "footprint" area on the pavement and allows Buick to utilize larger diameter brake drums than any other U.S.-made car (except Cadillac, which also uses 12-in. drums).

Buick brakes often have been praised by CL. The Buicks we have

CAR LIFE ROAD TEST

CALCULATED DATA
Lb./bhp (test weight)	13.1
Cu. ft./ton mile	132
Mph/1000 rpm (top gear)	23.6
Engine revs/mile (60 mph)	2530
Piston travel, ft./mile	1530
Car Life wear index	38.9
Frontal area, sq. ft	23.4
Box volume, cu. ft	512

SPEEDOMETER ERROR
30 mph, actual	30.5
40 mph	40.5
50 mph	49.5
60 mph	59.0
70 mph	69.0
80 mph	79.0
90 mph	89.0

MAINTENANCE INTERVALS
Oil change, engine, miles	6000
trans./diff.	24,000/as req.
Oil filter change	6000
Air cleaner service, mi.	12,000
Chassis lubrication	6000
Wheelbearing re-packing	as req.
Universal joint service	6000
Coolant change, mo.	24

TUNE-UP DATA
Spark plugs	AC 44S
gap, in.	0.035
Spark setting, deg./idle rpm.	2.5/550
cent. max. adv., deg./rpm.	30/3900
vac. max. adv., deg./in. Hg.	19.5/12
Breaker gap, in.	0.019
cam dwell angle	30
arm tension, oz.	19-23
Tappet clearance, int./exh.	0/0
Fuel pump pressure, psi.	5.5
Radiator cap relief press., psi.	15

PERFORMANCE
Top speed (5050), mph	120
Shifts (rpm) @ mph	
3rd to 4th ( )	
2nd to 3rd (4400)	70
1st to 2nd (4200)	40

ACCELERATION
0-30 mph, sec.	3.0
0-40 mph	4.2
0-50 mph	5.9
0-60 mph	8.2
0-70 mph	10.7
0-80 mph	13.9
0-90 mph	18.4
0-100 mph	24.6
Standing ¼-mile, sec.	16.7
speed at end, mph	87
Passing, 30-70 mph, sec.	7.7

BRAKING
(Maximum deceleration rate achieved from 80 mph)
1st stop, ft./sec./sec.	22
fade evident?	no
2nd stop, ft./sec./sec.	21
fade evident?	slight

FUEL CONSUMPTION
Test conditions, mpg.	10.2
Normal conditions, mpg.	10-13
Cruising range, miles	220-286

GRADABILITY
4th, % grade @ mph	
3rd	14 @ 74
2nd	23 @ 53
1st	36 @ 41

DRAG FACTOR
Total drag @ 60 mph, lb.	223

ACCELERATION & COASTING (graph: MPH vs ELAPSED TIME IN SECONDS, showing 1st, 2nd, 3rd gears and SS ¼)

RIVIERA GS

HEADLIGHTS SWING down into place when light switch is pulled "on," retract upward when it's pushed "off." Cross-flow radiator lets Riviera have a low hoodline.

IN-AND-OUT ventilation system draws fresh air in through cowl vent, sends it to five outlets, then it pulls it out through a flap-protected opening below rear window.

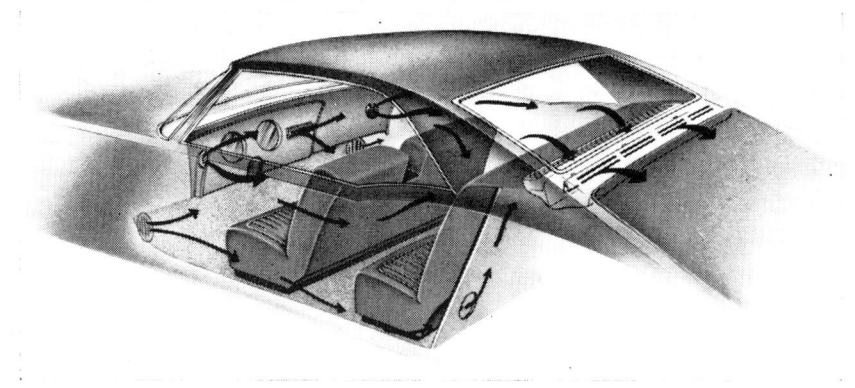

BUCKET SEAT interior features central console. Massive lever is automatic transmission control. Note how fascia slopes away from driver and passenger, giving added knee-space.

tested usually stopped well with minimum fade (though such is not the case with the smaller Buicks which seem to have just as bad brakes as the larger cars have good brakes). For one reason, Buick makes its front brake drums of aluminum, puts fins around their outer edge to aid cooling and bonds in an iron liner for a friction/rubbing surface. The combination of the larger diameter and the greater heat rejection properties of aluminum has given Buick significantly better brakes than those of manufacturers still using duo-servo drum-type brakes. CL testers generated maximum stopping power of 21-22 ft./sec./sec. for five consecutive stops from 80 mph before incipient fade became noticeable.

GOOD AS THESE brakes are, and they certainly represent the best of their type, they still cannot match the performance of disc brakes being used by competitors. Buick once upheld the banner of leadership in brakes, but must now be relegated to mediocrity because of the available superiority of disc brakes. Reference CL's tests of the Ford 7-Litre (Jan. '66 issue), the Corvette (Aug. '65), the Mustang GT-350 and Barracuda S (June '65), and the Thunderbird (Nov. and Dec. '64). The Riviera, and more particularly the Gran Sport variation, needs to have the best of everything.

Over-the-road handling of the Riviera GS is, for the most part, satisfactory. The heavy understeer on tight cornering is masked by the power steering and good roll resistance of the stiffer springing. If really pressed, the GS gives every indication of plowing head-first off the outside of the corner, which it would no doubt do if an imprudent driver continued his pressure. Once the GS owner learns the limits of adhesion, he can attain reasonably rapid velocities even on the twisting sort of roads. CL's biggest criticism in this area was for firmer shock damping. We know of several GS owners who have augmented their springing with such devices as Air-Lifts, or Delco Superlifts, and vastly improved their cars' appetites for non-straight roads.

Thus the Riviera GS in its 1966 form emerges as a satisfyingly adequate performer, capable of pleasing all but the most exacting driving enthusiast. And, with sufficient attention to detail modification, it could even please him. Of course, the Riviera can never really be as purely personal as the closer-coupled Corvette, but then the latter can't be a 4-6 passenger sedan, either. Here, then, is the Riviera's greatest appeal: It is a well-designed, well-finished, good-performing medium-sized sedan; one that can give its master pleasure in both driving and ownership. ■

TORONADO vs. RIVIERA
AN ON-THE-ROAD COMPARISON

AT FIRST LOOK, the only logical reason for buying an Oldsmobile Toronado over the Buick Riviera might be to obtain the mechanical novelty of front-wheel drive. Size, styling, passenger accommodation and performance, at least between Riviera and Toronado, are nearly on a par. But, where the Riviera retains tried-and-true, traditional front engine/rear-wheel drive, the Toronado offers a new front engine/front-drive arrangement. It's a powerful selling point, but is it a justifiable one?

Car Life sampled two early-production versions of the Toronado and Riviera and concluded that the Riviera is the better planned and finished car and that the Toronado is more roadable and stable under varied conditions.

In this latter context, the Toronado is outstanding. It has styling distinctive enough to make it stand out in any parking lot, and that styling shouts, "This is a front-wheel drive!" In a time when the outpouring of U.S. automotive design not only looks very much similar but is virtually identical in mechanical specification, the Toronado at least offers its buyer relief from the endless similitude.

The Riviera, too, has a distinctive styling and CL's reviewers found it the more refined and tasteful. But the Riviera has a drive-train just like that of every other Buick produced, so can offer no special appeal in this area.

Different people prefer different things. Good taste is good taste, no matter who likes or dislikes a design. The Riviera is a good example of good taste and good design. The Toronado is reasonably good design, but because of less refinement of its lines is not necessarily an example of good taste; it isn't gross enough in trim, proportion or finish to be in bad taste, it just doesn't come off as gracefully curved and pleasingly proportioned as does the Riviera. Side-by-side, or nose-to-nose, comparison quickly reveals the differences. The Riviera proclaims by purity of line and understatement that its occupants have enough confidence in their tastes to eschew ostentation.

Interior fittings tell the biggest story. The Riviera has all the elegance and attention to detail one must expect in a $5000 car. The Toronado appears to have been short-changed in this area in order to offset the expense of the much-costlier drive-train.

The Toronado with its flat floor develops one distinct advantage over the Riviera. With the standard bench front seat, the Toronado easily accommodates six adults. With the same seat, the Buick also seats six, but the two in the middle have to be either short-legged or uncomfortable. Otherwise, seating, knee-room, head-room and leg-room dimensions are virtually identical.

Straight-line accelerations are roughly comparable, unless weather or road-surface conditions are added to the consideration. Then the Toronado's greatest single advantage is immediately apparent. Wheelspin on takeoff is virtually impossible, even when Toro's front wheels are inches-deep in water. Traction on muddy, rain-slick streets is phenomenal —every bit as good as Olds claims it to be. On the other hand, the Riviera's rear-wheel drive skitters and slips all over the place when the throttle is injudiciously applied on even dusty pavement. The reason is obvious: Toronado has 61% of its test weight on its drive wheels where the Riviera has only 45%.

Over-the-road handling is the final major consideration and here again the Oldsmobile comes out ahead. Though a driver needs some experimentation before he can get the most out of the car, he will find the Toronado drives much like a normal car. On the other hand, the Riviera handles like a normal car in all situations; straight-line driving is comfortable and non-traumatic, curves taken too fast result in the car plowing off the road nose-first. The Toronado, has the great understeering nose-plow, too, but something can be done about it. When the driver finds he has entered the turn too fast and is being led head-first off the outside of the curve, he can slant his front wheels toward the inside of the curve, back off and then stand on the throttle and let the front wheels pull the car on around the turn. But, on straight, or mildly curving expressway, few non-enlightened drivers could tell the difference between the front and rear-wheel drives.

The Riviera scores mightily over the Toronado in the braking tests, achieving deceleration rates of 22 and 21 ft./sec./sec. in the first two all-on stops from 80 mph. The best the Toronado could do was 18 and 12 ft./sec./sec. and that was accompanied by rapidly building brake fade. Riviera went to five consecutive stops from 80 before fade made the brakes temporarily unreliable. Here, the hefty forward weight bias works against the Toronado.

The strong points for the Riviera, then, are quality of finish and esthetic appeal and good brakes. For the Toronado, advantages are a soundly engineered drive system which produces outstanding traction for both handling and adverse road conditions, and better utilization of interior space.

Either car should prove reliable and durable in the hands of the owner-driver. Both have a mechanical quality far above many cars in the same price range. But, the choice still comes down to whether or not the buyer with $5000 to spend wants the conversationally prestigious attributes of front-wheel drive over the esthetic appeal of the rear-wheel drive model. ■

BUICK RIVIERA GS ROAD TEST

THE RIVIERA IS BOUND *to change the driving habits of thousands of Americans* — they no longer will have a window-vent frame to cling to. ☐ This may distress many, but Riviera has more than enough that's new to make up for this reversion to the past. Three types of seating are now available: standard bench seats for 6-passenger capacity, optional buckets with center console that holds a new shift handle, and the new "Strato-Bench" notch-back seats with center arm rest and bucket-like looks. ☐ The dash, also redesigned, uses real gauges plus a new drum-type speedometer. However, we do wish they'd put some markings (like numbers maybe) on gauge faces to permit accurate readings. Except when the tank is "½" full, you can only guesstimate its content. A bin-type glove compartment doesn't spill things on the floor when opened, but, like the trunk, it's a bit small and lacks real carrying capacity. ☐ The "Strato-Bench" seats proved quite comfortable for long or short trips. There's an optional reclining feature for the passenger's side, and our test car's 4-way power plus tilting steering wheel gave a wide range of driving positions. Head room, leg room, and knee- and foot room were adequate, front and rear, with nice, wide-opening doors and tilting seatbacks to allow easy rear-seat entry and exit. ☐ These same doors, though, create problems when parked close to another vehicle in a parking lot. They're very heavy and getting in or out in close quarters is a chore. Opening them uphill takes a real effort. ☐ Looking back for parking or backing turned up another problem — that of rear vision. A smallish rear window, plus large rear-quarter blind spots and optional head rests restrict your view severely. ☐ But the real joy of owning the Riviera GS (that's "Buickese" for heavy-duty suspension, 15-to-1 quicker steering, a 3.23 performance axle with positive traction, and ornamentation) comes from driving it. It's fast — should top 120 mph easily. It handles very well for a 4400-pound automobile on a 119-inch wheelbase. And its big, 12-inch brakes, with finned aluminum drums in front and finned cast-iron drums in the rear, give it excellent stopping control. Add to this a set of 8.45 x 15 premium red-line tires with 32 psi up front and 30 psi in back — and you've got a luxurious 6-seater that'll adhere quite well to a winding road. ☐ Buick doesn't offer the twin-4-barrel setup as a factory option this year, but 340 is still a lot of horses when all 4 barrels of the single big Rochester are open. Zero to 60 mph in 8.6 seconds and an 84-mph quarter-mile run in 16.4 seconds spell performance with a capital "P." Buick calls this a "tuned" automobile, and it's very well tuned indeed, with all components working toward a common goal — a very uncommon automobile. ☐ We've mentioned its ability on corners. On fast straightaways it tracks unswervingly, actually feeling better as speed increases. And, when the end of the straight is reached, those husky, finned brakes give a great feeling of security as they bring this 4400-pound fastback to a straight stop, time after time. ☐ Whisper-quiet at 80+ mph, the ventless Riviera gives good ventilation via new intake openings and exhaust vents just behind the back window. It works best when all windows are closed. ☐ A real attention-getter, it attracted admiring glances wherever we went. No one asked if it was a Toronado. Comments such as "sharp, wild, and sexy" were heard about its new styling. We also received many compliments on the car's tastefully executed interior. ☐ Stretched out to 63 inches, the wider rear track aids handling. The car is also 3 inches longer, 2 inches wider and has gained 2 inches in wheelbase, plus more inside room. ☐ The Riviera GS is one of the most exciting new cars for 1966. It's a driver's car that handles, stops and goes like it seated two in the open rather than six in relaxing, closed comfort. How about that, sports-car fans? — R.M.

LEFT FRONT TIRE FOLDING OVER IS ONLY INDICATION THAT EDITOR MC VAY IS CORNERING WITH VERVE. GS SUSPENSION REALLY STICKS.

Comprehensive instrumentation is marred by casual calibrations. You're "F-½-E."

Riviera shares GM "E" body shell with Olds' Toronado, but Buick stylists managed to make it look tastefully different. No American car has a lower, easier-to-look-over hood.

Thanks to a new perimeter frame, tunnel is much less pronounced than it appears in this picture. Medical opinion is still split on protection provided by optional head rests.

Stylish rear quarter abets looks but not parking ease. Tail lights aren't sequential.

BUICK RIVIERA GRAN SPORT   2-door, 6-passenger coupe

ACCESSORY PRICE LIST

360-hp engine (dealer-inst.)	$254.71
*Automatic transmission	std
4-speed transmission	—
Overdrive	—
Limited-slip differential	incl. w/H-D susp.
*Heavy-duty suspension	176.82 pkg. (GS)
Whitewall tires	std
Disc brakes	—
*Power brakes	std
*Power steering	std
*Power windows	105.25
Power seat	69.47
*Radio AM	88.41
Radio AM/FM	175.24
*Air conditioning	421.00
*Tinted glass	42.10
*Bucket seats	std
*Adjustable steering wheel	std
*Clock	std
Tachometer	47.37
Automatic headlight dimmer	—
Automatic speed regulator	63.15
Vinyl roof cover	—
Head rests (with reclining seat)	84.20

*On test car
Dash (—) — not offered

MANUFACTURER'S SUGGESTED LIST PRICE: $4424 (incl. taxes, safety equip't & PCV device)
PRICE OF CAR TESTED: $5503.31 (incl. excise tax, delivery & get-ready charges, but not local tax & license)
MANUFACTURER'S WARRANTY: 24,000 miles and/or 24 months

SPECIFICATIONS FROM MANUFACTURER

ENGINE IN TEST CAR: Ohv V-8
Bore and stroke: 4.3125 x 3.64 ins.
Displacement: 425 cu. ins.
Advertised horsepower: 340 @ 4400 rpm
Max. torque: 465 lbs.-ft. @ 2800 rpm
Compression ratio: 10.25:1
Carburetion: 1 4-bbl
TRANSMISSION TYPE AND FINAL DRIVE RATIO: Automatic, Super-Turbine, 3-speed w/torque converter; 3.23:1

SUSPENSION: Coil springs at each wheel, ball joints at front; tubular shocks used with springs
STEERING: Recirculating ball nut, integral w/power piston
Turning diameter: 44.0 ft., curb to curb
Turns lock to lock: 4.0
WHEELS: Disc type; steel
TIRES: 8.45 x 15 tubeless rayon
BRAKES: Hydraulic, duo-servo, self-adjusting
Diameter of drum: front, 12 ins.; rear, 12 ins.
SERVICE:
Type of fuel recommended: premium-grade
Fuel capacity: 21 gals.
Oil capacity: 4 qts.; with filter, 5 qts.
Shortest lubrication interval: 6000 mi.
Oil- and filter-change interval: 3000 mi.
BODY & FRAME: Cruciform-type construction
Wheelbase: 119.0 ins.
Track: front, 63.5 ins.; rear, 63.0 ins.
Overall: length, 211.2 ins.; width, 78.8 ins.; height, 53.4 ins.
Min. ground clearance: NA
Usable trunk capacity: NA
Curb weight: 4400 lbs.

PERFORMANCE

ACCELERATION (2 aboard)
0-30 mph .... 3.1 secs.
0-50 mph .... 5.2 secs.
0-60 mph .... 8.6 secs.
TIME & DISTANCE TO ATTAIN PASSING SPEEDS
40-60 mph .... 4.5 secs., 330 ft.
50-70 mph .... 5.0 secs., 440 ft.
STANDING-START QUARTER-MILE: 16.40 secs. and 84 mph
BEST SPEEDS IN GEARS @ SHIFT POINTS
1st .... 44 mph @ 4800 rpm
2nd .... 73 mph @ 4700 rpm
3rd .... 114 mph @ 4700 rpm
MPH PER 1000 RPM: 24
SPEEDOMETER ERROR AT 60 MPH: .05%
STOPPING DISTANCES: from 30 mph, 28 ft.; from 60 mph, 154 ft.

NA — Information not available at presstime

BUICK RIVIERA
beauty only skin deep?

Since its introduction in 1963, the Buick Riviera has certainly had what publicity men would call "a good press". Although it blazed no new engineering trails and could only be called conventional in all respects except body styling, the car was clasped to the automobile magazine bosom and almost smothered with affectionate adjectives.

Why?

In the first place, the Riviera slipped into a segment of the automobile market which was thinly covered: The luxury two-seater, or 2 plus 2 class. This "sporty" type of big car was pre-eminent in the days of the classics. It throve during the period of big money and general affluence but expired during the depression and, with the notable exception of the Thunderbird, was never really revived. So it was something new.

Secondly, the Riviera wasn't all bad. It certainly wasn't the answer to everything wrong with cars or as unbearably glorious as some reports would have you believe, but it succeeded in most of its aims and could be driven with some confidence. Third, this is exactly the kind of prestigious car that the young executive, or even not-so-young, (such as automobile magazine editors) would go for as personal transportation. It is strikingly handsome to most tastes; has a lush interior; can be fitted with every comfort and convenience group spawned by the fertile industry and is in a price bracket not every buyer will venture into.

In 1966 Buick added to the car's market appeal by enlarging it a bit and giving it another styling twist. This move was made in order to take advantage of the new Toronado body shell basically but it reacted well as far as the Riviera was concerned. The 1966 chassis is on 119 inch wheelbase, instead of 117 and wheel track has been increased to 63.5 inches, front, and 63 inches rear (from 60.5 front and 59 rear) which puts it right next to the wide-track models. The car also gained over 200 pounds since last year making it right there with the T-Bird at nearly 4800 pounds with air and normal equipment.

IN T-BIRD COMPANY

The Riviera is smack up against the Thunderbird in the market and pretty competitive with the Toronado. It might also be the choice of the potential Cadillac owner who has an interest in performance and handling. In price, you can come out with a T-Bird and the same equipment for about $125 less than a

Riviera (retail before shipping, tax and license). A Toronado will cost you $200 more than a Riviera.

This leaves the buyer a fairly clean cut choice based on worth, rather than price (after all, what is a couple of hundred dollars when you are investing $5,500?). So how does the Riviera stand comparisons?

Well, it depends on which Riviera you are talking about. You can get a stock Riviera; you can pay $175 additional for the "Gran Sport" package or, you can add a couple of Buick options to the stocker for about $50 that will achieve a great deal.

In showroom form, the Riviera has very satisfactory highway manners for a car of this size and intent. This is especially true on the super-highway, or any smooth thoroughfare with sweeping curves. Its suspension reacts well to gradual changes of direction and 8.45 x 15 tires on the 6L ("Safety") rim provide enough tread patch to maintain good traction up to about .4-.5g. Above this the front end begins to plow, so it is not possible to throw the Riviera around really twisty roads with the abandon of a sports car. In addition, shock control and roll stiffness are not sufficient to prevent wallowing during transition. Sharp S-curves and the like are not this car's meat. Steering is a little quicker than average.

The Gran Sport's suspension package makes a great deal of difference. It won't turn the Riviera into a Corvette, but the higher spring rates, different shock valving and larger anti-roll bar stiffen the car enough to make it quite acceptable for touring. It also reduces the tendency to bottom on sharp dips.

For approximately $50.00 you can add H.D. springs and Positraction to the Riviera. Combined with some proprietary replacement shock absorbers such as Gabriel Silver E, Delco Superlift, etc. this will give you the best part of the Gran Sport package at less cost. Actually, it would probably be more satisfactory in one respect inasmuch as the Gabriels or whatever will outlast the stock Delcos by several thousand miles and will be better in the first place as far as damping goes. (The stock shocks on the 1964 Riviera owned by photographer Bob McKay were replaced at 30,000 miles and had been sick for a long time.) You have to order the springs and shocks with the car to take advantage of the $3.75 cheap price. Dealer-installed after the car is delivered would run $80 or so. While there are enthusiasts who prefer to set the car up like this using proprietary items, the fact that Gran Sports are bringing up to $200 more retail and $150 wholesale around the Los Angeles area used car marts makes it a more attractive deal to buy the GS initially.

BRAKING ABILITY

We have dwelt on the handling of the Riviera because it is one of the better features and certainly a factor which sets it off from the Thunderbird. In the realm of brakes, which should go right along with handling it is only so-so where it could be great with a little more effort on the part of the company. A top grade lining is used (Inlite 8818-L) and metallics are not an option. Drum swept area is 320 square inches versus 328 for Oldsmobile and 414 for Chrysler models which are in this gross weight bracket, so it is not exceptional but, by using finned aluminum muffs over cast iron 12 inch drums at the front, the Riviera's brakes are able to dissipate more heat and do retain stopping capability longer under duress than the more conventional type.

In action, as opposed to theory, the Riviera will maintain a 22 ft/sec.^{2} deceleration rate from 60 mph in a straight line. It takes constant attention to brake pedal and steering wheel, but you can bring the car to a halt in 180 feet this way. At anything over 22 ft/sec.^{2} the rear wheels lock up and the car wants to go sideways. We have read reports which alleged that this sort of deceleration rate could be maintained from 80 mph for five stops but our tests did not bear out this contention.

On the subject of tires: Extra capacity on the Riviera is not high. The 8.45s have a rating of 1280 pounds each. This gives the front end pair an extra load availability of 160 pounds, total, over curb weight. When the car is at its travelling weight with four passengers and luggage, it is right on the edge of the 720 pounds allowable before tires exceed their rating. You can fit 8.85s (which come with Electras) and gain an extra 360 pounds of capacity. Your dealer, who should be anxious to cultivate you in a sale of this magnitude, can accomplish the switch.

POWER, PERFORMANCE & ECONOMY

There is no doubt that the Riviera has plenty of power for most occasions. The 425 cubic inch, 360

Cornering sequence shows Riviera out of shape. GS package greatly improves handling of this lush car.

Front bumper offers no protection. Close to six-inch offset makes entire front end vulnerable to attack.

Dials are self-contained in box on dash. Barrel-type speedometer is hard to read, has no fixed reference.

Braking tests revealed tendency to lock up rear wheels and slide. 22 ft/sec² was best repeated figure for car.

horsepower engine coupled to the torque-converter/ 3-speed planetary transmission, (manual is not available), and a 3.23 final drive doesn't allow fantastic acceleration in a car of this weight, but the combination is quite responsive at highway speeds. The Buick's torque peak is at 2800 rpm, equivalent to 67 mph, so all of the whomp is available in this range for passing.

The GS engine is fitted with two Carter AFB (aluminum four-barrel) carburetors instead of the single Rochester four barrel on the regular Riviera. This, with the modified exhaust system, ups the horsepower rating to 360 but has no noticable effect on performance.

As far as fuel economy goes, economy is hardly the word to apply to a car in this category since no buyer will be seriously concerned. The 1963 and 1964 staff-owned models have a lifetime average of around 11 mpg. The 1966 is in the same target area with 10-11 mpg. Oil consumption is one quart to each 1800 miles, approximately. This seems to be standard and doesn't change much with mileage up to the point of ring failure. The 1964 model had an initial ring-seating problem and used excessive amounts of oil during the first 12,000 miles and carboned up the top end. This was cheerfully corrected by the dealer under warranty.

UPKEEP AND REPAIRS

At first, both of these engines would run without pinging only on Standard Supreme (white pump). As they matured, they would tolerate 90 plus octane, but lost a little snap in acceleration. The 1963 has been exemplary in maintenance, requiring only normal attention and infrequent service. The 1964, on the other hand, is difficult to keep in tune. Within 500 miles after plugs are cleaned or replaced, points gapped and timing set, it loses sharpness. This isn't an isolated owner-complaint, but it isn't remarkably frequent either.

Tire mileage on a 1966 can be estimated at about the 20,000 miles per set attained by the 1963 if driven and loaded conservatively. The increased tire size of the later models just about keeps pace with their weight increase. So we have a 17,800 mile average for the 9 tires used on the 1964 in 40,000 miles. However, this car has been driven several thousand miles over more abrasive roads than those found in the United States, primarily in Mexico.

Buick recommends 6,000 mile service intervals on this car (oil, filter and lubrication). To this can be added a tune up and sparkplugs if you want to keep it sharp. The big problem with most Rivieras and other cars in this bracket is the formation of carbon in the combustion chamber because the engine is seldom blown out. It has so much mid-range power, gearing is so high and it is generally used so much at

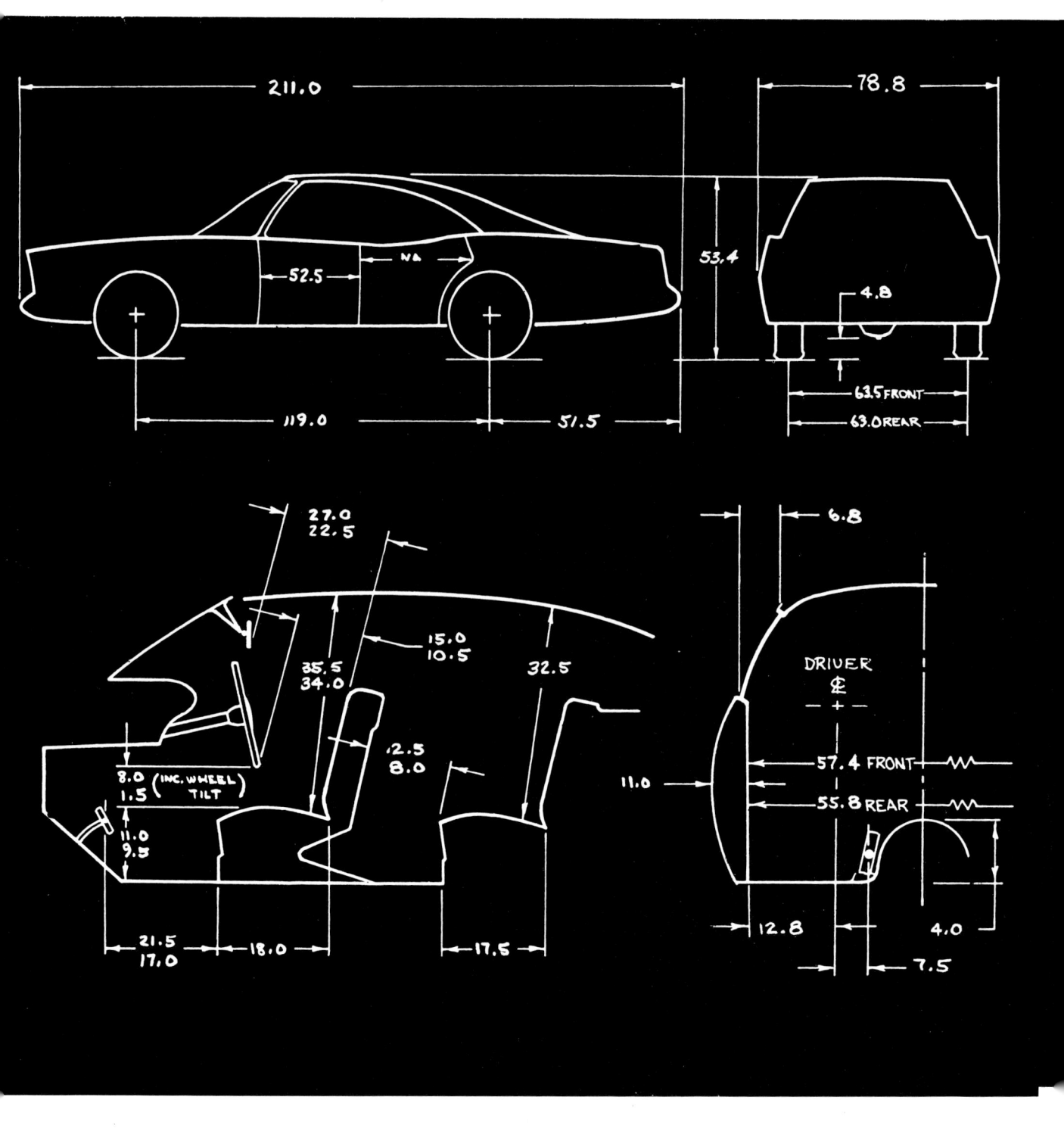

SPECIFICATIONS
Curb weight 4316
Weight dist. 55/45
Brake type . . . . drum
Swept area, sq. in. 320
Steering, turns 3.0
Turning circle 39.7
Std. ratios (automatic)
3rd 1.00:1
2nd 1.48:1
1st 2.48:1

Engine
Type . . . . V-8 ohv
Bore 4.31
Stroke 3.64
Disp. cu. in. 425
Comp. ratio 10.25:1
BHP @ rpm 340/4400
Torque @ rpm 465/2800
Clutch dia. . . . .

Acceleration
0-30 mph, sec. 3.7
0-40 . . . . 5.1
0-50 . . . . 7.5
0-60 . . . . 10.0
0-70 . . . . 13.6
0-80 . . . . 17.0
0-100 . . . . 31.6
50-70 . . . . 6.7
60-80 . . . . 7.3
Tire size . . . . 8.45 × 15

low speeds that this condition is a natural by-product. For this reason we tend to discount the complaints of many owners about dull performance or early engine repairs.

HOW DOES IT STACK UP?

The Riviera's long suit is comfort. Like the T-Bird, it accents deep dish seats and opulent appointments. We tend to rate its interior higher than the Bird because there is two inches more legroom for the front seat passengers. Also the bench seat with center armrest is actually usable by either two or three. The transmission hump is markedly low and gives a more spacious feel to the front compartment. Rear seat legroom, thanks to the increase in wheelbase, is pretty fair. The front seat track (with power seat) is somewhat short, but with it fully rearward, there is still knee room. Headroom in the rear is adequate for the person up to 5' 11" at which point there is only two inches of headroom and a good bump will bounce him off the roof (assuming that he isn't wearing the standard-equipment seat belts).

The ventilation system like the Toronado and others, is first rate. There is sufficient air circulation to remove the smoke generated by four chain-smokers but never the sensation of a draft. In hot weather, this feature is dispensed with in favor of the air conditioning unit with which dealers tell us, 95% of all Rivieras are ordered. Manually-controlled air costs $418, the thermostat-controlled type is an extra $62. This investment is repaid at Bluebook-looking time with a $275 allowance on the wholesale side.

The storage space is minimal for a car of this size, as it is in all domestics, but at least the glove box is fully usable. It tilts out like a bin and retains all the small objects deposited therein.

Visibility is excellent thanks to several styling ideas. Sloping hood and tilting wheel, combine to make forward vision unobstructed. The thin, angled pillars almost eliminate this near blind spot and side vision is no better in the blister of a PBY, because of the extreme tumblehome in the windows. Rearward, the slanted top obtrudes somewhat into the mirror, but very few cars are attacked from above, so this isn't serious. The only real blind spot is the off side rear quarter . . . and it isn't as bad as the Toronado.

Although the car is luxurious in trim, upholstery and hardware, the examples we have been able to study closely are no better in workmanship than average. On the 1964, the power window motor fell off early on in its lifetime and the windows have been improperly (and permanently) regulated so that the doors won't open if the windows are up. If the doors are closed with the windows up, the top edge of the glass is outside the channel. You'll find the same factory assembly miscues as on the Chevrolet or Ford but, of course, they'll be on more handsome material.

In short, the Riviera is not a supercar. However, it is considerably ahead of the Thunderbird or Toronado in all respects and it really stacks up as a better-than-average machine because of its road manners and comfort. Braking ability could definitely be improved but it isn't that much worse than other cars of this weight and is way ahead of the Toronado.

You can make a pretty fair deal on a Riviera, discounts are going up to around $800 or so on a load and you might even do better. The dealer has about $1,000 going in on the base price and $400 plus on the average list of accessories. Depreciation (off list) in a year is about $1,200, so you won't come off too badly.

The Riviera is, altogether, a fairly decent way to go. Given the GS modifications it rides and handles well without being harsh and is, by all standards, the best-feeling car in this size range. In the opinion of the ROAD TEST staff, if this type of car suits your fancy you couldn't do any better on the present market. ∎

Front seats are lush and comfortable. Upholstery is very good; armrest separates bucket-type seats.

Photos/Jim Gilbert

HOW THEY COMPARE

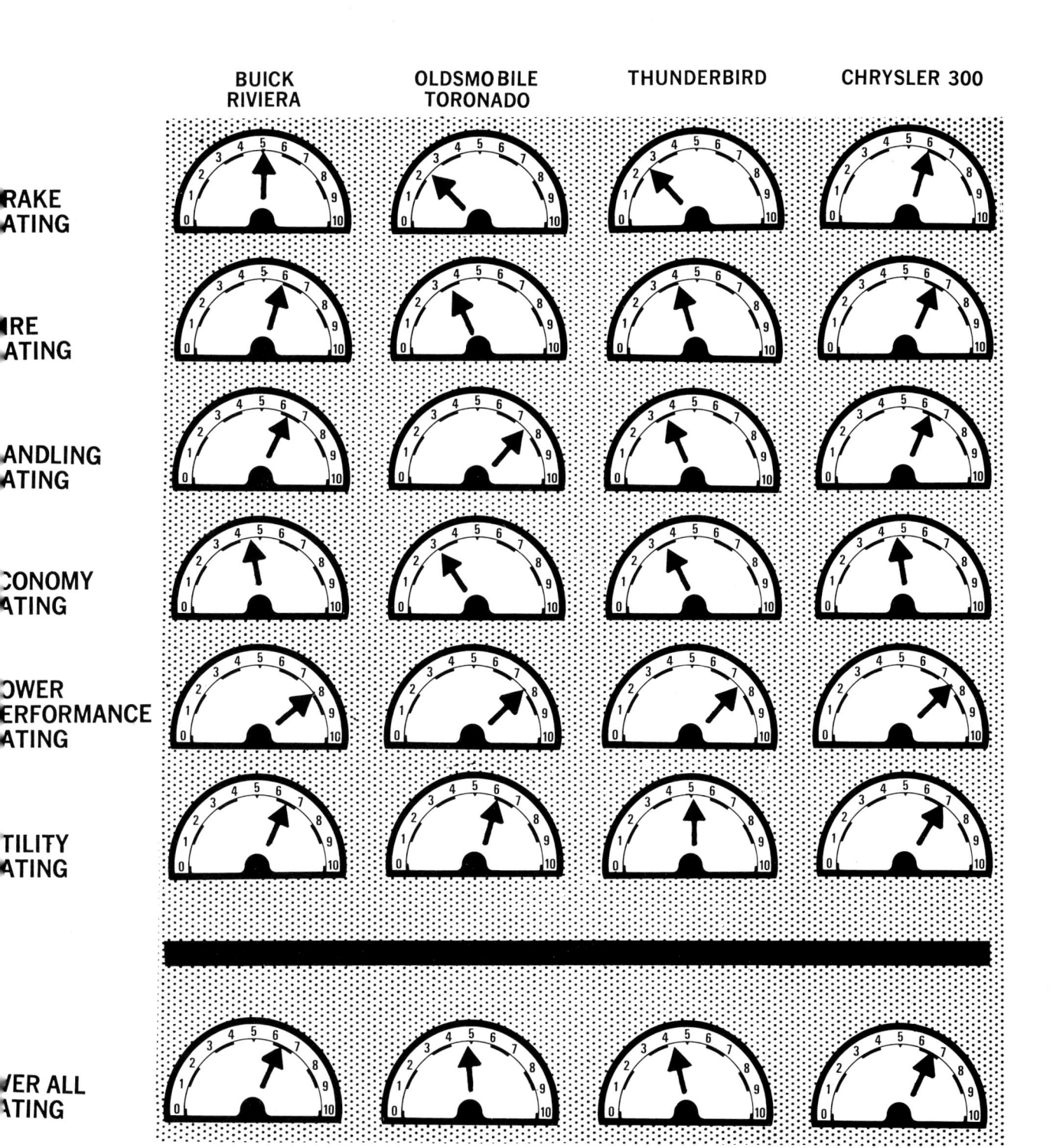

	BUICK RIVIERA	OLDSMOBILE TORONADO	THUNDERBIRD	CHRYSLER 300
BRAKE RATING	5	3	3	6
TIRE RATING	6	5	4	6
HANDLING RATING	6	7	4	6
ECONOMY RATING	5	3	3	5
POWER PERFORMANCE RATING	7	7	7	7
UTILITY RATING	6	6	5	7
OVER ALL RATING	6	5	5	6

* SEE PAGE 3 FOR EXPLANATION OF ROAD TEST RATINGS.

Toronado vs Riviera

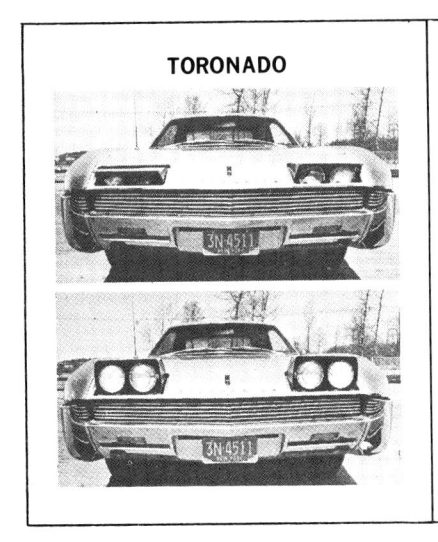

TORONADO	RIVIERA

Both cars feature now-you-see-them-now-you-don't blinkers. Toro's rest under faired-in, lift-up eyebrows, while Riviera sports drop-down units. Exposed units ruin the frontal appearance of the Toro. Test car's blinkers were slightly out of sync. Both cars rest on 119-inch frames, with the Riviera's being the sturdier of the two.

CARS ROAD TEST

IT ALL STARTED like this: "C'mon chief, you must be kidding! Spend two weeks testing what? A Toronado and a Gran Sport Riviera? Like we have a Plymouth street hemi with Stahl "tubes", 4.10's, Goodyear "cheaters" and a lot of trick stuff between the rails, and a new factory built D/Stock Dodge Dart just waiting for us. Charlie and George at Pacers are just about finished with both of them and the weather looks real good for strip stompin'. What do you want with reports on those flakey *plushmobiles?* Man, barges are out, supercars are in!"

Since the guy at the other end of the horn has some influence on the writing of checks each Friday and touring around the countryside isn't really that bad, we stashed out street hemi and D/Dart plans for another time and packed up all necessary test goodies.

Test plans called for one week with a Toronado and the following one with a Riviera. Since there are no performance options listed for the Toronado we settled for a stocker from the local zone office pool.

GM's Grandest Touring Rigs battle it out for the Number One spot in the Heavyweight Division of the Musclecar Sweepstakes

1966 OLDSMOBILE TORONADO SPECIFICATIONS

ENGINE

Type	OHV V-8
Displacement	425 cubic inches
Compression Ratio	10.5 to 1
Carburetion	Single Rochester Quadrajet
Camshaft	Hydraulic, .431/.433 inches lift
Horsepower	385 @ 4800 rpm
Torque	475 foot/pounds @ 3200 rpm
Exhaust	Dual pipes, resonators & mufflers
Ignition	Single point

TRANSMISSION

Make	Turbo Hydra-Matic
Control	Column shift lever

REAR END

Type	Beam axle, front wheel drive
Ratio	Drive planetary 3.21-to-1

BRAKES

Front	11 x 2.75-inch drums, power assisted
Rear	11 x 2-inch drums, power assisted

SUSPENSION

Front	Independent, ball joints, torsion springs, stabilizer links
Rear	Solid axle, four shocks, single leaf springs
Steering	Power-assisted
Overall Ratio	17.8-to-1

GENERAL

List Price	$4800
Price As Tested	$5900
Weight	5000 pounds
Wheelbase	119 inches
Overall Length	211 inches
Tire Size	8.85 x 15 US Royal Laredo

PERFORMANCE

0 to 30 mph	3.3 seconds
0 to 60 mph	9.0 seconds
Standing ¼ mile mph	85 mph
Elapsed Time	17.9 seconds
Top Speed	125 mph
Economy	10 mpg

We were much more fortunate, when we went to pick out a Riviera. We lucked out and located a dual quad-equipped full Gran Sport model, which also carried a full array of power and luxury options.

Upon completion of the two week test we had racked up approximately 600 miles on each car's odometer. This included stop and go city traffic, high speed Thruway hauling, hill climbing in the Catskills and a few passes through the traps. Since we were deprived of our MoPar toys for two weeks, we managed to take in a couple of days of local drag racing. We ran the Riviera through the eyes at New York National Speedway, without any fanfare on a busy Saturday night, and repeated the play on Sunday at the Madison Township track in Englishtown, New Jersey. Since these cars were not designed for quarter mile charging and performance packages are a rarity, we will not go into detail on their quarter-mile potential. The results of our trips to the track can be found in the specification charts.

By the time we were finished testing our respect for these heavyweight GT fastbacks skyrocketed. Handling and performance proved to be on par with lighter, smaller musclecars and the appointments and overall appearance of the Toro and Riviera are obviously far superior.

In every sense of the word the Toronado and Riviera Gran Sport are genuine high performance cars. They were not designed for brute force acceleration, unreal top end or road racing handling. They are in truth, genuine high performance grand touring machines. They're capable of scatting away from a traffic light ahead of most of the average stop light Grand Prix machines, cruising all day at speeds 30-40 over the legal limit and lapping a sports car handling course a shade slower than the all-out musclecars. Besides all the performance plus-features, both cars boast the sexiest styling to hit the domestic market since the 810 Cord and the plushest interiors this side of Cadillac. When you wrap all the above mentioned

---

Both cars boast fully-instrumented clusters with roller ribbon speedos, integrated air conditioning vents and aircraft-type rocker safety switches. Riviera, however, boasted sportier all-vinyl interior, while Toro was adorned with fabric & vinyl. Slotted wheels on Toro aid brake cooling, no options are available. Steel styled wheels are optional at extra cost on Riviera and add that "supercar" touch.

TORONADO

RIVIERA

1966 BUICK RIVIERA GRAN SPORT SPECIFICATIONS

ENGINE

Type	OHV V-8
Displacement	425 cubic inches
Compression Ratio	10.25 to 1
Carburetion	Dual Carter AFB quads
Camshaft	Hydraulic, .439/.441 inches lift
Horsepower	360 @ 4400 rpm
Torque	465 foot/pounds @ 2800 rpm
Exhaust	Dual pipes, reverse flow mufflers
Ignition	Single point

TRANSMISSION

Make	Torque Converter, three-speed
Control	Column shift lever
Ratios	Salisbury, limited slip 3.42-to-1

BRAKES

Front	12 x 2.25-inch finned aluminum drums
Rear	12 x 2.00-inch cast drums, power assisted

SUSPENSION

Front	Independent, HD coil springs, HD shocks, sway bar
Rear	HD coil springs, HD shocks
Steering	Power assisted
Overall Ratio	16.6-to-1

GENERAL

List Price	$4400
Price As Tested	$5900
Weight	4700 pounds
Wheelbase	119 inches
Overall Length	211 inches
Tire Size	8.45 x 15 Firestone Deluxe Champion

PERFORMANCE

0 to 30 mph	3.0 seconds
0 to 60 mph	8.3 seconds
Standing ¼ mile mph	86 mph
Elapsed Time	16.8 seconds
Top Speed	125 mph
Economy	9.5 mpg

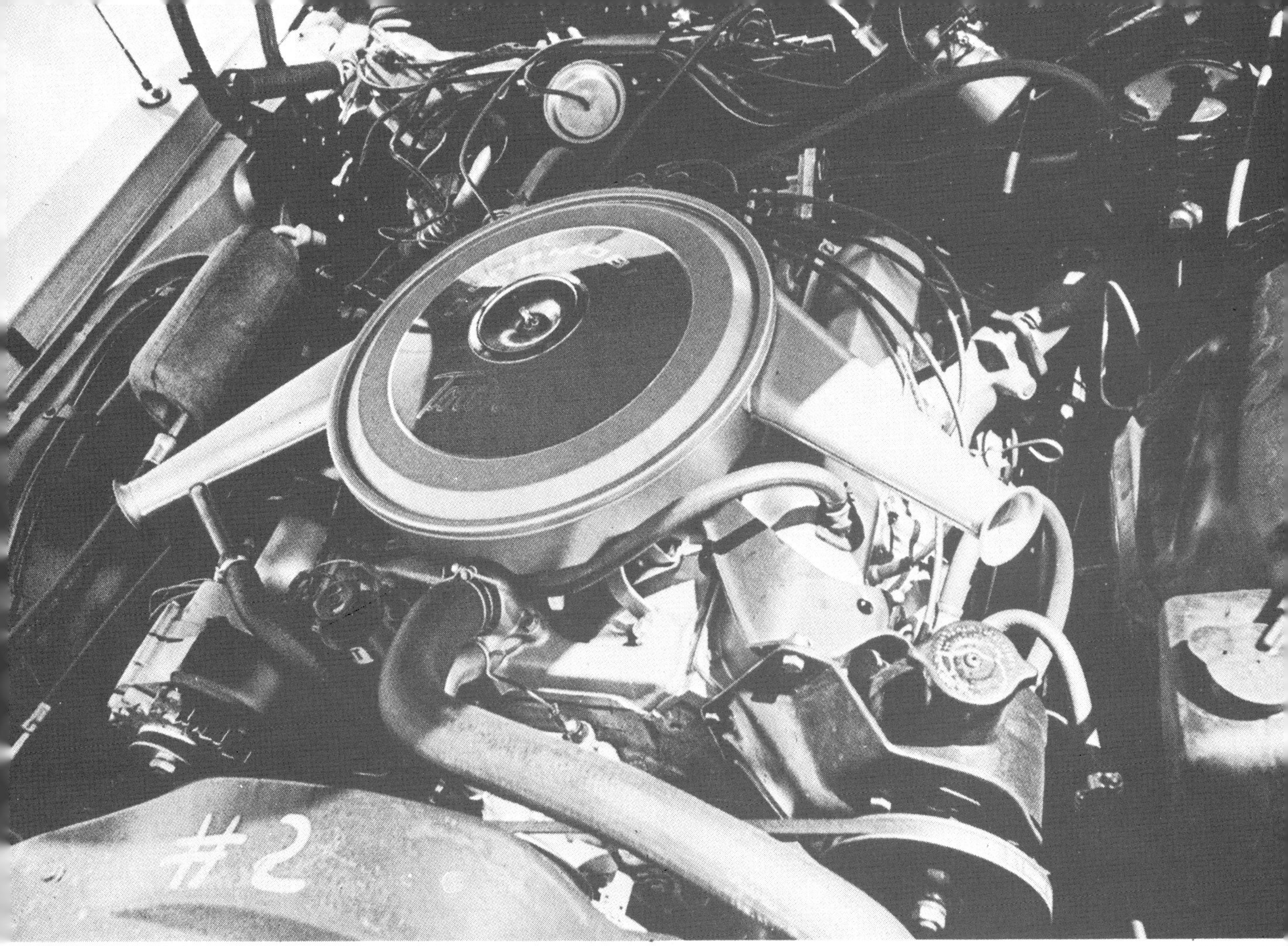
#2

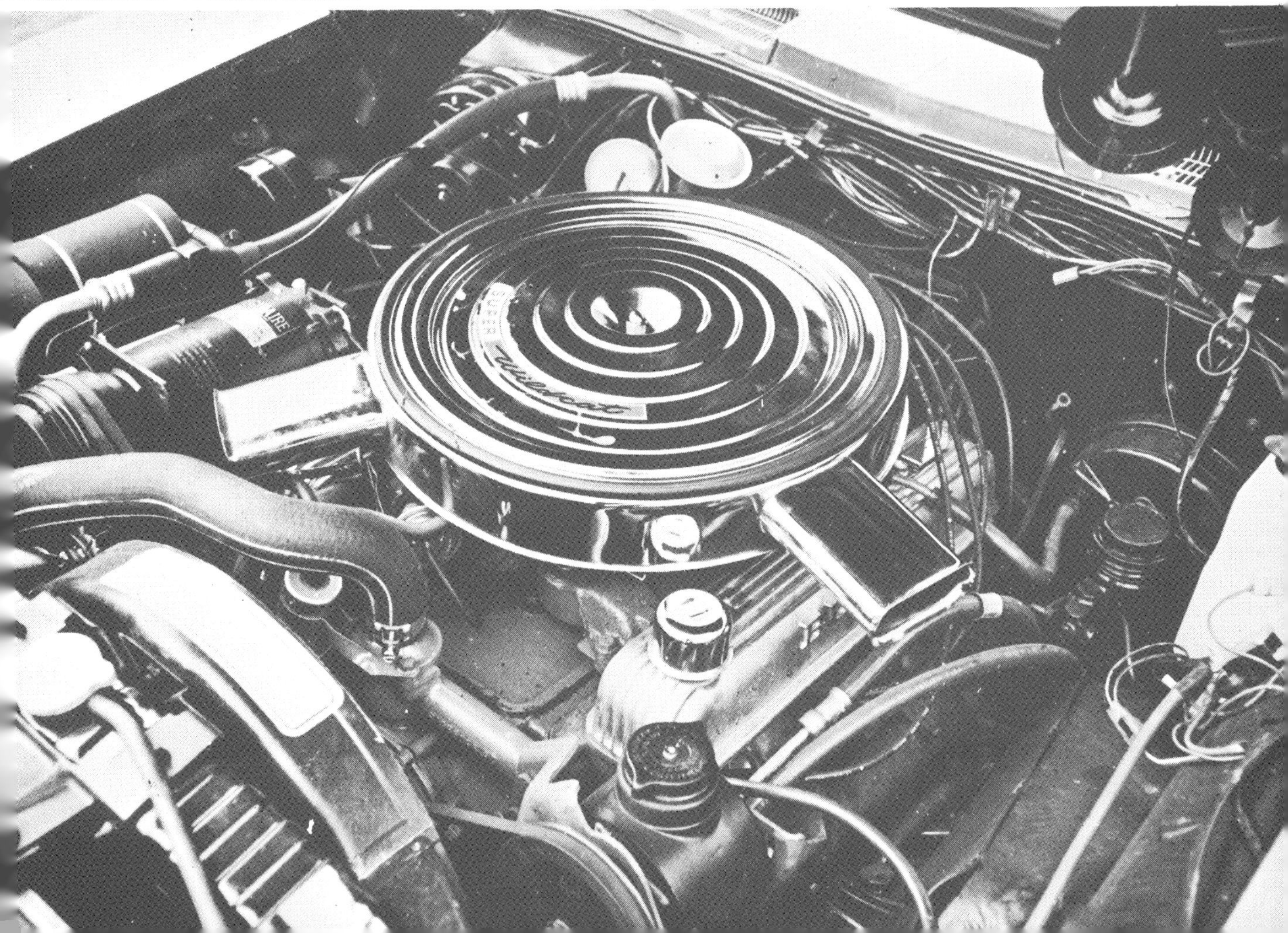
SUPER
Wildcat

features into two sleek shells you have GM's grandest touring rigs, the Toronado and Riviera GS.

In the power department both cars are as evenly matched as possible. The Gran Sport has the edge as far as options go, as the Toro is available in standard engine trim only. On paper the Toro seems to have the edge with 25 extra horses and ten extra foot pounds of torque. In the final analysis, however, the Riviera outshines the Toro. It's our guess that the front wheel drive drain might be responsible for a more than average horsepower drain.

Both engines displace 425 cubes and feature single point ignition systems, dual exhausts and basic wedge-shaped combustion chambers. The main differences lie in the carburetion and camming departments. Intake on the GS mill is ably handled by a matched pair of Carter AFB quads (dealer installed) which boast approximately 7 square inches more throttle bore area than the single Rochester Quadrajet fitted on the Toro. The dual quad engine really comes alive at mid-range and wails clear up to valve float which pops up just under the 5000 rpm marker. The GS mill also sports a slight camming advantage with a hydraulic stick rated at .439/.441 inches lift. The Toro's hydraulic cam checks out at .431/.433 inches lift. Both engines start to float the "poppers" at approximately 5000 rpm.

The engine used in the Toro is slightly different than the versions that appear in the more utilitarian Rockets. It features a superior porting layout, different heads and a new manifold. These heads are also utilized on the high preformance 442 400 cubic inch engines. There are no options listed for the Toro's 425. However, a few Toro's have been spotted (George Hurst drives one) with tri-power manifolds. You can recognize these cars immediately as the air cleaners extend through the low hood!

Performancewise the Riviera GS seems to have a slight edge over the Toro. This showed up both in the quarter-mile tests and the accepted standard 0-60 mph bash. The GS's superior performance can be directly attributed to its 300-pound weight advantage and slightly lower gearing. Buick lists options for its Riviera (3.42 vs 3.21) while the Toro buyer must settle for 3.21's only at this time. In the near future I'm sure Olds will iron out the gear ratio problem. Acceleration and performance in general is ultra smooth in both cars. Flooring the go pedal in either car produced a minimum of noise and roughness and a maximum of power transfer. The Toro rates slightly higher in engine noise level as the dual quads make a little music when all eight barrels are opened at once.

Both cars are available in automatic transmission trim only for obvious reasons. It would be just about insane to saddle the driver of an air conditioned Toro or Riviera with four-on-the-floor, as both engines were not designed for high revving and each car weighs in at approximately 5000 pounds. Today's automatics, even the two-speeds, are quite adequate for all but the highest performance engines available.

All it takes is a trip through the mountains or a few laps around a handling course to realize that GM has done a fantastic job designing suspensions for the GS and the Toro. One is a front-engined, front wheel drive car, while the other reflects the more accepted front engine, rear wheel drive engineering. There's no point in ranting and raving about the Toro's drive assembly, as it is no longer considered news-worthy. Basically it works like this. A torque converter bolted to the engine's flywheel flows power through a silent chain drive to a three-speed *Continued on next page*

Riviera offers dual quads, finned aluminum valve covers and chrome air cleaner with GS package. No power options are available on the Toro. Both engines displace 425 cubes and utilize Rochester quadrajet carbs and auto shifters in standard trim.

OLDS-RIVIERA continued

Turbo Hydro and then to a spiral bevel gearset. The gearset in turn transfers power to an all-spur geared differential. Axle movement is insured by ball-splined inboard joints. All this adds to up pull not push, a flat floor and a rather unique handling automobile.

The Riviera is not as fortunate as its new brother. It can't boast of such engineering innovations as front wheel drive, just superb handling, super superb braking and one of the finest compromise rides on the market. It makes you sort of wonder if all that engineering is really necessary!

Backing up the Toro's unique front boiler room is a rather utilitarian rear end which looks as though it belongs on the front of an early Ford product! Supporting the rear tires is a I-bean straight steel axle, two standard slightly sea-legged shocks and two extra shocks mounted parallel to the single leaf springs. These shocks are insurance against braking windup because of the front wheel drive location.

On the flat open road or when negotiating Hollywood Boulevard it's almost impossible to detect the Toro's front wheel drive. It's smooth, quiet and not unlike the ride of most 5000-pound luxury cars. On mountain roads or when winding a series of bends you notice immediately that the Toro handles like no other 5000-pound plushmobile, except, of course, for the Riviera GS. Since 60 percent of the Toro's weight rests forward of the cowling, there's an obvious understeering quality about the car. Cornering at high speed requires a complete re-education in handling and steering control. The car tends to pull itself through the wildest of bends and corners by simply getting off the go-pedal when the sleek ferocious front end starts to make tracks for the outermost arc of the bend and then back on it when the car falls back into your plotted course. The rear end, which comes along just for the ride, follows orders from the front drive. Thus you can't rely on the tried and true technique of powering the rear wheels around the corner, as those rear wheels just don't think for themselves. Super accurate steering control is a must when pushing the Toro over the ragged edge.

The Riviera GS is nowhere near as romantic as the Toro, suspensionwise but it gets the job done. At the rear of the GS is a typical live axle Salisbury-type rear axle with four locating links and coil springs. The GS option indicates that stiffer shocks replace the boulevard jobs and the coil springs are much beefier than the stockers. Stock ride rates are 130/110 lb./in. while GS rates are 180/160 lb. in. In the GS's favor is an ultra-study, rigid, self-supporting frame which is used in *(Continued on page 80)* the GM kingdom only by Riviera and Caddy (Limousine). Between the semi-unit body construction and the archaic rigid frame, the Riviera rates as one of the beefiest automobiles on the market. The stock Riviera outhandles most of its competition and the GS is an equal match for the finest handling Detroit products.

Another plus feature is the GS's quick steering ratio. With 15-to-1 at the box and 16.6-to-1 overall, the GS is second in line to the Sting Ray as far as quick, positive steering goes. Gilding the lily is three turns lock-to-lock.

Fitted with the standard GS suspension package and 8.45 x 15-inch wide shoes our test machine cornered flat, steering where it was pointed and took any and all bends in stride. It also understeers and always seems like it's going off the outward arc of each wild bend. It doesn't take very long to learn and master the understeering qualities of both the Toro and the Gran Sport. Except for the stiffer shocks and springs the Gran Sport handled and rode as well as the Toro.

When you pack enough power and sporty handling qualities in a 5000-pound car to qualify it as a genuine Grand Touring car you must also upgrade the brakes. The Riviera excells in this department. All Rivieras are factory-fitted with 12-inch drums and 15-inch wheels. Up front the drums are cast of aluminum for maximum heat dissipation and at the rear they are of cast steel. All drums are finned and the aluminum ones are fitted with iron liners for a friction surface. Fitted with wide footprint tires the GS tested stopped better than any other GM car except for the four-wheel, disc-braked Sting Ray. As far as we are concerned there's no need to fit the GS with discs as the aluminum-iron wide drum combo affords more brake power than the average driver could ever use. Repeated stops from legal highway speeds produced next to no brake fade and ruled out the need for discs. If the car was to be used for road racing, mountain climbing or other fun and games activities disc brakes would be a welcomed addition.

Our test Toro did not stop as well as the Gran Sport did during the panic stop fade tests. It seemed that we were running out of boost after a few stops and brake-ability simmered down. The Toro utilizes smaller 11-inch brakes, which seem inadequate by Riviera standards, considering the ready to roll weight of the Toro. The factory has remedied this for '67 with a new disc brake package available on more than one Olds product.

It was almost impossible to pick a winner during this runoff for top dog spot in the Heavyweight Division of the Musclecar Sweepstakes. Both cars are sexy, both cars perform and both offer the ultimate in luxury. We find the Riviera to be a better assembled, quieter and better performing car as compared to the Toro. The Toro has a slight edge in the sex department and far more HTP (Head Turning Power) than the Riviera.

Since we found it almost impossible to pick an eliminator, we decided to pick the best parts from each car, combine them and have GM build the ultimate GT car. The ideal body would have a Riviera front end and a Toronado rear end. Under the hood would be a Gran Sport dual quad mill coupled to the Toro front wheel drive assembly. We would retain the Toro suspension and add the Buick 12-inch drums or if available the '67 disc brake package. Either interior would do. We're taking orders for '67 delivery, so air mail deposits and orders now and avoid the rush!

DRIVING THE HOT '67s | BUICK RIVIERA

...styling unblemished by change with numerous improvements under the skin

THE NEW 430-CUBIC-INCH, 360-hp engine and the standard Riviera GS 3.42 rear axle combine to give the car noticeably more snap than last year's model, which had less power and a 3.23 ratio. (For those who want even more, there's an optional 3.91 gearset which should make for really scorching performance. Those interested in economy should take the non-GS Riviera, which has a 3.07 rear end.)

The Riviera's standard brakes, shared with the Wildcat and Electra, are improved over last year's which were themselves above average. The number of fins on the front aluminum cast-iron drums has been doubled to 90 and the inside lip has been extended .50-inch to reach further into the cooling air. A new lining material having more fade resistance and a greater thickness for longer life has been adopted.

Finally, the vacuum booster has been increased in size to give 40% greater power assist. In driving the car there's not much difference in pedal feel, apparently because the harder lining offsets a good part of the increased boost. We experienced no fade or unevenness after several abrupt stops and got the feeling that only severe abuse would cause these brakes to falter.

Ventilated Kelsey-Hayes discs are available in the Riviera and all other large Buicks for those who want the ultimate in stopping power, however.

The 1967 Riviera retains the responsive handling, which stems from somewhat higher than ordinary wheel rates, combined with a quiet luxurious ride – and these, along with good looks, make it a perennial favorite.

WITH GREAT WISDOM, RESTRAINT BUICK OPTED TO LEAVE RIVIERA'S STYLING LARGELY UNCHANGED. SCRIPT EMBLEM REPLACES BLOCK LETTERS.

UNMISTAKABLY RIVIERA FROM EITHER FRONT OR REAR, STYLING RELIES ON FORM AND SHAPE RATHER THAN GEWGAWS OR FANCY DETAILING.

STORY BY JOHN ETHRIDGE   COLOR BY BOB D'OLIVO

5 LUXURY SPECIALTY CARS

☐ Before the advent of the Luxury Specialty car (T-bird was first), the buyer who wanted something with more spice than the stolid domestic cars could offer, even in their most jazzed-up forms, had to go to something from overseas. These classy imports had strong esthetic appeal and stood out like Brigitte Bardot in a line of Twiggys at a bikini show. ☐ But all was not wine and roses with these machines because their creators hadn't taken conditions in this country into account. It was always with great trepidation that the luxury import owner left his pride and joy stand on an urban street or parking lot, because likely as not some nice old lady, parking with all the tenderness and care of a destroyer ramming a U-boat, would de-flower it before his errand was accomplished. ☐ Besides having to replace and straighten flimsy bumpers and sheetmetal, frequent trips to the repair shop were necessary because these cars were very finicky compared to most of the domestics. And all too often garage owners, assuming anyone who would drive such a car to be rich and foolish — and hence fair game, turned into Black Barts in shop coats and indulged in outright banditry. ☐ In addition to this group whose contretemps with foreign thoroughbreds in the '50s and '60s reverted them toward Detroit iron, there was a much larger number with esthetic leanings but who were too firmly attached to the American way of motoring to consider an import. Walk-in doors, flower vases, lap warmers, and general stodginess of the home product were not qualities that endeared a car to a member of the latter group. It was things like reliability and durability, power accessories, air conditioning, and automatic transmissions that kept them buying American. ☐ The Luxury Specialty car that came to fulfill this market could, with a great deal of truth, be said to be the kind of car everyone would own provided it were cheap enough and there were no special space or use requirements. Motorists of just about any stripe can find among our test group a *now* car with pleasing and distinctive lines, good performance, and all the things that go to make a car enjoyable. ☐ The erstwhile exotic import fancier may give up a few mpg and, perhaps, some maneuverability for something otherwise much easier to live with. Likewise, the big luxury car driver will have to do with smaller luggage space and comfortable seating for four or five instead of five or six in some cases. But neither has to make any painful adjustments, and both readily agree that the Luxury Specialty car is an excellent compromise. ☐ The five cars in this class compete with one another in a sense but nothing like the head-on, feature-for-feature struggle we find in the Low-priced Specialty cars. Each has its own individuality or personality, so to speak. This holds true in spite of the fact that three of them — the Toronado, Riviera and Eldorado — share the same basic body shell and two — the Toronado and Eldorado — have almost identical fwd and suspension systems. ☐ Also there's a large price differential, depending on what optional equipment is ordered between the Grand Prix at the lower end and the Eldorado on top. So, strictly speaking, all don't compete pricewise, either. But this doesn't mean that one prospective buyer wouldn't consider all five before narrowing down his choice. In this class more than any other, buyers will unhesitatingly go up or down several

5 LUXURY SPECIALTY CARS

clockwise
from top left:
eldorado
thunderbird
toronado
riviera
grand prix
eldorado

thousand dollars to get the styling or some particular feature they want.

POWERTRAIN & PERFORMANCE

Since the Thunderbird and Grand Prix offer optional engines, we chose engines for them that were the nearest equivalent to sole engine offerings of the Toronado, Eldorado and Riviera. The resulting engine line-up is pretty evenly matched — within 5-cu.-in. displacement and 45 advertised hp. The Grand Prix, which comes standard with a 3-speed manual transmission and offers a 4-speed manual as an option, was ordered with the optional 3-speed automatic because all of the others have this type with no options.

The Riviera GS is the outstanding performer of the group, tested chiefly because of its 3.42 "performance" axle ratio. The standard 3.07 ratio produces performance more in line with that of the others. The Riviera lost none of its quietness, and the engine remained unobtrusive as ever in spite of the considerably higher numerical ratio. Undoubtedly the Star Performer would be a Grand Prix with the 428 HO engine (376 hp @ 5100 rpm). Maybe a GP with this optional romping, stomping powerplant and an automatic would still be tame enough to be considered in the Luxury Specialty class, but it definitely would be something else with a 4-speed and heavy clutch.

As can be seen from the spec table, all cars are highly satisfactory performers, although performance *per se* is not an overriding factor in this kind of car. Thunderbirds with the smaller 390, and GPs with the 400 engine, give somewhat improved economy and performance that is still more than adequate. With any optional or standard engine on any of the cars, relaxed cruising rpm with plenty of reserve power — both for accessories and passing — is the order of the day.

We almost forgot to mention that the Toronado and Eldorado do their driving with the front wheels. And that's a good indication of how noticeable it is. Only under unusual conditions like cornering much faster than normal do you feel anything different. Also, we noticed the fwd cars would move out smartly from a standstill on rain-drenched streets, while their conventional brethren tended to lag behind with churning rear wheels.

There was nothing in our experience with Ford's automatic transmission in the Thunderbird and GM's Turbo Hydra-Matic in the other cars to make us prefer one over the other. Each went about its business with quick, barely detectable shifts.

HANDLING, STEERING & STOPPING

With the exception of Thunderbird all cars in this group either come with stiffer-than-usual suspensions (Toronado and Eldorado) or offer some option in this department (Riviera's GS package and the GP's Ride and Handling package). Whether loyal T-birders would go for some sort of handling kit we can't say, but the car suffers in comparison to any of the others in this respect. It is *very* softly sprung and has almost no roll stiffness.

But such a suspension does have its virtues. At city speeds it smoothed out potholes, railroad crossings, etc., like none of the others. The Toronado and Eldorado suspensions tended to show their teeth under similar conditions.

The Grand Prix with standard suspension had an excellent ride, yet was stable and had reasonable steering response. To our way of thinking, the handling kit would make it more fun to drive, but the car is quite acceptable as is.

We can't decide whether the Riviera GS or Toronado has the best ride/handling combination, but the two of them are clearly ahead of the others in this regard. Both are truly superb road cars that beg to be cruised around 100 mph. They feel very secure and stable at high speeds and are practically immune to crosswinds, undulating surfaces, and other perturbations.

The Eldorado's suspension differs from the Toronado's in that it has lower rate (less stiff) rear springs paired with a load-leveler as standard equipment. Thus riding height and natural frequency stay pretty much constant with varying loads. Because tires are as much a part of the suspension as the springs, there's another difference. The Toronado uses a special low-profile tire while the Eldorado uses the same tire as the rest of the Cadillacs.

The Toronado tire has a wider tread, and the low section height is more stable. Hence this tire puts more rubber on the road and keeps it there. The Eldorado has noticeably less cornering power and all-around traction than the Toronado for this reason. Disc brakes are practically a necessity on the Eldorado as stops from 60 mph in less than 200 feet are hard to come by with drums and these tires. The drum-braked Toronado stopped in about the same distance as the disc-braked Eldorado due to the difference in tires. From all indications a Toronado with discs should be a super stopper. Also, the rear wheels on the Eldorado had an annoying tendency to lock very early and cause fish-tailing when braking on wet surfaces, and again we can think of no reason except the tires.

The standard Thunderbird disc/drum combination is very well balanced and produces the ultimate in stopping power. What we've said that discs could be expected to do for the Toronado applies to some extent to the Grand Prix and Riviera, too: a further improvement in stopping, even though performance of their drums was very creditable.

SPACE, COMFORT & SAFETY

Space and comfort for a stated number of passengers is practically the name of the game with this class of car, and taken as a group they are probably safer than the average car on the road today. They are very kind to occupants — especially the driver — on extended trips, and it's pretty generally conceded that the fresh, alert driver is a safer driver.

Either fastback design and/or smallish rear windows tended to limit rearward visibility on all except the Grand Prix. But none was, in our opinion, restricted to the point of being hazardous, and with use of outside mirrors and the pivots in our neck, we had no difficulty determining when the coast was clear for lane changing.

BEST & WORST FEATURES

Trying to be objective about these cars proves to be as elusive as trying to do the same with another class of beguiling creatures — women. In looking back on our encounters with them we tend to remember not so much which was best or worst, just that in some ways some were better than others.

The big doors of the Riviera, Toronado and Eldorado qualify for both categories. They give good access to the rear seat, but need lots of room to swing open.

The best feature of the Eldorado, which has many nice accessories including a fine AM-FM Multiplex Stereo, has nothing to do with any of these. It's the awesome respect and prestige value accorded it by persons from all walks of life. After observing the effect it had on a great many onlookers we're convinced that, in this country at least, there's no car made anywhere at any price that equals it in this respect. Its worst features are the tires and the bent rear window that puts a sinister sneer on the grille of any car approaching from behind.

The T-bird's flabby suspension is its biggest drawback, and the good brakes and availability of a smart appearing 4-door are the best things it has going for it. The Grand Prix is the only one of the bunch offering a full choice of engine and driveline options as well as a convertible body style.

Flow-through ventilation (which we're sold on) and absence of front vent panes was a feature on all five cars. The missing vents and placement of the door-locking buttons on some of the cars probably won't stop a determined thief, but it will tend to separate the professionals from the joy-riders.

ELDORADO   GRAND PRIX
THUNDERBIRD   RIVIERA
TORONADO

Leather buckets are optional on Eldorado but bench shown here has fold-down center armrest, serves same function and has proved most popular. Grand Prix, shown with standard buckets, offers bench option. T-bird 4-door brings you luxurious expanded-vinyl tufted fabric, vinyl trim. Vinyl-interiored Riviera comes standard with tilt wheel — a needed option on others for complete comfort. Toronado in leather-textured vinyl has neat, designed-for-this-car look about its interior furnishings.

PHOTOS BY BOB D'OLIVO, GERRY STILES

	Eldorado	Grand Prix	Riviera GS	4-Door Thunderbird	Deluxe Toronado
PERFORMANCE					
Acceleration (2-aboard)					
0-60 mph (secs.)	9.5	8.4	7.8	9.0	8.9
1/4-mile (secs.)	17.0	16.1	15.9	16.8	16.6
Speed at end of 1/4-mile (mph)	81	87	86	86	85
Mph per 1000 rpm	23.7	27.0	22.6	25.0	25.3
Stopping Distances					
From 30 mph (ft.)	41	40	38	40	38
From 60 mph (ft.)	165	167	165	143	168
Speedometer Error (%)	+3	+2	0	0	+3
Gas Mileage Range (mpg)	10-13	10.5-14.5	10-13.5	10-13.5	10-13
SPECIFICATIONS					
Engine Type	V-8	V-8	V-8	V-8	V-8
Bore & Stroke (ins.)	4.13x4.00	4.12x4.00	4.19x3.90	4.13x3.98	4.12x3.97
Displacement (cu. ins.)	429	428	430	428	425
Horsepower @ rpm	340@4600	360@4600	360@5000	345@4600	385@4800
Torque (lbs.-ft. @ rpm)	480@3000	472@3200	475@3200	462@2800	480@3200
Compression Ratio	10.5:1	10.5:1	10.25:1	10.5:1	10.5:1
Carburetion	1 4-bbl	1 4-bbl	1 4-bbl	1 4-bbl	1 4-bbl
Transmission Type	3-spd. Auto	3-spd. Auto	3-spd. Auto	3-spd. Auto	3-spd. Auto
Final Drive Ratio	3.21	2.93	3.42	3.00	3.21
Steering					
Type	Variable-Ratio Power	Power	Power	Power	Power
Turning Dia. Curb-to-Curb (ft.)	41.3	42.8	42.3	42	43
Turns Lock-to-Lock	2.6	4.2	3.57	3.68	3.4
Wheel Size	15x6JK	14x6JK	15x6L	15x5.5JK	15x6JK
Tire Size	9.00x15	8.55x14	8.45x15	8.15x15	8.85x15
Brakes	Opt. Disc/Drum	Drum	Drum	Std. Disc/Drum	Drum
Fuel Capacity (gals.)	24	26.5	25	24.1	24
Usable Trunk Capacity (cu. ft.)	13.46	19.4	10.32	12.3	14.1
Curb Wt. (lbs.)	4680	4400	4420	4640	4800
Dimensions					
Wheelbase (ins.)	120.0	121.0	119.0	117.0	119.0
Front Track (ins.)	63.5	63.0	63.5	62.0	63.5
Rear Track (ins.)	63.0	64.0	63.0	62.0	63.0
Length (ins.)	221	215.6	211.3	209.4	211.0
Width (ins.)	79.9	79.4	79.4	77.3	78.5
Height (ins.)	53.8	54.2	53.2	53.8	52.8
PRICES AND ACCESSORIES					
Manufacturer's suggested retail	$6277.00	$3549.00	$4791.88	$4858.25	$4869.00
Optional Engine		(428 V-8)		(428 V-8)	
	—	78.99	—	90.68	—
Air Conditioning	515.75	419.60	421.00	421.49	421.28
Automatic Transmission	Std.	226.44	Std.	Std.	Std.
AM Radio	161.60	82.25	NA	NA	86.89
AM-FM Radio	187.90	124.20	175.24	89.94	173.78
AM-FM Stereo	287.90	225.00	266.81	163.77	238.03
Stereo Tape	NA	116.00	115.00	128.49	128.49
Vinyl Roof	131.60	105.32	115.78	Std.	110.59
Power Windows	Std.	104.00	105.25	103.95	104.00
Power Seat	83.15	94.79	94.73	97.32	94.79
Power Steering	Std.	105.25	Std.	Std.	Std.
Disc Brakes	105.25	110.50	78.94	Std.	78.99
Speed Control	94.75	44.95	63.15	129.55	84.26
Tinted Glass	50.55	42.10	42.10	47.49	47.39

'68 NEW BUICKS AND PONTIACS

BUICK and Pontiac are the first U.S. manufacturers to announce their 1968 models. The changes are all of a styling or detail nature with nothing new in terms of engineering apart from the energy absorbing front bumper for the Pontiac GTO.

Buick have revised the complete body shape for their Special, Skylark and GS models with a theme of longer bonnets and shorter tails like the bigger cars (Wildcat, Electra and LeSabre) started last year. There is also a new 5,736 c.c. vee-8 for these new cars, the 7-litre remaining the engine for the Wildcat, Electra and Riviera. All 35 models in the Buick range will have extra side lamps which are literally on the sides of the front wings to improve visibility; they work in parallel with the headlamps.

New Bumper

Pontiac have changed their main front-end theme with a new peripheral bumper for the Catalina, Executive and Bonneville. There are 34 models in the Pontiac range and each of these will have front and rear seat belts and extra padding across the top of the facia, down the windscreen pillars and across the backs of the front seats. A novel device is a buzzer which sounds if a door is opened with the ignition key still in its slot, but in the off position; it is a reminder to take the key out and is called an anti-theft package. ■

Far left: Tail of the Buick Riviera has been revised with new bumpers and recessed lamps. At the front there are marker lamps on the sides of the wings which work with the headlamps. Below left: The Buick GS has been completely restyled for 1968 with a shorter wheelbase and a longer nose. The standard engine is a new 5-7 litre with 285 b.h.p. gross. Below: Front quarterlights have been eliminated on the 1968 Pontiac Firebird which now has a new ventilation system with positive air extraction. Bottom: The new Pontiac Le Mans four-door hardtop has pillarless sides above the doors and features all the new safety items.

RIVIERA

A Superb Combination of Styling, Performance, Ride and Comfort

ENJOYMENT OF A Buick Riviera starts long before the ignition key is turned. It starts even before one enters the car. In fact, it starts with that first good look. The 1966-1968 Riviera is a beautiful car. Seldom has any car achieved such widespread acceptance of styling. The 1968 Riviera features a new grille which many believe is a step in the wrong direction. The clean, lithe look of 1966-1967 Rivieras is cluttered somewhat by the new front end treatment. Still, the 1968 Riviera is very attractive, and continues to display the basic contours which have been lauded in automotive publications throughout the world.

Riviera has received a new instrument panel for 1968, and Dr. Haddon's efforts are visible throughout the new design. Wherever practical thumb wheels have replaced push-pull or toggle switches. A huge padded ledge extends over the upper portion of the panel. Standard on all Rivieras is a tilt-adjustable steering column. This is a valuable feature, which eases entry and egress, and permits a low wheel position for comfortable long-distance driving. Seats also have been redesigned for 1968, and this brings up two points, one pleasant and one most undesirable.

Driving position and driver comfort are exceptionally good in the 1968 Riviera, as compared with other domestic passenger cars. The traditional GM wheel-in-the-chest driving position has been altered to a point at which Riviera drivers should be quite comfortable, and should be able to maneuver the automobile without ball-jointed elbows. *CAR LIFE*'s test car was equipped with a 4-way power-adjustable driver's seat. Though seatback angle was slightly more vertical than *CL* testers prefer, general seat contour and cushioning were excellent. The right front seat incorporated a reclining seatback which was very peculiar in operation. The seatback pivot point was well above the intersection point between seatback and seat cushion. This caused the lower edge of the seatback to move forward and upward in tilting rearward, to bear heavily

CAR LIFE ROAD TEST

RIVIERA

against the reclining occupant's lumbar area. A lower seatback pivot point would provide much greater comfort in the reclined position, admittedly at the expense of a small amount of rear seat knee room.

Riviera's new spade-handle, console-mounted transmission selector is delightful to use. Gear changing is precise, and a simple depression of the handle permits selection of Reverse, Park, First or Second. This is a welcome change from knob-mounted pushbuttons, ragged side detents, and the like.

Chassis alterations for 1968 are confined to rear suspension modifications. The 1968 Riviera features a lowered Panhard rod and relocated rear suspension trailing arms. Essentially, the new rear suspension geometry provides a lower roll center and longer effective trailing arm for less wheelbase change through jounce and rebound. These changes are intended to provide less understeer during hard cornering, and to improve ride comfort over large bumps.

The test car did ride smoothly and quietly. Small bumps, tar strips, etc., were traversed in almost complete silence, without harshness. Large undulations, however, were not so pleasantly accommodated by the Riviera. Buick claims to have increased shock absorber control for 1968, but the test Riviera did little to exhibit this increase. A very soft, vertical oscillation was dominant over rolling roads. To the Riviera's credit, this up and down jounce and rebound caused no difficulty in maintenance of directional control. Comfort provided by this sort of soft, flexible suspension is questionable.

AMERICAN MANUFACTURERS long have maintained that an automobile cannot be suspended too softly, at least if ride quality is of prime concern. This definitely is not true, and the 1968 Riviera is a case in point. Lack of harshness is commendable. Almost complete absence of road noise over smooth roads is remarkable. However, minimal control of large-amplitude oscillations and almost total dissimilarity between vehicle motion and road contour are neither comfortable nor desirable. Driver control suffers, and occupants are subjected to a floating sensation that can cause motion sickness. It would seem that adequate shock absorber control of large-amplitude motion is within the capability of an engineering staff that produces an otherwise excellent automobile.

If the 1968 Riviera has been modified to reduce understeer, the test car kept this fact a secret. Its abundance of understeer was only slightly masked by power steering. The Riviera exhibited a large degree of roll, even in moderately hard cornering, although occupants were not bothered by the roll angle. The Riviera is not a race car, and in violent maneuvering around tight bends the car felt clumsy and unmanageable. To the Riviera's credit, however, handling remains completely predictable. Driven reasonably, on the large-radius highway curves for which the Riviera is most suitable, handling is quite acceptable, safe and very forgiving of poor driving technique.

Riviera's power train was well matched to the general character of the car. The 430-cid/360-bhp engine provided smooth, strong torque and excellent flexibility. Acceleration was brisk, but not electrifying. Wheelspin could not be provoked by flooring the accelerator pedal from idle, but takeoff was rapid. A quarter-mile elapsed time of 16.5 sec. is not outstanding, in this day of enormous engines in light cars, but it will keep Riviera drivers well ahead of the mainstream of traffic. High-speed acceleration was more than adequate for passing. The Riviera was capable of cruising comfortably at speeds well above any speed limit in the U.S. Throughout all full-throttle tests, noise level in the Riviera was very low, and a feeling of effortless performance prevailed. Even at speeds of over 5000 rpm, engine noise remained almost nonexistent.

Two minor deficiencies marred performance testing. For some reason, the engine suffered intermittent loss of power. This was noticed on an occasional acceleration run, and appeared to be due to vapor lock and/or percolation. When this phenomenon occurred, the Riviera was reluctant to accelerate beyond 60 mph. Coming to a stop and revving the engine a few times seemed to clear the fuel system of whatever blockage it had incurred, and normal power returned. Unfortunately, there was not sufficient time during the test period to investigate the exact cause of this occasional power loss.

Transmission shift quality, normally excellent in the Buick Super Turbine 3-speed automatic transmission, was erratic in the test car. An occasional slipping 2-3 shift was noted, and 1-2 shifts of the slide-bump variety were felt occasionally. It must be emphasized that the test car was the second production Riviera to come off the assembly line. Also, the car had undergone extensive testing and evaluation before *CL*'s test period. Thus, transmission adjustment may have been incorrect, or the transmission may have been abused.

At the other end of the scale, puttering around in city traffic was smooth, silent and completely enjoyable. The space-capsule concept of automotive design was evident in the Riviera. A Riviera driver need not be aware of his mechanical environment. No trace of drive-train vibration could be detected. Buick engineers have gone to great lengths to insure against drive-line shudder and high-speed vibration, as evidenced by the incorporation of double-Cardan, constant-velocity universal joints in the propeller shaft.

A LARGE PART of the feeling of effortless performance and silence of the Riviera undoubtedly is attributable to the strong cruciform chassis structure. The Riviera's combination of substantial body structure with a very rigid frame provides a high degree of total vehicle integrity. This became obvious in driving over a stretch of broken pavement. In comparison with other domestic passenger cars, the Riviera felt like the proverbial rock. Shake and body flexing were pleasantly absent. A feeling of complete solidity was apparent, creating an impression of durability and strength. Rivieras should remain free from rattles longer than the majority of other cars, another sound reason for buying this automobile.

Brakes long have been a Buick strong point. The 1968 Riviera test car was equipped with optional front disc brakes, in place of the excellent finned-aluminum drum units standard on all full-sized Buick models. Fade resistance and brake effectiveness were not noticeably superior to previous Buicks equipped with drum brakes. The Riviera's maximum deceleration rate of 23 ft./sec.^{2} is only fair. The third 80-0 mph panic stop produced 17 ft./sec.^{2}. This represents adequate fade resistance, although other disc/drum combinations have been tested that were substantially better. A road

THUMB WHEEL and flat knob controls, greater expanses of padded surface, spade-handle shift lever mark the 1968 Buick Riviera.

STRONG, SMOOTH and flexible, the Riviera's 430-cid/360-bhp V-8 delivered 16.5-sec. e.t.

test of the 1966 Riviera, with drum brakes all around, showed that car to have superior fade resistance to the 1968 disc/drum version, though maximum stopping power on the first stop is slightly improved in the 1968 Riviera.

The test 1968 Riviera displayed one really commendable trait during braking tests. Directional stability during hard braking was almost perfect. No conscious effort was required to maintain a straightline stop. Rear wheel lockup could be easily obtained, but was also fairly easy to avoid. Even when one rear wheel locked, the Riviera had no tendency to dive to the side of the road. A driver faced with a highway emergency should be in no danger of losing control of a Riviera. As stated, this is a commendable quality, and one that is unfortunately rare in current domestic automobiles.

Occasionally, when writing a road test, the question "what good is it?" is posed. In the case of the 1968 Riviera, this question is readily answered. The 1968 Riviera is a businessman's express, a logical extension of the luxurious pseudo-sporting theme favored by Detroit product planners. Interior room is comparable to intermediate-sized passenger cars, but comfort and appointments are in the luxury car class. The 1968 Riviera is not a large car, by 1968 Detroit standards, but it

1968 BUICK
RIVIERA 2-DOOR HARDTOP

DIMENSIONS
- Wheelbase, in................119.0
- Track, f/r, in............63.4/64.0
- Overall length, in............215.2
- width.......................78.8
- height......................53.4
- Front seat hip room, in......23.3 x 2
- shoulder room...............58.7
- head room..................38.1
- pedal-seatback, max..........44.2
- Rear seat hip room, in.......54.3
- shoulder room...............56.4
- leg room...................36.6
- head room..................37.4
- Door opening width, in......41.3
- Ground clearance, in.........5.5
- Trunk liftover height, in....30.2

PRICES
- List, FOB factory..............n.a.
- Equipped as tested............n.a.
- Options included: Automatic climate control; cruise control; power windows, seats, antenna; deluxe wheel covers; wsw tires; deluxe interior with console; am/fm radio.

CAPACITIES
- No. of passengers..............5
- Luggage space, cu. ft........10.3
- Fuel tank, gal..................21
- Crankcase, qt..................4
- Transmission/dif., pt.......22/4.2
- Radiator coolant, qt..........17.0

CHASSIS/SUSPENSION
- Frame type: Cruciform.
- Front suspension type: Independent by s.l.a., coil springs, telescopic shock absorbers.
  - ride rate at wheel, lb./in.....127
  - antiroll bar dia., in.........0.781
- Rear suspension type: Live axle, 4 trailing arms, coil springs, Panhard rod, telescopic shock absorbers.
  - ride rate at wheel, lb./in.....109
- Steering system: Recirculating ball nut gear with integral assist, parallelogram linkage behind front wheels.
  - overall ratio...............19.0:1
  - turns, lock to lock...........3.57
  - turning circle, ft. curb-curb..42.3
- Curb weight, lb...............4550
- Test weight..................4930
  - distribution (driver),
  - f/r....................54.3/45.7

BRAKES
- Type: Two-line hydraulic, vented disc front, cast iron drum rear.
- Front rotor, dia. x width, in.....n.a.
- Rear drum, dia. x width.....12.0 x 2.0
- total swept area, sq. in........n.a.
- Power assist: Integral, vacuum.
  - line psi at 100 lb. pedal......1100

WHEELS/TIRES
- Wheel rim size...............15 x 6JK
- optional size.................none
- bolt no./circle dia. in.........5/5.0
- Tires: Goodyear Power Cushion.
  - size......................8.45-15
  - normal inflation, psi f/r.....24/26
- Capacity @ psi......6060 @ 24/26

ENGINE
- Type, no. of cyl........ohv, 90° V-8
- Bore x stroke, in.........4.188 x 3.90
- Displacement, cu. in........429.690
- Compression ratio..........10.25:1
- Fuel required...............premium
- Rated bhp @ rpm...........360 @ 5000
  - equivalent mph..............132
- Rated torque @ rpm.....475 @ 3200
  - equivalent mph................85
- Carburetion: Rochester 1x4.
  - throttle dia., pri./sec....1.38/2.25
- Valve train: Hydraulic lifters, pushrods and overhead rocker arms.
  - cam timing
    - deg., int./exh......14-104/88-47
    - duration, int./exh.........298/315
- Exhaust system: Dual, reverse flow mufflers and resonators.
  - pipe dia., exh./tail......2.0C/2.00
- Normal oil press. @ rpm...40 @ 2400
- Electrical supply, V./amp......12/55
- Battery, plates/amp. hr........66/70

DRIVE TRAIN
- Clutch type:
  - dia., in....
- Transmission type: Three-speed automatic with fixed pitch torque converter.
- Gear ratio 4th (   ) overall......
  - 3rd (1.00:1)...........3.42:1
  - 2nd (1.48:1)...........5.06:1
  - 1st (2.48:1)...........8.48:1
- 1st x t.c. stall (2.30:1).....19.50:1
- Shift lever location: Console.
- Differential type: Hypoid, semifloating.
  - axle ratio................3.42:1

is heavy. Fortunately, a large portion of the 4560-lb. curb weight has been utilized to improve structural integrity.

The 1968 Riviera is a perfect automobile for transportation of 4 passengers for long distances over high-speed thoroughfares. During the test, a persistent thought kept recurring. The Riviera is what Ponycars might be, when they grow up. Or, taken from another viewpoint, the Riviera is what Ponycar buyers can look forward to when their bank accounts permit purchase of a higher priced automobile. The Buick Riviera has long been a favorite with *CL* staffers, largely because the car is a superb combination of styling, performance, ride, comfort and solidity. As they are more handling-oriented than the average consumer, the GS handling package option would be specified by staff members. However, the standard suspension can do an acceptable job.

The 1968 Riviera is a good-looking car. More than that, it is a smooth, quiet transporter that features all of the modern conveniences intended to make long-distance driving as pleasant as possible. No 1968 price information is available at press time, but the Riviera will probably remain in the $6000 range when equipped with all of the desirable options. This is a lot of money for lots of sound, well-styled automobile. ∎

CAR LIFE ROAD TEST

CALCULATED DATA
Lb/bhp (test weight)............13.7
Cu. ft./ton mile...............114.0
Mph/1000 rpm (high gear).....26.5
Engine revs/mile (60 mph)....2260
Piston travel, ft./mile........1470
CAR LIFE wear index..........33.2
Frontal area, sq. ft............23.3
NHRA-AHRA class....D/SA-D/SA

SPEEDOMETER ERROR
30 mph, actual................28.4
40 mph........................37.5
50 mph........................47.9
60 mph........................60.0
70 mph........................70.0
80 mph........................80.4
90 mph........................90.9

MAINTENANCE
Engine oil, miles/days.....6000/60
oil filter, miles/days....6000/180
Chassis lubrication, miles..6000/180
Antismog servicing, type/miles....
 replace PCV valve, 12,000; tuneup, 12,000.
Air cleaner, miles.......clean, 12,000
Spark plugs: AC 44TS.
 gap, (in.)....................0.030
Basic timing, deg./rpm.........n.a
 max. cent. adv., deg./rpm 32/4600
 max. vac. adv., deg./in. Hg.
 ....19.5/25
Ignition point gap, in.........0.016
 cam dwell angle, deg........29-31
 arm tension, oz.............19-23
Tappet clearance, int./exh......0/0
Fuel pressure at idle, psi.......6.0
Radiator cap relief press., psi....15

PERFORMANCE
Top speed (4620), mph...........118
Test shift points (rpm) @ mph......
 3rd to 4th ( ).................
 2nd to 3rd (5000).............89
 1st to 2nd (5000).............54

ACCELERATION
0-30 mph, sec..................4.8
0-40 mph......................6.5
0-50 mph......................8.5
0-60 mph.....................10.7
0-70 mph.....................13.5
0-80 mph.....................17.1
0-90 mph.....................21.6
0-100 mph....................28.0
Standing ¼-mile, sec..........16.5
 speed at end, mph...........79.5
Passing, 30-70 mph, sec........8.7

BRAKING
Max. deceleration rate from 80 mph
 ft./sec.^{2}...................23
No. of stops from 80 mph (60-sec. intervals) before 20% loss in deceleration rate..................2
Control loss? None.
Overall brake performance.....good

FUEL CONSUMPTION
Test conditions, mpg...........n.a
Normal cond., mpg..............n.a
Cruising range, miles..........n.a

GRADABILITY
4th % grade @ mph..............
3rd........................17 @ 48
2nd........................24 @ 31
1st........................32 @ 18

DRAG FACTOR
Total drag @ 60 mph, lb........190

ACCELERATION & COASTING
(Graph: MPH vs. ELAPSED TIME IN SECONDS, showing 1st-2nd, 2nd-3rd shift points, SS¼)

Buick Riviera

ENGINE CAPACITY 430 cu in, 7,046.41 cu cm
FUEL CONSUMPTION 12.7 m/imp gal, 10.5 m/US gal, 22.3 l × 100 km
SEATS 6 **MAX SPEED** 132 mph, 212.5 km/h
PRICE IN GB basic £ 3,580, total £ 4,402
PRICE IN USA $ 4,589

ENGINE front, 4 stroke, slanted at 5°6'; cylinders: 8, Vee-slanted at 90°; bore and stroke: 4.19 × 3.90 in, 106.4 × 99.1 mm; engine capacity: 430 cu in, 7,046.41 cu cm; compression ratio: 10.2; max power (SAE): 360 hp at 5,000 rpm; max torque (SAE): 475 lb ft, 65.5 kg m at 3,200 rpm; max engine rpm: 5,200; specific power: 51.1 hp/l; cylinder block: cast iron; cylinder head: cast iron; crankshaft bearings: 5; valves: 2 per cylinder, overhead, in line, slanted at 45°, push-rods and rockers; camshafts: 1, at centre of Vee; lubrication: gear pump, full flow filter; lubricating system capacity: 8.27 imp pt, 10 US pt, 4.7 l; carburation: 1 Rochester 4 MV downdraught 4-barrel carburettor; fuel feed: mechanical pump; cooling system: water; cooling system capacity: 27.81 imp pt, 33.40 US pt, 15.8 l.

TRANSMISSION driving wheels: rear; gearbox: Super Turbine automatic, hydraulic torque convertor and planetary gears with 3 ratios + reverse, max ratio of convertor at stall 2, possible manual selection; gearbox ratios: I 2.480, II 1.480, III 1, rev 2.080; selector lever: steering column; final drive: hypoid bevel; axle ratio: 3.070.

CHASSIS X box-type frame; front suspension: independent, wishbones, coil springs, anti-roll bar, telescopic dampers; rear suspension: rigid axle, lower trailing arms, oblique upper torque arms, coil springs, anti-roll bar, telescopic dampers.

STEERING recirculating ball, servo; turns of steering wheel lock to lock: 3.57.

BRAKES drum, dual circuit, servo; area rubbed by linings: total 320.50 sq in, 2,067.22 sq cm.

ELECTRICAL EQUIPMENT voltage: 12 V; battery: 70 Ah; generator type: alternator, 42 Ah; ignition distributor: Delco-Remy; headlamps: 4.

DIMENSIONS AND WEIGHT wheel base: 119 in, 3,023 mm; front track: 63.45 in, 1.612 mm; rear track: 63 in, 1,600 mm; overall length: 215.20 in, 5,466 mm; overall width: 74.85 in, 1,901 mm; overall height: 53.40 in, 1,356 mm; ground clearance: 4,85 in, 123 mm; dry weight: 4,259 lb, 1,932 kg; distribution of weight: 52.5% front axle, 47.5% rear axle; turning circle (between walls): 46.9 ft, 14.3 m; width 6"; tyres: 8.45 × 15; fuel tank capacity: 17.4 imp gal, 21 US gal, 79 l.

BODY coupé; doors: 2; seats: 6; front seats: bench.

PERFORMANCE max speeds: 56 mph, 90.2 km/h in 1st gear; 94 mph, 151 in 2nd gear; 132 mph, 212.5 km/h in 3rd gear; power-weight ratio: 11.9 lb kg/hp; carrying capacity: 1,058 lb, 480 kg; speed in direct drive at 1,000 rp mph, 43 km/h.

PRACTICAL INSTRUCTIONS fuel: 100 oct petrol; engine sump oil: 6 pt, 8 US pt, 3.8 l, SAE 5W-20 (winter) 10W-30 (summer), change every 6,00 9,700 km; gearbox oil: 19.18 imp pt, 23 US pt, 10.9 l, ATF Dexron; final d 3.52 imp pt, 4.25 US pt, 2 l, SAE 80; greasing: every 6,000 miles, 9,700 kr timing: inlet opens 14° before tdc and closes 104° after bdc, exhaust op before bdc and closes 47° after tdc; normal tyre pressure: front 24 psi, rear 26 psi, 1.8 atm.

VARIATIONS AND OPTIONAL ACCESSORIES 3.910 or 3.420 axl front disc brakes (diameter 12 in, 305 mm), internal radial fins; cleaner air air conditioning system.

CAR LIFE ROAD TEST

RIVIERA
FOR THE FREEWAYS

Buick engineers have been able to adapt some of their new suspension geometry thinking to the Riviera—and it paid off.

HANDLING PACKAGE isn't quite the right description for the Buick Riviera's new suspension and steering. What the Buick Division engineers had in mind—and built—is a quick lane-change kit.

The Riviera is not a sports car, nor is it supposed to be. A handling package, in the sense of stiffer springs and bigger shock absorbers, would have given the Riviera firmer, more predictable handling, and a harsher ride than Riviera owners expect, or want.

Instead, Riviera chassis changes are intended to promote stability and maneuverability. The front suspension change represents a reversal, literally, of the path that other makers have been following since the independent front suspension was adopted 30-plus years ago.

Everybody else designs suspension geometry so there is a camber gain, that is, as the car leans in a turn, the outer wheel tilts in. On the Riviera, and on all 1969 Buicks, it tilts out.

In theory, the Buick system would produce massive understeer, with the front outside wheel losing its grip much earlier than would the wheel on a standard car.

In practice, it doesn't. Camber gain seldom keeps pace with body lean, and few, if any, domestic cars keep their outside wheels upright during hard cornering, so the Riviera's loss is a matter of degree. Buick engineers say that tilting the wheel out doesn't reduce cornering power, while it

RIVIERA

makes the car much more stable over bumps and ridges in the road. When the front wheel hits a bump, the car moves away from it, the engineers say. As the wheel rises, it moves in and pulls the car back. The two forces work against, and cancel, each other.

The Riviera's variable-ratio power steering is shared with other General Motors cars. Straight ahead, the steering is slow, so that fractional motions by the driver won't be translated into swerves. As the steering wheel is turned, it moves the steered wheels faster and faster. In parking, or in trying to turn quickly, the response is very quick. Sports car drivers have complained for years that domestic steering is too slow, and drivers of standard cars have complained that sports car steering is heavy and twitchy. The variable-ratio power steering combines the virtues of domestic ease and European speed.

On the highway, the Riviera is beautifully stable, easy to control in a straight line, and to snake through traffic from lane to lane. It's very responsive on sweeping turns, and in the parking lot. On twisting roads, where Riviera drivers probably don't try to set speed records anyway, there's more understeer than, say, showed up in the Thunderbird tested on page 38. The engineering changes for 1969 improve the Riviera's handling where buyers will notice it, and decrease grip only during situations the buyers aren't

PHOTOS BY GORDON CHITTENDEN

1969 RIVIERA
2-DOOR COUPE

DIMENSIONS
Wheelbase, in.	119.0
Track, f/r, in.	63.4/63.0
Overall length, in.	215.2
width	79.2
height	53.2
Front seat hip room, in.	58.0
shoulder room	58.8
head room	37.9
pedal-seatback, max.	44.0
Rear seat hip room, in.	54.0
shoulder room	56.1
leg room	36.7
head room	37.2
Door opening width, in.	47.0
Trunk liftover height, in.	29.0

PRICES
List, FOB factory	$4683
Equipped as tested	$6555

Options included: Disc brakes, $53; sonomatic radio, $118; stereo tape player, $117; air conditioner, $421; power seat, $99; power windows, $111.

CAPACITIES
No. of passengers	6
Luggage space, cu. ft.	10.3
Fuel tank, gal.	21.0
Crankcase, qt.	5.0
Transmission/dif., pt.	23.0/4.3
Radiator coolant, qt.	16.7

CHASSIS/SUSPENSION
Frame type: Cruciform (separate).
Front suspension type: Independent by s.l.a., coil springs, telescopic shock absorbers.
  ride rate at wheel, lb./in. 111.0
  antiroll bar dia., in. 0.812
Rear suspension type: Live axle, trailing arms, coil springs, telescopic shock absorbers.
  ride rate at wheel, lb./in. 104.0
Steering system: Integral assist recirculating ball; parallelogram linkage behind front wheels.
  overall ratio 17.4-11.6
  turns, lock to lock 2.9
  turning circle, ft. curb-curb 41.7
Curb weight, lb. 4610
Test weight 4905
Distribution (driver),
  % f/r 54.2/45.8

BRAKES
Type: Ventilated disc front; drum rear.
Front rotor, dia. x width, in. ..... 11.0 x 1.875
Rear drum, dia. x width ..... 12.0 x 2.0
  total swept area, sq. in. 320.5
Power assist: Integral.
  line psi at 100 lb. pedal 1100

WHEELS/TIRES
Wheel rim size ..... 15 x 6.0JK
  optional size ..... none
  bolt no./circle dia. in. 5/5
Tires: Goodyear Power Cushion.
  size 8.55-15
  normal inflation, psi f/r 24/26
  Capacity, lb. @ psi ..... 6480 @ 24/26

ENGINE
Type, no. of cyl. ..... ohv V-8
Bore x stroke, in. ..... 4.19 x 3.90
Displacement, cu. in. 430
Compression ratio 10.25
Fuel required ..... premium
Rated bhp @ rpm ..... 360 @ 5000
  equivalent mph 131.0
Rated torque @ rpm ..... 475 @ 3200
  equivalent mph 83.8
Carburetion: Rochester 1x4.
  throttle dia., pri./sec. 1.38/2.25
Valve train: Hydraulic lifters, pushrods and overhead rocker arms.
  cam timing
    deg., int./exh. 14-104/88-47
    duration, int./exh. 298/315
Exhaust system: Dual, reverse-flow mufflers with resonators.
  pipe dia., exh./tail 2.0/2.0
Normal oil press. @ rpm ..... 40 @ 2400
Electrical supply, V./amp. 12/55
Battery, plates/amp. hr. 66/70

DRIVE TRAIN
Transmission type: Three-speed automatic with torque converter.
Gear ratio 3rd (1.00:1) overall .3.07:1
  2nd (1.48:1) 4.54:1
  1st (2.48:1) 7.61:1
  1st x t.c. stall (2.05:1) 12.6:1
Shift lever location: Steering column.
Differential type: Hypoid, limited-slip.
  axle ratio 3.07:1

likely to get into. A big improvement for a slight loss is a good bargain.

As a minority report, if not a dissenting opinion, one tester reported that he thought he could feel the Riviera's suspension hitting bumps, and reacting to them a split-second later. He read the Buick engineer's report before he drove the car. The other testers, who drove the car before they read the book, didn't notice this.

The Riviera's 430-cid engine is virtually unchanged from last year. Most noticeable feature is that it's never noticed. Turn the key, and drive. At full speed, engine noise reaches the level of a faint hum. Power is more than adequate for traffic, and there's plenty in reserve for passing on the highway or cruising at any possible speed. The three-speed automatic transmission, too, is quiet and smooth.

The first all-out stop in CAR LIFE's series of braking from 80 mph recorded a deceleration rate of 23 ft./sec./sec.—about average. The rear brakes showed a tendency to lock and fade, so that the latter cancelled the former. By the eighth stop, with the front brakes doing most of the work, the rate was back up to 22, after a low at mid-test of 14. Buick's disc/drum system isn't the best on the market, but the Riviera will stop once in a hurry, and repeatedly within an acceptable time.

As a luxury car, the Riviera has a long list of convenience items. One, the cruise control, we did not like at all. It's supposed to keep the car at a steady speed, selected by the driver. That's fine, especially on a long trip. The controls, though, scared us.

The first driver to run afoul of the

CAR LIFE ROAD TEST

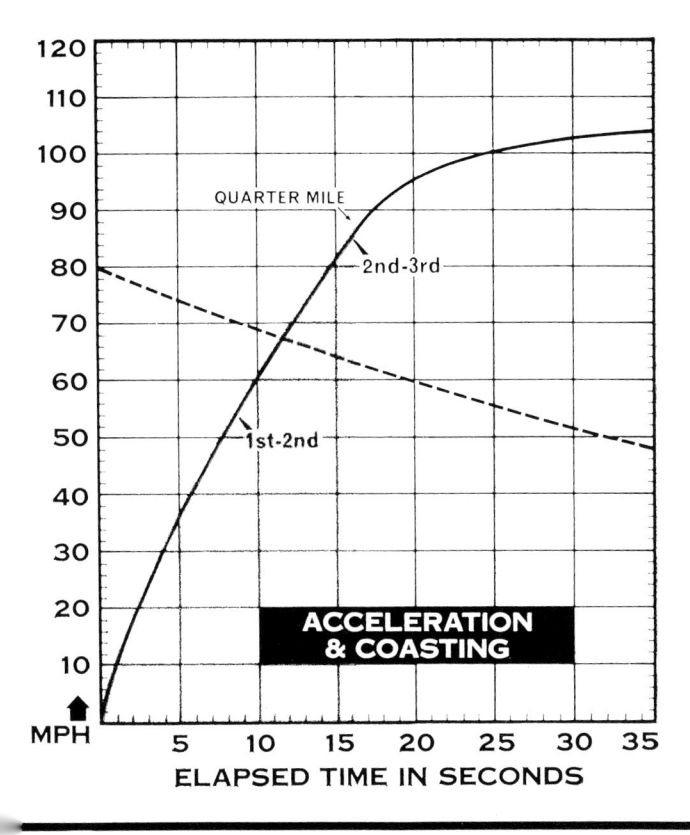

CALCULATED DATA
Lb./bhp (test weight)..........13.63
Cu. ft./ton mile................116.4
Mph/1000 rpm (high gear)......26.2
Engine revs/mile (60 mph).....2293
Piston travel, ft./mile........1490.6
CAR LIFE wear index...........34.2
Frontal area, sq. ft............23.4

SPEEDOMETER ERROR
30 mph, actual.................30.0
40 mph.........................41.3
50 mph.........................51.1
60 mph.........................60.8
70 mph.........................69.9
80 mph.........................78.7
90 mph.........................88.1

MAINTENANCE
Engine oil, miles/days......6000/120
 oil filter, miles/days....12,000/240
Chassis lubrication, miles......6000
Antismog servicing, type/miles..
 tune-up, check and replace PCV valve/12,000
Air cleaner, miles.....replace/24,000
Spark plugs: A.C. R44TS.
 gap, (in.)...................0.030
Basic timing, deg./rpm....TDC/550
 max. cent. adv., deg./rpm.32/4600
 max. vac. adv., deg./in.
 Hg........................19.5/25.0
Ignition point gap, in.....0.013-0.019
 cam dwell angle, deg........29-31
 arm tension, oz..............19-23
Tappet clearance, int./exh.......0/0
Fuel pressure at idle, psi.....5.5-7.0
Radiator cap relief press., psi.....15

PERFORMANCE
Top speed (4735), mph..........124
Test shift points (rpm) @ mph
 2nd to 3rd (5000)............85.2
 1st to 2nd (5000)............52.8

ACCELERATION
0-30 mph, sec...................3.5
0-40 mph........................5.3
0-50 mph........................7.4
0-60 mph.......................10.0
0-70 mph.......................12.2
0-80 mph.......................14.4
0-90 mph.......................17.6
0-100 mph......................24.0
Standing ¼-mile, sec.........16.51
 speed at end, mph..........86.71
Passing, 30-70 mph, sec........8.7

BRAKING
Max. deceleration rate from 80 mph
 ft./sec./sec...................23
No. of stops from 80 mph (60-sec. intervals) before 20% loss in deceleration rate...................4
Control loss? None.
Overall brake performance......fair

FUEL CONSUMPTION
Test conditions, mpg............9.0
Normal cond., mpg..........10-12.5
Cruising range, miles........190-238

RIVIERA understeers strongly when driven at its cornering limit.

OUR MEAN GUYS of the month award goes, this month, to us, in recognition of the malevolent way we pushed the plush Riviera around the handling circuit. As the picture shows, Buick engineers didn't have this sort of thing in mind when they designed the car.

We had our reasons. The reversal of everybody else's ideas by the Buick designers intrigued us. As part of the announcement of the new concept, Buick sent out sketches of the suspension and the way the wheels tilted in what has been for years the wrong direction.

We looked at the above picture closely, and were reassured. Changes in geometry are measured in degrees, and fractions of degrees. We suspect that the sketches exaggerated the amount of wheel tilt, either way. As pictured, the Riviera is leaning severely, about as far as it will go on its springs. The front wheels are turned toward the inside of the corner, a sure sign of understeer: The front end is trying to plow forward in a direct line, and the wheels have been turned to resist the car's momentum. But. The outside front wheel, the one doing all the work, is nearly parallel to the side of the car. Ideally, the tire has its best hold on the road when it is vertical to the road. The path of most front wheels is laid out so the wheel leans less than the car does, and so stays nearly upright. In practice, very few cars achieve this.

We've tested many cars in the recent past that tipped their outside front wheels the wrong way, without intending to, to the same degree that Buick does deliberately. On one test car, the wheel tipped further.

One auto engineer now at work testing cars as part of the federal government's testing program, was distressed at Buick's idea. Buick already has too much understeer, he said, and this change will make it worse.

We think that he, like us, saw the sketches, and had visions of the outside wheel heeled over like a sailboat in a strong wind, or the rear wheel of a car with swing axles. It doesn't happen, not to a degree that can be seen by the untrained eye. The 1969 Riviera certainly does understeer, but so did the 1968 Riviera, and so do all the new models in the Riviera's class. The difference is a matter of degree. Or two.

RIVIERA

system is a hard-rock fan, who was drumming along with The Association when the accelerator suddenly leapt from under his foot, and pressed itself against the floor while the Riviera picked up speed at a great rate. Usual cure for a jammed throttle is to turn off the ignition.

Not this year. GM has a steering column lock built into the ignition switch. The switch has five positions—accessory, lock, off, on and start—and the driver couldn't remember which was where. The thought of the steering lock did cross his mind. He mashed down on the brake, determined to let the brakes and engine fight it out, there was a soft click from under the dash, and the accelerator came back up.

The cruise control switch is inside the turn signal stalk. Push in on the stalk, or drum against it, and the control tries to speed the car up. We learned later that the column won't lock unless the transmission is in "park," but we didn't know it when it was important.

Another CAR LIFE staffer did the same thing. Testers, who spend most of their driving time in unfamiliar cars, are prone to this, and we wouldn't have mentioned it in a road test except that one of Buick's representatives said the same thing happened to him, and he was going to let the head office know how he felt about putting the switch where it is. Now, they know

94

ELECTRA was also stable at speed and understeers in turns.

ELECTRAS, and the other full-size Buicks, get suspension changes front and back for 1969. The new rear suspension, like the front-end geometry, isn't intended as a boost for sheer cornering power, or handling.

When Buick owners travel, they go on trips, with luggage. Buick has provided ample storage space for years, and Parkinson's law seems to apply. Luggage expands to fill available trunk space.

The engineers say that with the trunk loaded the weight distribution changes and with it, handling characteristics. The rear of the car tended to sway sideways on turns. The rear axle has coil springs, and is located by control arms, which keep the axle from moving back and forth, or side to side. For 1969, the big Buicks have their arms mounted at a wider angle. Last year, they were trailing arms, running almost straight back. This year, each arm is at an angle of 45° to the car's center line, for a total angle of 90° to each other. (The Riviera has two trailing arms and a Panhard rod keeping its axle in place.)

The change for the big cars was easily done. They received new bodies this year. The Riviera is restyled, and mildly at that. It may be given a similar rear axle system when it gets a completely new body. We don't expect that to happen until 1971, but we wondered what difference the rear suspension change would make, so we borrowed an Electra.

In brief, the Electra drives like a slightly bigger Riviera. The variable ratio power steering and the new front suspension makes another quick-lane change kit. We were at a loss when we tried to compare the Electra to previous models because we didn't drive one last year. With full tank and a family of six in the car, the back didn't sway. On curves, there was strong understeer, like the Riviera. The Electra could be kept in hand under any sort of normal driving. We couldn't feel any difference in handling with the car full or with driver-only and the tank nearly empty.

Our conclusion, then, is that the Buick engineers have achieved their aim. The Electra is an excellent car to drive on long trips, over the smooth roads available for most long trips, and the suspension capacity matches the trunk's capacity.

we don't like the location, either.

The Riviera interior is the sort of luxury to which it's easy to become accustomed. The semi-bucket seats are comfortable, and adjust to accommodate almost any shape. The seat belts adjust themselves. An inertia reel in the outboard strap lets the occupant pull the belt out. When it's snapped, the reel takes up the slack automatically. The instrument panel is thoughtfully done, with the myriad controls labeled and within reach. The Riviera has the latest thing in warning lights: The temperature warning comes in two stages. If the engine overheats, a red light comes on. There's a second switch, reading the temperature of the engine metal, not just the coolant. If the metal temperature goes higher than it should, a flashing red light tells the driver to "stop engine."

The Riviera has an electric fuel pump, mounted inside the gas tank. The Riviera shares a skid plate, in the headliner just above the windshield, and an improved version of the collapsible steering column, with other GM cars. (The electric fuel pump is such a good idea that the rest of the GM line will surely adopt it.)

Fuel mileage is average for a car with the Riviera's engine size and weight. The cost isn't important, not for buyers considering a $6500 car. But the cruising range isn't far, a handicap for those who like to cover long distances non-stop.

We haven't said very much about driving the Riviera. There's not much to say. Smooth, comfortable and quiet, the Riviera doesn't lend itself to sporting motoring. The driver has it so easy, though—he doesn't care. ■

BUICK RIVIERA

The Riviera is by far the most successful of GM's luxury/speciality cars, outselling both Toronado and Eldorado by a factor of two to one or more. It has not, however, become popular enough to seriously threaten Thunderbird's current lead, perhaps because the T-bird has since it got into this class always offered more than one body style.

The GM "E" body shell, which Riviera uses along with Toronado and Eldorado is roomier than its lone FoMoCo competition. It is, in fact, one of the few coupes on the market in which four adults will find comfort on a day-long trip. In standard form it is obviously a luxury car, making the $168 custom trim option seem redundant. Power brakes, steering and automatic transmission are included in the base price, as is a fully-adjustable steering wheel. For those who don't care for Buick's traditionally spongy ride, a handling package is offered that includes a fast-ratio (15 to 1) steering gear.

Motivation comes from a 430-cubic-inch V8 with 4-barrel carburetion and a 10.25 to 1 compression ratio that requires premium fuel. Transmission is Buick's excellent 3-speed Super Turbine which this year has a fixed rather than a variable stator. Aside from nippier acceleration and less complication, the new design allows part-throttle downshifting. You can drop into second in the 15 to 40-mph range without the uncomfortable and sometimes dangerous surge that occurs with full-throttle shifting. Another improvement common to all GM makes is a switch to a new transmission fluid containing chemicals to keep the intricate passageways and parts clean.

Either drum or disc-front brakes are available, but before spending money for the disc option, it should be remembered that Buick-built drum systems are probably the best in the business. Some comparative figures are given in the section on the Electra 225 which shares the same system as the Riviera. Other detailed improvements include hidden wipers that have a new parallel motion that wipes 20 percent more glass surface. More importantly, most of this increase is in front of the driver where it counts. The left-hand blade is articulated to reach within an inch of the vital left "A" post. Another convenience item is the spade-handled shift lever that is much easier to grasp.

1. Buick's Riviera comes in this 2-door hardtop body style only, but there is a Gran Sport model available which has heavy duty suspension and a "GS" nameplate

2. Riviera's tail lights are concealed almost as well as its headlights. Did you notice there are no windwings?

Vital Statistics	
Horsepower	360
Torque, lbs-ft	475
Axle ratios	3.07-3.91
Wheelbase	119.0 ins.
Length	215.2 ins.
Width	78.1 ins.
Height	53.2 ins.
Curb to curb	44.1 ft.
Fuel tank	21 gal.
Brakes	drum/disc opt.
Tires	8.45 x 15/rad opt.
Service	2 mos/6000 miles

RT/TEST REPORT

RIVIERA... A Buick That Lives Up to Its Slogan

"When better cars are built, Buick will build them" is a familiar theme that sometimes has been more fiction than fact. The new Riviera, though, is THE better Buick.

It's very seldom that advance word leaks out on a new Buick, not so much because their security is any tighter than the others, but because it just hasn't become a habit to look to Buick for innovation. They lost the performance image of the old Century years ago. Succeeding generations of Buicks have come and gone, notable mostly for their increasingly soft ride, non controversial appearance and plush interiors. Even the latter-day GS 455 was a much too genteel looking hot rod to convince anyone that Buicks really could be made to perform.

Then there was the Riviera which gradually evolved into a quite strikingly good looking car. There are many who will argue that the '70 Riviera was the best looking car on the road, but these fans are also the first to admit that there was nothing about its handling that appealed. Wallowing down the highway behind the wheel of a recent Riviera is undeniably comfortable, perhaps almost soporific, but the experience is not calculated to generate oneness with the machine. On a reasonably smooth road, a passenger could close his eyes and believe he was standing still. That represents a high standard of engineering in the sense that Buick has

The Riviera's front wheels have been moved ahead three inches to give nice balance to the clean new frontal appearance. The bumper in front would seem highly practical.

managed to make its big cars the nearest thing to a mobile living room on the market. However, quite a bit that some people like in their cars was sacrificed in the process.

Whether the old design team was transferred to Cadillac en masse or not, we don't know, but the '71 Riviera is now a handling jewel without losing too many of its former characteristics on the straight. Maybe a management that we know is new allowed the existing design team to follow their true instincts, which is more probably what happened. In any case, there is much about the new Riviera that will now appeal to the enthusiast, and the appeal started way back in July when sketches of it first appeared in this magazine.

First, though, we should take note of certain styling features that affect the driver. That vast expanse of glass which carries the spreading boattail theme up into the roof is fine for rearward visibility of distant objects. Backing into a parallel parking space, however, is another matter. The raised, or boattail, portion of the trunk makes it hard to judge close distances

photos by Bob Benyan

Here a demonstration Riviera with Max Trac turned off shows the futility of accelerating with wheels spinning on specially soaped test track.

With Max Trac in operation, the car moves off surely if sedately on the same soaped track. The optional electronic device is a Riviera exclusive for 1971.

and there's also that brutally sharp projection in the rear bumper. Owners of Volkswagens and other lightly protected cars would be well advised to ignore a parking space adjacent to a Riviera and Riviera owners, in turn, hopefully be aware of the lethal weapon in their hands. If a Riviera owner asks for a push, loan him your Auto Club card instead.

The rear glass has a very complex curvature and this necessitated stress relief to prevent it from fracturing during installation or during extreme body stress such as caused by climbing a curb. Much like the present Eldorado, you can see this stress line quite clearly in the rear view mirror and it tends to separate a following car into two halves. That's a little disconcerting but it can't be considered a safety hazard. Then, as we've noted elsewhere, the glass doesn't extend far enough over the rear passengers to cause them discomfort from the sun.

The trunk itself is claimed to be 20% larger than the previous model, giving it a capacity of about 12 cubic feet. However, the extra space is all

Another advantage of Max Trac is to ease the transition between dry and slippery surfaces which is the time when the average driver loses control.

From a little distance the boattail shape and pronounced bumper projection of the '71 Riviera isn't too noticeable but avoid them in parking lots.

under the boattail bulge, and packing so this can be used is sort of like trying to check to see if the refrigerator door light goes out when the door closes. You have to slam the lid without disturbing the precarious balance of the top-most duffle. There's also some problem with accumulated water entering the luggage area when the lid is opened.

The orientation of the instruments, or rather the warning lights and accessory controls, to the driver is excellent and this is one of those new-type GM panels where you can change a bulb in a few minutes without standing on your head. The fan-type speedometer is right in front of you and the other items wrap around on either side. On the passenger side, the glove drawer has a concave padded shape.

All Rivieras have the three-speed Series 400 Turbo Hydra-Matic as standard equipment but our test car included the optional console. The unusual feature of this is that it slants in toward the driver, which makes the lighted quadrant easier to read. The wheel slant was a little steep for our tastes, but this could easily be remedied by ordering the optional tilt column. The panel and interior utilizes softly finished metal trim, rather than the ubiquitous imitation wood so often found in cars of this class. This wood may look well for a year or so, but being a veneer, will sooner or later tend to fade and fray at the edges.

A hangover from Buick's all-out-for-comfort past is the jelly-smooth action of the brake and accelerator pedals. We'd really prefer a little more resistance in both of them. You tend to overbrake because of the small gap in the pressures required for normal and panic stops. Then, with the soft accelerator, you can't just rest your foot to maintain speed. It will increase that way so you have to rather tiresomely keep lifting pressure on your throttle leg. A driver used to other makes might have a little trouble with over-controlling the throttle in parking maneuvers at first.

The standard steering is variable-ratio power, which, as far as we're concerned, is the best solution yet to give big American cars a reasonable degree of feel. Both extremes of the ratio are unusually fast, ranging from 16.5 to 14.56 to one. In fact, we know of no other Detroit product with a ratio as fast as that lower one. Even at the risk of repetition, it should be pointed out that the lower (numerical) ratio holds forth during most road maneuvers. The higher ratio comes in near the lock point on each side for easier parking and negotiation of hair-pin turns. You won't believe this, but the Riviera requires only 2.94 turns of the wheel from lock to lock. That figure is within a fraction (.04) of the turns required in a Corvette and need we add that the latter is generally conceded to be a true sports car.

From steering wheel to cornering is a logical progression and here the '71 Riviera shines, the first Buick to do so in our memory, which dates back to testing '55 models when they were new. Of necessity, because it was way before official introduction time, our present test took place at GM's vast Milford proving grounds about 50 miles Northwest of Detroit.

The Riviera dash is all-new, plush but still emphasizes warning lights. Any bulb, instrument, control or the radio may be removed in minutes for service.

Buick has a better idea with its new tie-down for the seat belts. This accessory comes when the custom seat belt option is ordered.

There are disadvantages to this in that test mileage is limited and you don't get the chance to "live" with the car in day-to-day use. On the other hand, these proving grounds condense every kind of bad road imaginable within their 3,400 acres. From a handling standpoint, you learn more in an afternoon than you would on a trans-continental trip.

In any case, there's one particularly nasty reverse camber curve with an even nastier increasing radius that you descend upon from a 20% grade. The Riviera took this with no lean and very little tire squeal at 70 miles per hour. We've been around this particular turn before in other GM prototypes, but never faster. Part of the freedom from tire squeal is due to the fact that Riviera tires are one-of-a-kind that are engineered for the Riviera. Essentially, they're the ordinary 4PR belted variety, but tuning ply angles for a specific car has an obvious advantage. These tires, however, are not the secret of the new handling.

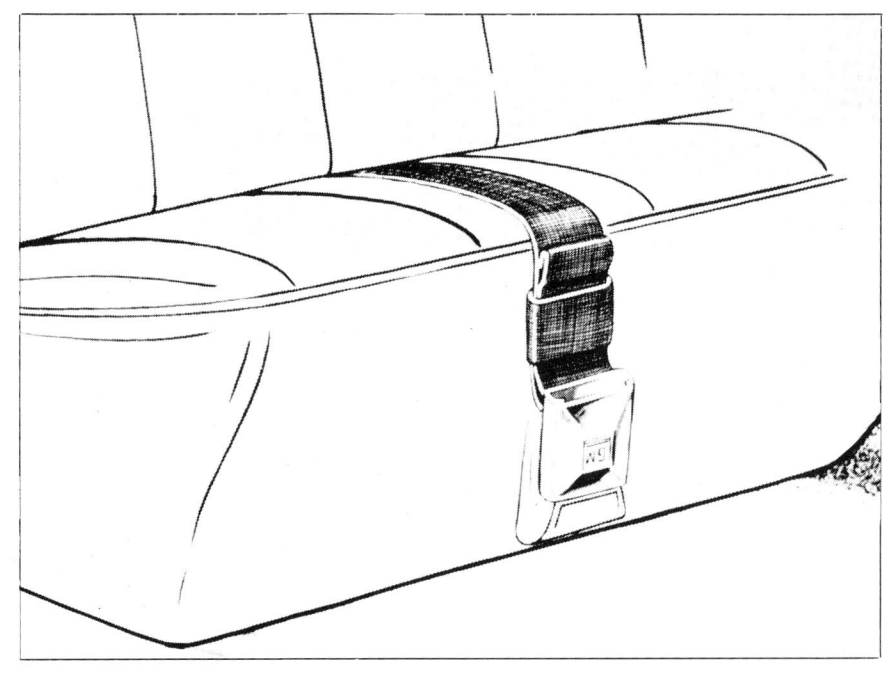

The level cornering is the result of "Accudrive," a name given to a suspension geometry that reacts against centrifugal force. Up to a point, the harder you corner, the harder the suspension on the outside pushes back against the body's tendency to lean. The same principle also works on undulating straight sections of road, in gusty crosswinds and when you're passing or being passed by a large truck or bus. It's all in the geometry of how the wheels travel through their arc as the spring compresses. As viewed on a grease rack, the Riviera would seem to have the ordinary coil springs fore and aft that have been Buick fixtures since 1938. What is the more remarkable is that a link-type stabilizer is used only in the front, not at the rear.

Accudrive does not affect the softness of the Riviera's turnpike ride but it feels like a handling package when the springs are working. It doesn't, though, serve up the harshness of the ordinary optional suspensions. Some of these, at their extremes, make you

100

Here the Riviera is just beginning a full throttle zero to 60 mph run. Note complete absence of wheel spin with Max-Trac in operation.

feel you should have ordered heavy-duty door handles, glove box and a bag of sand to keep the empty, chattering passenger bucket still. That latter is actually a pretty good though non-scientific test criteria. If you've got a car that corners to your satisfaction and doesn't rattle the seat on a freeway, you know that some talented engineers had a hand in the design.

The Riviera has two engine choices, both being variations of the 455-cubic-inch V-8 used in single exhaust form in the even heavier Electra and Centurion. The Riviera has standard dual exhausts which enables this engine to produce 315 horsepower at 4,400 rpm and 450 foot-pounds of torque at 2,800 rpm. These figures are arrived at by the more familiar gross rating method and reflect only the drop caused by de-tuning the engine for operation of low-lead, 91-octane fuels. The optional GS engine produces 330 horsepower and 455 foot-pounds of torque, thanks to a slightly hotter cam that peaks the horsepower at 4,600 rpm. Our test car had this engine which calls for a mandatory 3.42 axle ratio with a limited slip differential.

The detuning hasn't hurt performance too much because once a car can achieve zero to 60 miles per hour in 9 seconds or less, anything faster becomes a bit academic on the street. Screeching tires and clouds of rubber smoke will sooner or later net you a ticket for an "agressive display of performance." Our test car, with two aboard, managed this maneuver in 9.1 seconds which isn't much over what last year's premium fuel, 370-horsepower Riviera would do. We also don't know how much was gained or lost by the optional "Max Trac" installation which we'll describe in more detail shortly. The standing quarter came in 15.9 seconds at 88 miles per hour, again not bad at all for a car laden down with air-conditioning and every other accessory in the catalog.

In this day when anti-skid means electronically controlled braking on two or four wheels, Max Trac comes as a bit of a surprise. This system, which is electronic also, prevents the wheels from spinning under acceleration. It was demonstrated by equipping a Riviera with a cut-out switch and running it up and down a slick, soaped stretch of macadam with and without Max Trac in operation. Without the device in operation the car fishtailed wildly as the pictures show. With it turned on, progress from rest was steady and straight, although admittedly a bit sedate. There being only one car equipped with the device, it wasn't possible to stage a race so we don't know if Max Trac got you from A to B faster. At least, it got you there more safely as without it, you occupied more than just two lanes of road.

The device, which uses sensors in the front wheel and on the transmission shaft feeding through a computer to detect and control wheelspin at the rear, is primarily intended for use on slick surfaces although it is in operation as soon as the ignition is turned on under any circumstances. It would also, however, effectively prevent wheelspin on a dry pavement and the acceleration times cited above were obtained with Max Trac operating. We got the feeling we might have gone a little faster without, on dry pavement, but that could be pure imagination. Anyway, it is doubtful if this optional device will have much acceptance or crowd appeal at the local drag strip of a Sunday afternoon.

It is used in conjunction with, rather than replacing the normal locked differential. A locked differential only diverts traction from the wheel that's slipping to the wheel that's not. If both are spinning, the locked differential is of little assistance but, of course, Max Trac works better when it is combined with a locked differential. When the sensors detect a trace of wheel spin, you can pour on all the throttle you want to no avail. The car will proceed only as fast as there is traction. This trait might get a little hairy if you got caught on an ice slick while passing someone on a two-lane road. Wheel spin could possibly burn through a thin layer of ice and get you around. Max Trac would take its own sweet time.

Ideally Max Trac should be combined with Imperial's new four-wheel anti-skid brake system but the Riviera brakes are pretty good by themselves.

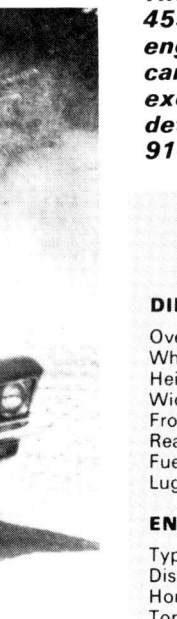

The 330-horsepower, 455-cubic-inch Riviera GS engine is essentially a carryover from last year except for a 40-horsepower detuning for operation on 91-octane gasoline.

Power assisted front discs are standard equipment and the rear drums are well modulated to prevent premature lock-up. The Riviera dives hardly at all when maximum pressure is applied and stops were straight and short. We couldn't measure them exactly but they looked to be in the neighborhood of 160 feet from 60 miles per hour.

The Riviera was a total and very pleasing surprise to us, as it will be to buyers whether they are used to past Buicks or not. Only in cars like the more expensive Jaguar XJ6 have

Never a Buick forte until this new model year, the Riviera now corners with the best of them. The rapid 2.94 steering lock matches Corvette.

we encountered a similarly happy combination of soft ride and fine handling. It performs agilely enough for any normal need and the appointments are luxurious. The styling? Well, that's a matter of personal opinion. We like it from the side and front, anyway.

Buick Riviera GS
Data In Brief

DIMENSIONS

Overall length (ins.)	217.4
Wheelbase (ins.)	122.0
Height (ins.)	54.0
Width (ins.)	79.9
Front tread (ins.)	63.6
Rear tread (ins.)	64.0
Fuel capacity (gal.)	25.0
Luggage capacity (cu. ft.)	12.4

ENGINE (in test car)

Type	OHV V-8
Displacement (cu. in.)	455
Horsepower (4600 rpm)	330
Torque (ft.-lb. at 2800 rpm)	455

WEIGHT, TIRES, BRAKES

Weight (lbs.)	4428
Tires	H78×15
Brakes, front	Power disc
Brakes, rear	Power drum

SUSPENSION

Front	Stamped A-frame upper and lower control arms, coil springs and ball joints. Link stabilizer
Rear	4-link, coil springs

PERFORMANCE

Standing quarter mile (sec.)	15.9
Speed at end of ¼ mile (mph.)	88
0-60 mph (sec.)	9.1
Braking from 60 mph (ft.)	160

ALMOST A LIMOUSINE

Riviera-Thunderbird-Toronado, three personal luxury cars for the junior executive who almost has it made

BY JIM BROKAW

The man who buys one of the three current personal luxury standards — Toronado, Riviera, Thunderbird — is like the quarterback who has a first down on the goal line. Success is just a couple of smart moves away. But, if you blow the chance, you have to settle for a field goal and quarterbacks don't get credit for field goals. (George Blanda excepted.)

These cars are expensive. If you have to check your budget to see whether you can handle the payments, you can't afford one. They're totally impractical for many family pursuits, which indicates that there is at least one other means of transportation sharing the garage. Beach trips with wet bottoms and sandy feet are out. Hauling around a couple of sweaty, dirty, teeny-weeny football players is out. Interior space is comfortable for four adults, adequate for five, and tolerable for six on a quick trip from the office to an expense account lunch.

Power won't peel rubber but it will get you around town quick enough to grab a ticket if you try. Handling is surprisingly good on all three, but not good enough to get careless on strange roads. Economy really isn't there in the true sense of gas mileage.

If these creatures seem to have all of the disadvantages of the other classes of cars and few of the advantages, what do they have that keeps them selling? Prestige. In spite of advertising claims labeling the mini-limos as sports-luxury, the thing that brings in the buyer is good old fashioned status. For something under $7,000 the owner can announce to the world that he has

ALMOST A LIMOUSINE

arrived, and will shortly move on to bigger things and out of the neighborhood.

Once upon a time, just because your car was luxurious, you didn't have to suffer poor handling. Cadillacs even raced at LeMans in the early 50's. But, in the last two decades, domestic luxury cars have grown fat and lazy, content in wallowing their way about corners as they tote up to a half-ton of options to keep their inhabitants oblivious to the fact that they're in a car rather than a living room.

But our test of this year's crop of instant envy machines came up with a surprise — handling that was unexpectedly good for luxury vehicles.

Our test cars were each ordered with the "whole shot" — big engine, all power, automatic transmissions — each representative of the way the cars are usually ordered by the big buck buyers in this class. The Thunderbird has the smallest engine, in terms of cubes, if you call a 429 V8 small, and the other two GM cars, the Riviera and Toronado, both had 455 cu. in. V8s, rated at 315 hp and 350 hp respectively. A higher horsepower version of the Riv, the Gran Sport, is available, but since there are no "hot" versions of the T-bird and Toronado, we did not order it. Gone is the mushy ride, and tire-scrubbing noises while you're turning, gone is the slow sway on the easy corner. Updated suspensions and the phenomenal recent success of Mercedes, have blessed the affluent with a firm but comfortable ride and the ability to hustle around a corner in a level attitude.

Both Toronado and Riviera have revised suspension systems. A wide span front lower control arm permits better dive control while the rear suspension on both units is completely redesigned. One of the reasons for a complete suspension revision is the switch to a full perimeter frame. The partial frame with a "floating" rear suspension has been abandoned. While both GM products have the full frame, the rear end treatment is unique to each model, primarily because the front-wheel-drive Toro has less weight to worry about in the back.

Toronado uses a fairly light coil spring with a trailing arm track bar. Transverse links retain lateral stability, but the rear axle actually pivots around the forward mount on the longitudinal track bar. This set-up very effectively eliminates the small bump of last year's dead axle/carriage-spring layout. Unfortunately, there is a slight penalty. While it handles the harsh bumps with disdain, the Toronado tends to loaf on the more moderately sloped rolling ones.

The Riviera does not have to contend with some rear end unsprung weight so the Buick engineers have taken a slightly different approach. The four-link layout is basically the same but the whole thing is beefier, including the springs, producing a different rebound effect than Toronado. The 1-inch anti-sway bar up front does a great deal to improve handling on the corners as well as dampening out any roll movement imparted to the rear end. Small, short amplitude bumps produce a slight harshness but the larger ones do not generate any unpleasant rebound. Under heavy cornering, the Riviera still tends to understeer and plow a bit, but much less than expected and not at all uncomfortable. Liberal use of body snubbers keeps the ride free of unwanted road noise.

Since both the Toronado and the Riviera are built by GM, albeit different divisions, the comparison of the handling characteristics is quite revealing. Like all the front-wheel-drive cars, the Toro has an inordinate amount of weight up front, tending to induce massive understeer, almost to the point that you would have to start turning at the corner grocery store to make it in the driveway. The anticipated trip to the outside of the turn never occurs, however, because the tendency to plow is overcome by the natural tendency of a powered wheel to proceed in the direction in which it is pointed.

Thunderbird also has four-coil suspension but the lateral and longitudinal restraints are handled a bit differently. The front end has drag-strut type bars to absorb high frequency vibrations, and high impact shock, which it does very nicely. The rear end has three trailing control arms, two below the axle and one above, and a lateral track bar. The net result is a slightly firmer ride than the Toro or the Riviera, but much less roll control than either. The T-bird takes a set position going into a corner which can be a bit disturbing if done at too high a rate of speed, but once it takes a tack, it holds what it has all the way through. The Bird requires a bit of attention going into a corner at high speed, but produces no surprises after the initial turn is passed. Small, rough bumps are felt, but not to an uncomfortable degree, and the larger ones are traversed unnoticed.

The most dominant impression when driving or riding in any of the three cars is the feeling of isolation you get — isolation from the road surface, isolation from any feeling of acceleration or braking. You could go from a concrete road, across a metal bridge grate, to a gravel road and there will be no vibrations coming to tell you that you're on a different road surface. While this will turn off "feel-of-the-road" buffs, this car-as-a-cocoon philosophy is great if you want to look upon your car as a place to unwind and relax, even while trying to drive 700 miles between sun-up and sun-down.

continued on page 106

Riviera instrument panel lacks gauges, b[ut] clusters controls in easy reach. Right si[de] dimensions are specifically tailored for a lad[y]

T-Bird dash is well instrumented and easy [to] read. Courtesy light under glare shield is e[x]cellent for map reading and other night game[s]

Toronado dash follows Riviera cockpit them[e] but lacks delicate balance and styling fines[se] of the dual curved approach favored by Buic[k]

viera's massive mpers, bulging fenders and at-tail rear deck nstitute a return to a more bstantial styling mode. Lateral tortion through ar window does not affect the iver's judgment of distance.

Thunderbird ains last year's yling with only niscule chrome anges to enable e salesmen to istinguish the fference in the dels. Durability design is a new end which may minate planned bsolescence.

onado bears a marked semblance to '70 Eldorado, not by accident. onado fans will y it and so will former Eldo tomers who do ot take to big ther's restyling 71, so hope the marketing managers.

ALMOST A LIMOUSINE

Interestingly, Thunderbird is the only American car offered with radial ply tires as optional equipment, although our test car had the bias-belted wide ovals, which are more consistent with the cushiony ride concept. But, if you want luxury driving *plus* feel of the road, order radials.

In spite of the sporty styling and mammoth engines, none of the three cars will turn drag strip times that will scare any supercar owners. The Riviera was fastest, up to 60, turning an 8.8-second time compared to the T-bird's 9.2. Still, in one of those phenomenons known only to quarter-mile racing, the T-bird was fastest "through the eyes," turning a 16.25-second e.t. at 86 mph while the Riviera could only get it down to a 16.60-second e.t. at 88 mph. The Toronado was up at 16.90 seconds at 84 mph.

Speedometer error was most pronounced on the T-bird, reading 7 miles per hour faster than you were actually driving. The other two cars read a mile above or below your actual speed. The fact that brand new cars can have off-register speedometers should motivate you to get yours checked for accuracy before an officer does.

We entered into the braking tests with trepidation. While driving two tons of luxury car is great for comfort, there comes a time when you're going to have to stop in a hurry. It's then when you wish maybe your car was a little lighter.

All three cars stopped in a straight line from 30 mph, the T-bird stopping the quickest, and the Riviera second in braking ability. The story was the same from 60 mph, the T-bird taking 129 feet to stop, compared to the Riviera's 146 feet and the Toronado's 182. It was in the maximum effort stop from 60 that the heavy weight on the front end of all three cars, particularly the Toronado, demanded its penalty in controllability. All three cars began to swing sideways when the brakes were applied hard at 60 mph and, while the Riviera and T-bird took only one steering correction from the driver to prevent a spin, the Toronado took two fast lock-to-lock maneuvers to keep the back end from coming around, not at all in keeping with the machine's generally highly engineered nature.

The styling of the cars is the primary point of distinction. Each has a different theme, each imparts a unique impression and each generates a completely different attitude or feeling on the part of the driver. The Toronado is a refinement of last year's Eldorado. This is not an accident nor is it a money-saving ploy. The old Eldo was quite popular and people who buy Eldos tend to be quite firm in their opinions. Retaining a taste of Eldo in the Toronado opens the field to two types of customer. The ones who do not like the new design of the Eldo and did like the old, will be pleased with the Toronado. The Oldsmobile customers who couldn't afford an Eldo but liked them, will now be able to possess the styling they have been hankering after the past.

Riviera is a statement of what's happening. In spite of the fact that the car is a bold departure from what is current and accepted, it is by no means new. The rear end boat tail treatment bears more than a passing resemblance to a '63 Corvette, but its ancestry goes much farther back than that. Remember the Cadillac LeSabre in 1951? With the exception of the tail fins and the loop nose, the general body outlines are almost identical. This, reflecting perhaps a return to some of the solid values of earlier times.

Thunderbird doesn't have anything really new to offer other than last year's Bunkie Knudsen redesign. One gets the impression that T-bird is about to move off in a new direction but is

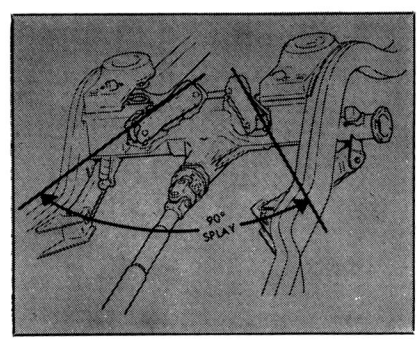

Riviera and Toronado share the same rear suspension design in different dimensions. Four link configuration permits greater roll and sway control with no sacrifice in comfort.

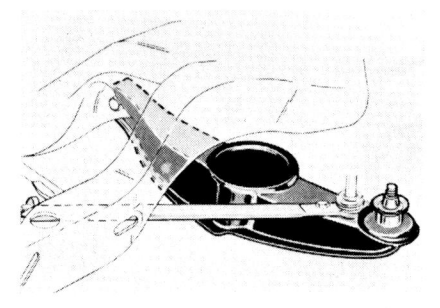

Above: Single mounted, narrow lower front control arm on Riviera has been replaced by heavier triangular piece (below) which reduces bump steer and increases stability.

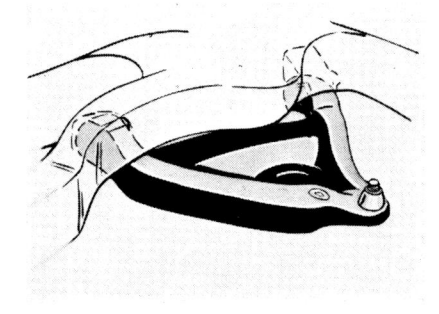

now in a period of transition and hasn't yet made up its mind as to the intended path. Then too, it is part of the current durability-of-design concept being touted in Detroit; make it good and keep it around for awhile. Rumor has it that the current design for the Toronado will be with us for a good four or five years as well.

Interior styling presented more contrast between the three cars than their exterior. The Toronado was almost Spartan-looking, with the passenger's side of the instrument panel bare as a bone (for safety and to accept air bags should they be required) and all the controls hidden away and activated by mysterious electric motors. The Riviera came across with a bit more pomp and circumstance in the interior, with more plumped-up upholstery and a double-dip dash panel which molds itself around both driver and passenger. The Thunderbird's interior, though, was the Grand Palace of the lot. With its button-tufted brocade cloth upholstery, wrap-around rear seat and tunnel-like Cave of Love cockpit, created by the elimination of the rear quarter windows – it looked like something befitting Mae West or maybe even "Broadway" Joe Namath. With all its pizazz, the T-bird's sumptuousness couldn't match the practicality of Toronado's flat front floor – the unique advantage permitted by front wheel drive. One "problem" with the T-bird's interior was noted by a Swede who was invited to ride in the T-bird. He commented that it was typical of the American puritan ethic that "you have a car that looks like a bedroom but the seats don't fold down."

Overall, we feel that any of these cars fill the bill as far as being good combinations of comfort conveniences, handling quality and performance. You couldn't be any more comfortable in a Lincoln or Cadillac unless someone else was driving. Their air conditioners wouldn't make you any cooler nor would their seats be any softer. But the bigger-is-better philosophy still rules at GM and Ford styling and lots of people will still go on thinking that a car the size of a Riviera, Toronado or T-bird couldn't be as luxurious as a car three feet longer. We would even like to see the luxury approach tried on something three feet shorter than our test cars.

While all the attention paid to the Vega, Pinto, et al would seem to give the impression that the auto-makers have abandoned their Queen Mary-sized cars and taken to the life-boat-sized compacts, there are still thousands of consumers to whom "bigger is better" is a viable concept. You may call them the "establishment" derogatorily but, for establishment cars, the three we tested were cars worth owning, and even saving for. Tradition is a good thing-sometimes. /MT

MOTOR TREND SPECIFICATION DATA

SPECIFICATIONS	RIVIERA	THUNDERBIRD	TORONADO
Engine:	90° OHV V8	90° OHV V8	90° OHV V8
Bore & Stroke — ins.	4.3125 x 3.90	4.362 x 3.59	4.125 x 4.250
Displacement — cu. in.	455	429	455
HP @ RPM	315 @ 4400	360 @ 4600	275 @ 4200
Torque: lbs.-ft. @ rpm	450 @ 2800	480 @ 2800	375 @ 2800
Compression Ratio	8.5:1	10.5:1	8.5:1
Carburetion	4V	4V	4V
Transmission	3-spd auto, turbo hydramatic	3-spd auto	3-spd auto
Final Drive Ratio	2.93:1	3.00:1	3.07:1
Steering Type	Power, variable ratio	Power	Power
Steering Ratio	16.5-14.56:1	21.9:1	17.9:1
Turning Diameter (Curb-to-curb ft.)	43.3	42.7	44.3
Wheel Turns (lock-to-lock)	2.94	4.0	3.4
Tire Size	H78-15 bias-belted	H78-15 bias-belted	J78-15 bias belted
Brakes	Power disc/drum	Power disc/drum	Power disc/drum
Front Suspension	Coil, shock, upper & lower A frame control arms	Coil, shock, upper & lower control arms	Torsion bar link stabilizer
Rear Suspension	Coil, shock, 4-link	Coil, shock, 3 control arms & lateral track bar	Coil, shock, 4-link
Body/Frame Construction	Body on full Perimeter frame	Body on full perimeter frame	Body on full perimeter frame

PERFORMANCE	RIVIERA	THUNDERBIRD	TORONADO
Acceleration			
0-30 mph	3.3	3.9	4.4
0-45 mph	5.5	6.4	7.2
0-60 mph	8.4	9.2	10.7
0-75 mph	12.6	13.3	15.5
Standing Start			
¼-mile mph	83	85.6	84.0
Elapsed time	16.9	16.4	16.9
Passing speeds			
40-60 mph	5.1	4.1	6.4
50-70 mph	5.5	5.0	6.5
Speed in gears*			
1st ....mph @ rpm	45 @ 4000	43 @ 4000	48 @ 4500
2nd ....mph @ rpm	77 @ 4000	74 @ 4000	80 @ 4500
3rd ....mph @ rpm	96 @ 3500	91 @ 3500	89 @ 3500
Mph per 1000 rpm (in top gear)	27.4	26	25.4
Stopping distances			
From 30 mph	29.8	27	30.0
From 60 mph	135.2	145	175.0
Speedometer error			
Electric speedometer	30 45 50 60 70 80	30 45 50 60 70 80	30 45 50 60 70 80
Car speedometer	31 46 51 62 72 82	37 52 57 67 78 89	28.5 43 48.5 59 69 79

*Speeds in gears are maximum speeds. (limited by the length of track)

1971 RIVIERA

Mfg. suggested retail price	$5,251.00
Max trac	91.57
Radio AM/FM	238.92
White walls	40.00
Climate control	515.73
Seat belts	26.32
Cornering lights	36.84
Speed alert	17.90
Fingertip windshield wipers	21.05
Tinted glass	49.47
Rear window defroster	31.58
Power seats (6-way)	105.25
Power windows	126.30
Cruise master	68.42
Electric door locks	47.37
Power brakes disc/drum	Std.
Power steering	Std.
Invoice	$6,667.72

1971 THUNDERBIRD

Two-door Landau base	$5,357.00
429-4V	Std.
Select shift Cruis-o-matic	Std.
Power steering	Std.
Power brakes disc/drum	Std.
Vinyl roof	Std.
Sequential turn signals	Std.
Remote mirror	Std.
Electric clock	Std.
Front cornering lights	Std.
Auto parking brake release	Std.
NOX emission control	Std.
Brougham cloth & vinyl trim	170.13
WSW tires H78x15	31.53
Convenience Check Group Courtesy lights & extra warning lights Seat back release — vacuum door locks	106.07
Tilt steering wheel	54.67
6-way power seat	103.89
A/C select-air	448.36
AM/FM stereo radio	157.47
Tinted glass	50.46
Power windows	115.46
Deluxe wheel covers	54.67
Invoice	$6,649.71

1971 TORONADO

Base price	$5,459.00
Corner lamps	36.86
A/C 4 season	437.08
Tinted glass	49.50
Belted WSW tires	36.86
AM radio	87.42
Rear speaker	18.96
Power trunk release	14.78
Convenience group Courtesy lights & vanity mirror Extra warning lights	21.80
Chrome door guards	6.32
Power windows	126.38
Power door locks	47.39
6-way power seat	105.32
Low fuel warning light	9.48
Automatic transmission	Std.
Power steering	Std.
Power brakes disc/drum	Std.
Dual Exhaust	Std.
Heavy duty battery	Std.
Clock	Std.
Rear cigarette lighters	Std.
Front center arm rest	Std.
Remote mirror	Std.
Invoice	$6,457.15

1971. Buick introduces a new set of values.

1971 Buick Riviera GS.

The things people expected out of a performance car a few years ago aren't the same anymore.

They want more than emblems in return for their money. They want more value.

And value is what has led more people to Buick's performance cars every year. A whole new set of values await you in your dealer's showroom now.

Our new Riviera GS is the ultimate in an American luxury performance car. Its styling alone will set a trend. But you want more than that. And we want to give you more.

The Riviera engine.

The new Riviera GS features a big 455 cubic-inch V-8 engine designed to run clean and smooth. We put in improvements like a new time-modulated carburetor choke that will give quicker warm-ups and a more consistent fuel mixture. And we've even added new, exclusive nickel-plated engine exhaust valves for smoother engine operation and longer valve life.

The transmission.

A specially calibrated 3-speed Turbo-Hydramatic 400. The shift lever can be mounted on an available between-the-seats console that is slanted toward the driver for ease of operation.

Suspension and handling.

New, longer wheelbase with improved AccuDrive directional stability system. Full-perimeter frame. Heavy, side-guard beams for added protection. A four-link rear suspension, specifically engineered fiberglass belted, white wall tires, heavy-duty springs and shocks, stabilizer bars and heavy-duty suspension bushings will give you ride and handling without peer. Positive traction differential (3.42 axle ratio standard).

The interior and braking.

More room inside. Even in the trunk. Driver cockpit includes new control center designed around driver for ease and convenience. New brakes have a unique valve that proportions braking force front to rear to help give you quick, smooth, straight-line stops. Standard equipment includes power front disc brakes, more nimble variable-ratio power steering and, of course, automatic transmission.

MaxTrac. Another Buick first.

We introduced MaxTrac for 1971. And you can order it for the Riviera. Listen to what it does. If you're on the ice or in the snow or in the rain, MaxTrac helps give you cat-like handling ability. A miniature on-board computer does it by controlling the power to the rear wheels to reduce slipping on slick surfaces.

One last point. Study a new Riviera GS in person at your Buick dealer's. Only a Buick Dealer can offer you our new set of values. And we want you to test them against your values. We say we build cars that are something to believe in. So, ask a lot of questions. Until there is only one question left.

Wouldn't you really rather have a Buick.

Something to believe in.

RT/TEST REPORT

PHOTOS BY DALE F. KLEE

One Of A Kind

Buick's Riviera combines unique styling, roomy, luxury level comfort and well above average performance capabilities.

Cockpit of Buick Riviera is comparatively unchanged from last year. Using aluminum with engine turned design gives instrument panel the flavor of race car or high performance sports car.

In the super-competitive U.S. auto industry, each manufacturer aligns most offerings toe-to-toe with those of the other makers in type, size, options and price — a practice called slotting. There are some notable exceptions to slotting, however. One of these is an offering from General Motors Corp.'s Buick Division — the Riviera.

Riviera is without direct competition. Available in only one body style — a 2-door hardtop coupe — it represents an almost unique combination of high styling with an innovative flair, plus a fairly strong emphasis on both luxury and a rather high level of performance. All that in the same package!

In some respects, Riviera shares certain attributes with the front wheel drive Oldsmobile Toronado. It therefore has some things in common with the Cadillac Eldorado, since that car is derived from Toronado. A potential Riviera buyer might also look at a Ford Thunderbird or a Lincoln Continental Mark IV, though the similarity is mainly that these are loosely classified as personal luxury cars with performance overtones. On a point-by-point basis however, all these autos have more in common with each other than with Riviera.

Some car enthusiasts may wonder for whom the Riviera is produced. The answer isn't complicated — this is a car aimed in particular at a comparatively young (usually under age 40) man (or woman) of above average income who wants a lively automobile with lots of distinctiveness and a fairly high level of luxury.

As a '72 model, Riviera doesn't reflect any major appearance changes since last year when the car got an all-new frame, a wheelbase 3-in. longer than previously and new inner-outer body sheet metal including the eyebrow-raising "boat tail" rear styling. Largest appearance change is the new die-cast chrome plated grille which has a predominantly rectangular theme. Rubber bumper protective strips (front and rear) have been added to the option list.

The extra-cost bumper guards have been redesigned for greater strength and durability and provide a higher level of frontal protection. The rear bumper center guard has been revised to better protect sheet metal from damage. The combination taillight, turn lamp and backup light has new treatment and body side molding with a color-matching vinyl insert added as standard. In short, there were a number of comparatively minor exterior appearance changes, with the grille the biggest. Larger ones are under the skin.

Base price tag on ROAD TEST's Riviera, nearly fresh off the assembly line, was only the beginning. The rest of the sticker total was a somewhat whopping example of what you may pay for one of these unique cars if well equipped. The base auto retails for $5,099.00, plus $15.05 Federal excise tax on the tires (an irritation which remained when the vehicle excise tax was dropped). To this was added $29.00 for transportation charges to Detroit from the factory in Flint, Mich. (about 80 miles northwest of the Motor City) for a total of $5,143.05.

In addition, there were enough optional items to buy another car, though not a Riviera to be sure. Specifically, $2,621.00 worth of them, bringing the total tab to a tidy $7,764.05. By adding local and sales taxes, plus a dealer preparation fee, this Buick will cost above $8000.

ROAD TEST's Riviera, obviously loaded with extras, may not be truly representative of the car most typically ordered. It was so fully fitted out for special demonstration use; the objective apparently was to incorporate every available feature. Much of the extra equipment will be recorded in the appropriate part of this report, but a few items can best be noted here.

For one thing, the car had special exterior paint called Skylark blue — $113.00 extra — a little steep, it would seem. There was also a custom vinyl top (white) for $125.00, white wall tires (instead of black) for an additional $35.00 and chrome plated wheels $70.00. A total of $343 for mainly appearance items.

Two versions of the Riviera are available: the base model and the GS option, which costs $195.00 extra. Differences are mainly in the driveline, particularly the power plant. Both use Buick's largest engine, the 455 cu in. 4-bbl V8, and get an extra measure of output from it via dual exhausts, which are standard on the Riviera.

The 455 CID engine with a compression ratio of 8.5 to 1 operates on regular grade fuel of 91 octane or better. SAE net (at the wheels) figures are now used to rate engines, rather than SAE gross, as was common practice for decades. In the standard Riviera the 455 produces 375 lb ft of torque at 2800 rpm and 250 hp at 4000 rpm.

The GS 455 has modifications to the carburetor, camshaft, spark advance curve, among others, to raise output slightly. Torque is 380 lb ft, also at 2800 rpm, and maximum output is up to 260 hp but at 4400 rpm, instead of 4000 rpm with the base power plant.

Both engines are off very slightly in output from last year, to meet the tighter '72 emission rules. For example, the GS powerplant was rated at 265 hp SAE net (also at 4400 rpm) as a '71 — five horsepower more.

For 1972 both 455 engines incorporate some important improvements. One of these — a revised time modulated choke control — enables the engine to run on the leanest possible fuel mixture consistent with smooth performance during warmup. (The lean mixture is for low emissions). The choke control has a deeper seated thermostatic coil; it's now located closer than previously to heated exhaust gases. Result is faster response to changing temperatures during warmup, the key to the leaner mixtures.

An even more significant change for 1972 in Riviera power plant design for those cars sold in California is exhaust gas re-circulation (EGR). This lowers the formation of nitrogen oxides by mixing a small amount of exhaust gas with incoming fuel-air mixture during certain operating modes, particularly hard acceleration and high speed driving.

Considerable merit of EGR is that it lowers emissions to legally required levels without compromising driveability, as other approaches have. With it and the improved time modulated choke control Buick '72 engines have generally avoided complaints of poor driveability while some other makes have been plagued with such difficulties.

Riviera buyers can get regular wheels and choice of special optional wheel covers, or the chrome plated sports wheels shown here which cost $70.00 extra and don't use covers. Tires are built to special Riviera specifications, being tuned to the car's suspension for sports auto feel.

Buick has also incorporated a solenoid switch in the throttle linkage of the 455 engine to replace the previously used dash pot. The solenoid promptly closes the carburetor throttle plate when the ignition is turned off, blocking air flow and thus preventing continued combustion. That phenomena, usually called "run-on" or "dieseling" has been a problem with many late model, lower compression engines operating on lean mixtures of regular grade fuel to meet emission rules.

Other improvements to Riviera (and other Buick) power plants for 1972 include a revised throttle linkage for more immediate response to accelerator pedal movement. This results in a faster opening throttle and a consequent improvement in power plant performance. In addition, camshaft modifications reduce intake and exhaust valve overlap for smoother engine idle and improved engine response at low speed.

The big 3-speed Hydra-matic 400 transmission (Buick's largest) is the only one available in a Riviera. There's a slight variation in axle ratios however, with the 250 hp 455 getting 2.93:1 as standard and 3.42:1 optional. With the 260 hp GS 455, the 3.42:1 ratio is the only one offered.

Important drive line option unique to Buick Division, introduced on the '71 Riviera only and now available on all the Division's full size cars (but nowhere else in the industry) is Max Trac. This comparatively low-cost ($89.00) computerized rear axle control was developed to prevent fish tailing before it starts during hard acceleration, especially if traction is poor. It does this by controlling power fed to the rear wheels.

When Max Trac (the words formed from "maximum traction") senses that a rear wheel is starting to spin — from a wheel sensor — it modulates the power to it. This feature helps maintain traction on roads made slippery by rain, ice or snow. An On-Off switch permits use of the system when needed and reversion to standard drive when it might be desirable to have wheel spin to keep the car moving. In such a situation, Max Trac would limit rear wheel motion to a slow spin — not enough to keep the car underway.

Main objective of Riviera's suspension design was to provide a very high level of roadability with minimal compromise to handling attributes. To do this engineers developed a set of components quite unique to this car alone — its own specification shock absorbers, coil springs, stabilizer bar and even suspension bushings. Sum total of all this special tailoring should please most drivers who want luxury car ride with handling that has a good bit of the sports car "feel."

Emphasis is pretty clearly on the kind of operation good, straight highways permit, rather than on roads which require fast direction changing, however. If the Riviera is pushed fairly hard in cornering, it goes where it is aimed tractably enough without undue protest but with some understeer. It also leaves an apparent amount of rubber on the roadway.

Still Buick engineers manage a fairly good combination of diverse roadability and handling needs via coil suspension on all wheels and a steering system which the Division calls AccuDrive. Here the geometry tends to equally counter centrifugal force working on the car in direction changing, and in cross wind situations during straight ahead driving. This without sacrifice of resiliency for normal cruising. In other words an absence of harshness during turnpike travel, something expected with typical heavy duty suspension.

One liked Riviera roadability and handling feature is fast and responsive steering. Only 2.93 turns are required lock to lock which is getting into the area reserved for true sports cars. Variable ratio, with power assist, is used here, with sufficient feedback provided for steering feel not usually expected from large luxury cars. The anti-spin (Max Trac) system makes a solid contribution to handling also, especially in hard acceleration, particularly in the wet, minimizing fish tailing.

In low speed maneuvering for parking and where space is restricted, Riviera is still a big auto. Curb to curb turning requires 43.3 ft, only 2/10-in. less than the Electra 225 4-door hardtop sedan, and 2.9 in. more than the Centurion 4-door hardtop sedan.

Everything considered, and while Riviera acquits itself rather well in moderately robust handling exercises, it is not for the driver who goes in for a lot of action on less than first-class roads. The car shows itself off best on the open highway.

In the power and performance category Riviera can be a deceptive car to a driver unfamiliar with its main characteristics. The somewhat flashy styling can be misleading since it doesn't suggest the performance muscularity which is one of this car's basic design and selling points.

The Riviera will really get up and go and more than meets the requirements of fast paced urban traffic and wherever else rapid acceleration is desired. In these situations, away from standstill, Riviera will surprise owners of cars with a larger performance reputation, outrun some of them and make quite a few others work hard to defend their image.

Under maximum throttle situations, with some transmission pre-loading Riviera jumps away from standstill with little hint of tire spin (thanks to Max Trac) but with a quite rapid acceleration rate. Zero to 30 mph takes under 4 sec with several test runs recorded at 3.8 sec. Zero to 45 mph requires 7.1 sec with preloading, around 7.5 sec without. Zero to 60 mph took 9.9 sec on the best run.

In the quarter mile, with half a tank of fuel and driver weight of 205 lb (no passengers) ROAD TEST's Riviera made the fastest trip in 16.8 sec (terminal speed: 82 mph) — 9/10 sec slower than our time in a well-tuned 1971 model (November, 1970 issue). From idle to 75 mph, we needed 14.7 sec with the engine turning at about 2500 rpm before the brake was released.

For the motorist, who wants a good measure of lively action in a luxurious full-size car, the Riviera with the base 455 engine and standard (2.93:1) axle ratio ought to be quite adequate.

In the brakes and safety department, Riviera measures up well. Ever since engineers put the first 4-wheel brakes on a

Highly styled "boat tail" design of Riviera trunk lid costs a few cubes of luggage space because of pronounced slope. Total of 14.6 cu ft is provided — a bit less than for any other full size Buick car. Space saver tire would help a little here but is not available on Riviera.

Buick way back in 1923 (a '24 model), years ahead of most autos, the Division has annually laid claim to having "the best stopping system in the industry." Tangible evidence to support this contention has often been cited — Buick probably has spent a bit more time, design effort and money on brake systems than a lot of the competition.

For '72 Riviera continues with power-assisted front discs and composite cast iron rear drum brakes. That's about the best combination short of discs front and rear. They are still a few years ahead except for the Chevrolet Corvette which, alone among U.S.-built cars, has had them since the 1965 model was introduced.

Riviera's braking system is so effective that until the driver familiarizes himself with its personality and becomes fully aware of the need for a light touch, it might seem to be too much so. Our car, at least, displayed a tendency to lock all four wheels with what we felt was not unduly high system line pressure. Lockup of rear drum brakes, when the trunk and rear seat are empty is expected of many cars. Lockup of front discs isn't — at least not on front engined cars. But this happened toward the end of a number of initial test stops from 60 mph, even with weight transfer plus the engine's mass and good traction provided by the extra-wide biasbelted H78-15 tires (which have a 2-ply sidewall and 4-ply tread).

Best 60 mph to zero stop without wheel lockup, which seemed to need less brake pedal pressure than many other late model cars, required 178 ft. All test stops were without notable hint of swerve. Fade resulting from a hard series of stops to heat the friction surfaces was minimal, in part no doubt because the composite design of rear drums provides better than average heat absorption and dissipation.

In other safety-related respects, Riviera gets overall good ratings. Visibility is more than adequate in most respects. It is better than expected rearward through the huge back glass which is of somewhat complex shape to mate it to the unique styling of car's trunk lid. The optional, and previously mentioned anti-rear wheel spin system, cornering lights, speed alert, front light monitor and electric door and seat locks all contribute to the Riviera's safety level. So do some other extra cost items not so far noted, such as a rear window defogger ($31.00), front bumper guards ($30.00) and bumper protective strips ($24.00).

The speed alert, as should be explained, is part of the speedometer, has a yellow needle adjusted with a small knob on the instrument's face. When a pre-set speed is exceeded, a buzzer sounds until rate of travel drops below the previously decided limit or the dial is adjusted for a higher speed.

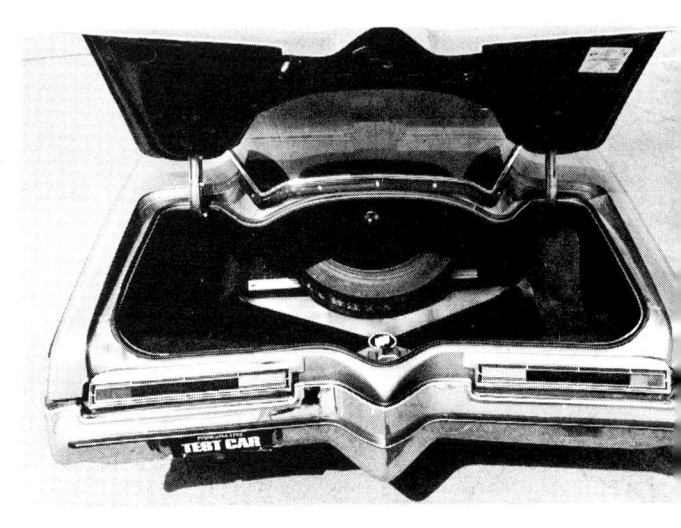

The front light monitor is an installation of light-transmitting (and bending) clear plastic cords which pick up illumination from headlights, turn signals and cornering lamps. They emerge in the form of indicators on the front fenders. This system provides positive indication when these lights are operating (or aren't) — a foolproof method far superior to the indicator system of separate bulbs which may (in some designs) glow even when a lamp has burned out.

In addition to intermediate and regular size classifications of cars, Buick has a third group, basically also full-size autos. These are the "upper series" vehicles — four models of the Electra, plus the Riviera hardtop coupe. One of the main things which distinguishes these cars from the other standard size autos (LeSabre, Centurion and the Estate Wagons) is the higher level of built-in comfort and convenience — in other words luxury — which Electra and Riviera get as part of the basic vehicle.

In addition to providing Buick's biggest engine and largest automatic transmission as standard equipment, the Riviera package includes some otherwise extra cost features at no charge. These include variable ratio power steering, power assisted brakes and a tilt steering wheel. Interior upholstering and trim is of higher quality. Among minor touches are a remote control outside left hand mirror and a clock.

Riviera is also eligible for a somewhat longer than usual list of extra comfort and convenience options. An electrically operated sun roof heads the list, cost-wise, at $589.00. That's in addition to the strictly-appearance vinyl top at $125.00 (which you don't have to order to get the sun roof, as is required for some make cars). Next was $405.00 extra for optional front seats — $200.00 for the split (60-40) type with a big center arm rest, custom cloth, vinyl notch back trim plus $205.00 for individual 6-way power for both passenger and driver sides.

In addition there was manual control air conditioning ($431.00), an AM-FM stereo radio with front and rear dual speakers ($233.00), power windows ($129.00), electric door and seat locks ($70.00), automatic cruise control ($67.00), tinted glass all around ($49.00), cornering lights ($36.00), front light monitor ($22.00), finger tip windshield washer control ($21.00), speed alert and trip odometer ($17.00) and door guards ($6.00). All this represents added-on comfort-convenience equipment listing for a total of $2075.00 — and this figure doesn't include that strictly-appearance vinyl top.

ROAD TEST's nearly month-long evaluation of the '72 Buick Riviera was during that period this year when Michigan weather was making slow and uncertain transition from Winter to Spring. This presented an opportunity to use all of

To meet 1972 Federal emission rules, both standard Riviera engine and the slightly more powerful GS version are off about five horsepower from last year, but the driver will find it difficult to detect the difference.

the car's extra features, from the anti rear wheel spin package following a light snowfall to the sun roof and even including (on one day) the air conditioning. This pointed up the fact that a fully equipped Riviera pretty much equals an out-and-out luxury car and in addition provides an extra measure of performance. But putting it all together does cost a fairly substantial sum.

To some motorists the Riviera will be found slightly lacking in one area of the convenience category. Rear styling costs somewhat in trunk capacity — its 14.6 cu ft compared to 17.0 cu ft for the Centurion 4-door hardtop sedan and 18.8 cu ft for all other full size Buick cars.

Riviera stands pretty much alone because it combines in one car an unusual group of attributes. These include unique styling, roomy, luxury level comfort and well above average performance capabilities in a comparatively low volume assembly line production car. The latter is important to motorists who avoid a car which looks like too many others. In most cases such a vehicle as this one commands a premium, price-wise.

Not so Riviera. It is no inexpensive car, but there's very tangible evidence of everything the sticker price includes — both as standard and optional equipment. This is in contrast to some makes and models for which the owner pays a substantial penalty for low-volume construction, too much of which is often hand work.

The current Riviera clearly represents the best yet for this model and total model year sales will undoubtedly reflect buyer awareness of this. While those sales will never be high compared with the volume offerings, that fact in no way suggests this is a lesser car than those built on assembly lines at a one-a-minute (or faster) rate. On the contrary, it's because Riviera is a special kind of better car for a special kind of motorist. ●

BUICK RIVIERA 2-DOOR HARDTOP

SPECIFICATIONS AS TESTED

Engine . . . . 455 cu in, OHV V8
Bore & stroke . . . . 4.31x3.90 ins.
Compression ratio . . . . 8.5 to one
Horsepower . . . . 250 (SAE net) at 4000 rpm
Torque . . . . 375 lbs-ft at 2800 rpm
Transmission . . . . 3-speed, automatic
Steering** . . . . 2.94 turns, lock to lock
43.3 ft, curb to curb
Brakes** . . . . disc front, drum rear
Suspension . . . . coil front, coil rear
Tires . . . . H 7.8x15, bias-belted
Dimensions (ins.):
  Wheelbase . . . 122.0   Rear track 64.0
  Length . . . . . 218.3   Ground clearance . . 5.5
  Width . . . . . . 80.0   Height 54.0
  Front track . . . 63.6   Weight . . . . . 4554 lbs
Capacities:
  Fuel . . . . . . 25 gals   Oil . . . . 4.0 qts
  Coolant . . . . 19.0 qts   Trunk . . . . . 14.6 cu ft

**Power assisted as tested

PERFORMANCE AND MAINTENANCE

Acceleration: Gears:
  0-30 mph . . . . 3.8 secs, 1st
  0-45 mph . . . . 7.1 secs, 1st, 2nd
  0-60 mph . . . . 9.9 secs, 1st, 2nd
  0-75 mph . . . . 14.7 secs, 1st-3rd
  0-¼ mile . . . . 16.8 secs at 85 mph
Ideal cruise . . . . 75 mph
Top speed (est) . . . . 123 mph
Stop from 60 mph* . . . . 171 ft
Average economy (city) . . . . 10.6 mpg
Average economy (country) . . . . 12.8 mpg
Fuel required . . . . Regular
Oil change (mos/miles) 4/4,000
Lubrication (mos/miles) 4/4,000
Warranty (mos/miles) 12/12,000
Type tools required . . . . SAE
U.S. dealers . . . . 3,300 total

*Anti-Spin installed

BASE PRICE OF CAR

(Excludes state and local taxes, license, dealer preparation and domestic transportation): $5,143.05 at Detroit
Plus desirable options:
$ 431.00 Air conditioning, manual control
$ 205.00 6-way power front seats
$ 200.00 60-40 front seat
$ 233.00 AM-FM stereo radio
$ 129.00 Power windows
$ 89.00 Anti-spin differential
$ 22.00 Front light monitor
$6,452.05 TOTAL

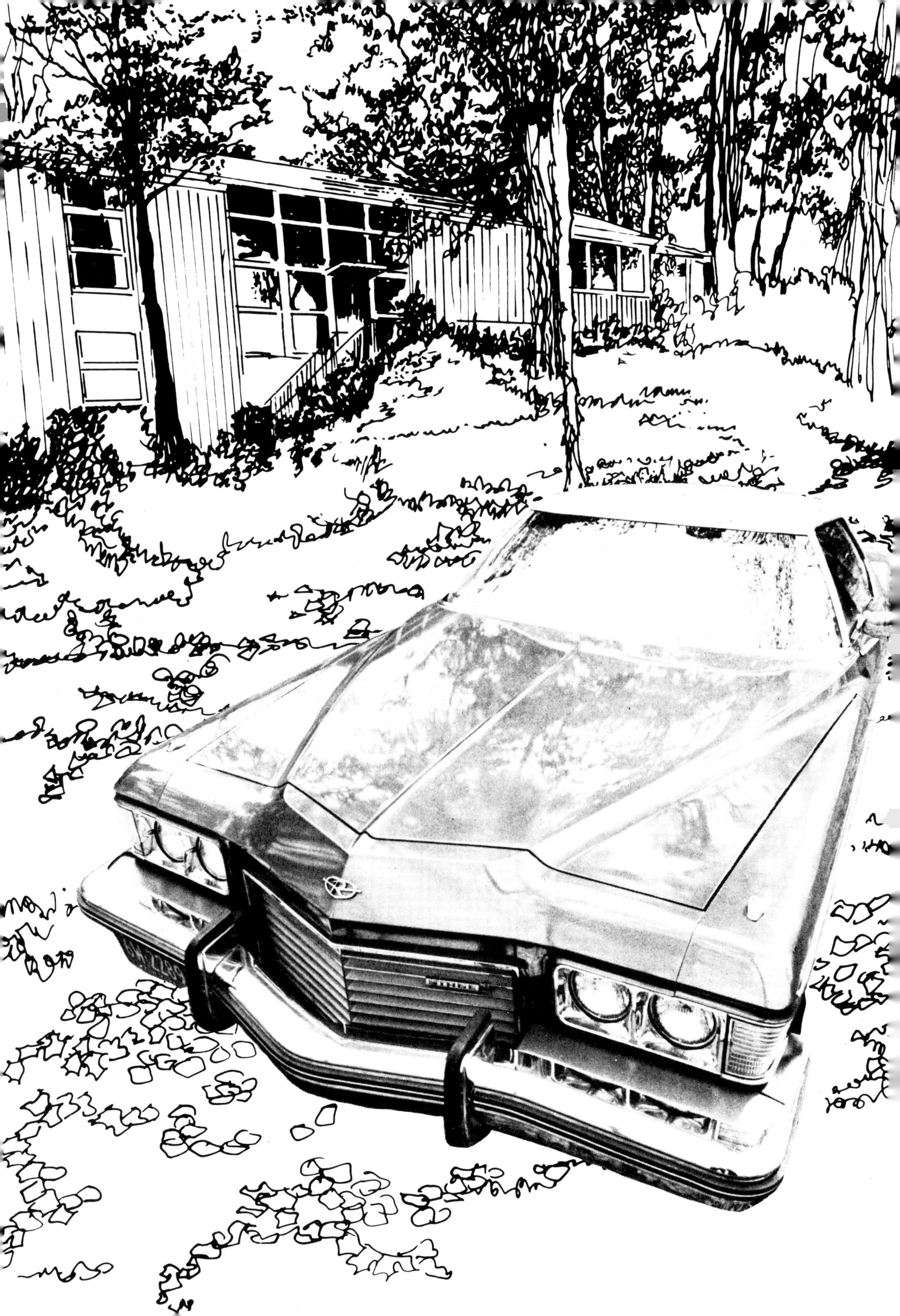

CARS ROAD TEST

While the Riviera has been known primarily as a "high-roller short" for the garment center sharpie (who usually refers to it as a Riv), it has for many years maintained the position of the top luxury/performance vehicle in this country. In its heyday there was nothing in its class that could stay with one from a traffic light, a dragstrip Christmas Tree or a twisty mountain road. Oldsmobile for a short while offered a W-32 Ram Air option in its Toronado, but very few were built. Before Oldsmobile entered this personal/luxury performance field, Buick had already discontinued pushing its dual four-barrel Gran Sport Riviera. The Thunderbird, a dead issue then and now, never really posed a threat to the GS' position in the marketplace. In fact, in 1965 the Gran Sport Riviera and its baby brother, the GS Skylark, shared the Top Performance Car of the Year Award from this magazine. As late as 1967 there was a performance Riviera available with 10.25-59-one compression and a 360-hp 430-inch engine. It was a helluva running car with the old 430 engine and a bitchin' handler with stock-type tires. Remember, those were the days before radial tires and 60-series ground grabbers!

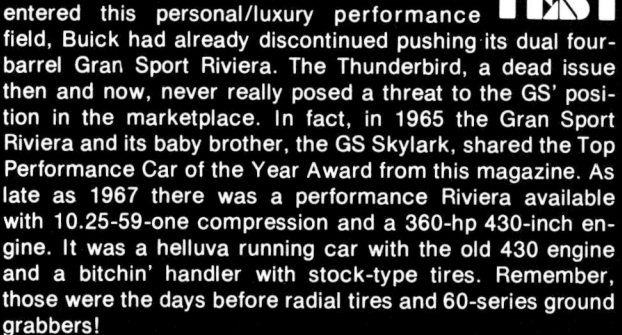

There are many rumors surrounding the original Riviera, many of which point out that GM styling's Riviera design wasn't even supposed to be for Buick. From what we could gather it was originally slated to be a Chevy II/Nova car but given at the last moment to Buick as it was going through a slump period. They needed the pick-me-up and they got the Riviera. How true this is we don't know. Because of our never-ending respect for Buick and what they have done in the performance car field (a field that is not their piece of the action), we couldn't resist trying out the latest in the Riviera Gran Sport Stage I. Because of the car appeals obviously to the Riv line up, the '73 its tariff and size

THE PRINCELY PACHYDERM

When bigger supercars are built, Buick will build them

set, but we've always been a sucker for a GS. So here it is.

For 1973 the Riviera GS has been re-engineered to make it even more desirable for the high rollers. It's smoother-riding and plusher than ever before thanks to a number of suspension modifications. The older GS and Stage I models had *genuine* HD suspensions that sacrificed boulevard ride characteristics for precise road manners. The kind of ride enthusiasts wanted. Well, them days are gone forever. Even with the new steel-belted radial-ply tires the ride and handling does not equal that of the GS in the good old days. The new suspension is composed of new front and rear springs with shocks valved for a low-deflation rate, front and rear sway bars, wide wheels and 70-series 15-inch radials. The net result is a luxurious ride with good roll control and positive handling characteristics. However, it doesn't offer that firmness and high-speed stability we used to love in the old GS. We found that the front end tended to bottom out negotiating bad roads and the car was quite susceptible to cross winds at highway speeds. Since the car does cruise effortlessly at speeds of 80-plus mph, you must pay careful attention at all times to make sure you don't wander out of your lane.

The old performance package that was part of the Gran Sport option is now known as the Stage I package. When you opt for Stage I you get the 455 engine used in the Stage I intermediate except this version has valve timing modifications designed to smooth-out low-speed-performance and idle roughness. With valve timing the engine does idle smoother than you would believe considering all the emission control devices and the camshaft. They've done a great job in that area. With Stage I you also get a beefed transmission and a performance axle ratio with limited slip. Our test car was equipped with a 3.23 gear set. We would have liked more positive bang-shift-type gear changes in the excellent Turbo-Hydro but they've been dampened out so as not to disturb the typical Riv buyer. Buick knows where the market is and they know as well as we know that catering to the youth market or the performance enthusiast with the Riviera is tantamount to a quick-trip to the poorhouse!

The new Riviera is obviously no longer our cup of tea. However, one must appreciate what Buick engineers have done to retain a decent degree of performance in a car of this type and still meet all emission requirements in all states. The Stage I engine produces 10 more horsepower at 400 more rpm than the standard engine and five more foot pounds of torque at the same rpm than the normal version. This represents approximately 10 hp and 10 foot pounds less than the rating of the same engine in the intermediate coupe. The engine is a super-smooth performer and doesn't bog, stumble, break-up or stutter (providing it's warmed up). It no longer offers snappy performance unless you constantly bury the loud pedal every time you want to move out. Using this type of driving   Continued on next page

PACHYDERM

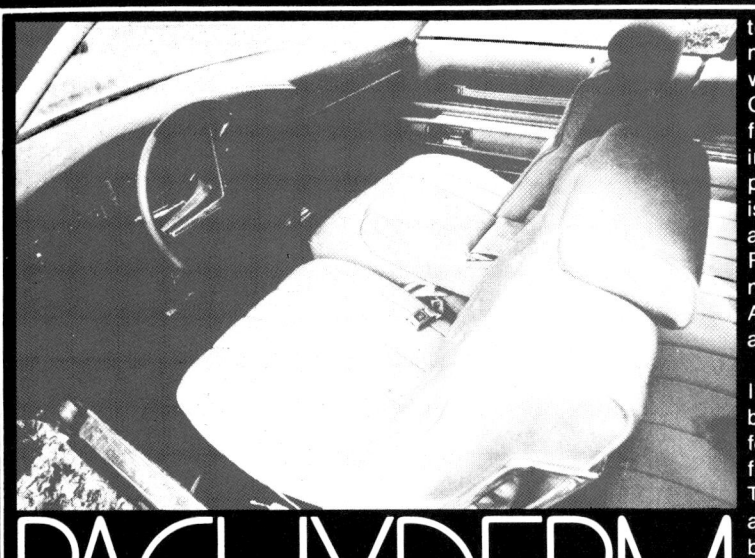

technique you will not only quickly meet every lawman in town but you will also become quite friendly with each and every gas pump jockey in the area. Gas consumption in general is terrible, but under full throttle conditions it becomes bank-breaking in scope. It just isn't worth it. When evaluating this powerplant we can't for one minute forget the 455 is now equipped with no less than seven devices associated with the emission problem: Exhaust Gas Recirculator, PCV, Time Modulated Choke, Thermac Air Pre-Heat System, Air Injection, Solenoid-Actuated Throttle Stop and a low-overlap cam. It's amazing that it runs at all!

The new Riviera is a big car and it feels like one. If it wasn't overstuffed enough before, the new bumpers ruin it forever. However it is rather agile for a car its size; the power front discs work beautifully and the power steering offers great road feel. The new radial tires do a lot for the handling without any ill effects. The most critical personal luxury car buyer will be pleased with the HD suspension package which is probably why the hard-core enthusiasts won't. We were also most impressed with the detailing and quality control on our test car. It was loaded with every conceivable power accessory and everything performed flawlessly. The infinitely adjustable semi-buckets offered a driving position for everyone, regardless of stature. Everything fit right. The car simply reeked of class.

If you're looking for a high-roller personal luxury car, look at the GS Stage I Riviera. If you're looking for a car in the tradition of the good old 1965-1967 GS you had better look in the used car lots. Buick doesn't build one anymore.

All appointments on the Riviera are First Cabin, right down to the distinctive emblems. Between the adjustable steering wheel and the power seats, there's a seating position for everyone. Wire wheels are simulated yet extremely effective. They're the best looking wire 'caps to come along in years. Somewhere under all the power takeoffs and emission control devices rests an engine—an impressive 455-incher. The forest used as a backdrop was supplied by our good friends Mary & Dick Sugatt of Rhinebeck, New York.

BUICK 455 RIVIERA GS SPECIFICATIONS

ENGINE
Type	OHV V-8
Displacement	455 cubic inches
Compression Ratio	8.50-to-1
Carburetion	Rochester Quadrajet
Camshaft	387/.445 Hydraulic
Horsepower	260 hp 4400 rpm
Torque	380 foot/pounds @ 2800
Exhaust	Headers, dual pipes
Ignition	Stock

TRANSMISSION
Make	Turbo Hydramatic
Control	Column

REAR END
Type	Limited Slip
Ratio	3.23-to-1

BRAKES
Front	11-inch power assisted discs
Rear	11-inch power assisted drums

SUSPENSION
Front	Independent HD springs, HD shocks, sway bar
Rear	HD coil springs, shocks
Steering	Power-assisted
Overall Ratio	Variable

GENERAL
Price As Tested	$6500
Weight	5047 pounds
Wheelbase	122 inches
Overall Length	223.4 inches
Tire Size	HR70x15

PERFORMANCE
0 to 60 mph	9.2 seconds
Standing ¼ mile	88.00
Elapsed Time	15.65
Top Speed	120
Fuel Consumption	5/10 mpg

Buick Riviera

Another Good Year Ahead

Buick's Riviera has always been a distinctive car. For '74, the Riviera has new external appearances, what Buick calls "greater refinement without loss of distinction."

The Riviera is built on the 122-inch wheelbase chassis and comes in a hardtop model only. A Gran Sport option package is available.

The Riviera has a 455 CID V8 with four-barrel as standard equipment, including the unitized high energy ignition system as standard also.

The Riviera GS and normal colonade hardtop (with trapezoidal windows) have a ride and handling package available that includes higher rate suspension springs, tighter controlled shock absorbers and a rear stabilizer bar. With the new GM Specification steel-belted radial-ply tires, the Riviera buyer can put together quite a nice handling package for such a big car.

An added technical change, seen on all intermediate and full-size Buicks, is a visual wear indicator on the lower ball joints. If wear should occur, the grease fitting at the top of the joint recedes into the end cap, eliminating the need for an expensive teardown to check the condition of the ball joint.

Max Trac, Buick's electronic system for preventing wheel spin, is again available on Rivieras and others in the full-size class.

The Riviera has been a standout in sales since its 1963 introduction as a model. With all the refinements and updates made thus far, plus the handful of new items, the Riviera seems assured of another good year.

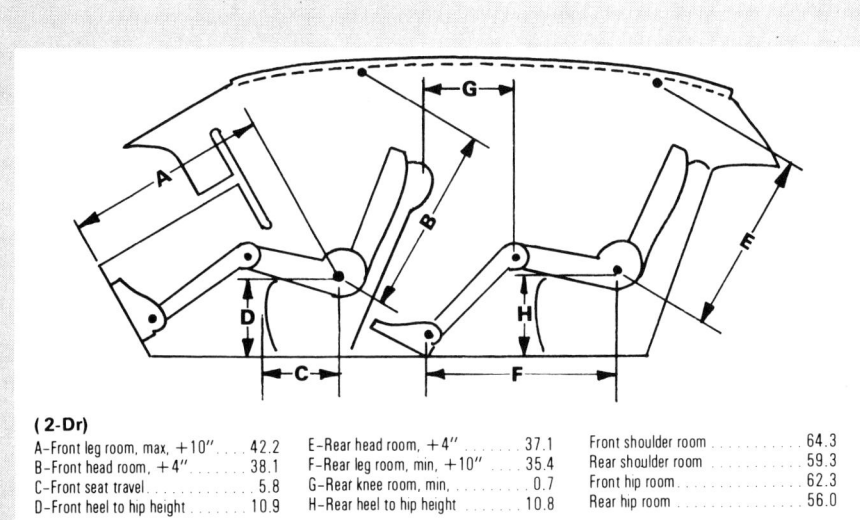

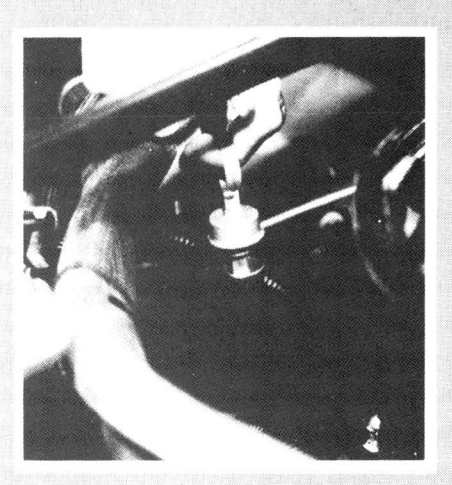

(2-Dr)
A–Front leg room, max, +10" 42.2
B–Front head room, +4" 38.1
C–Front seat travel 5.8
D–Front heel to hip height 10.9
E–Rear head room, +4" 37.1
F–Rear leg room, min, +10" 35.4
G–Rear knee room, min, ... 0.7
H–Rear heel to hip height 10.8
Front shoulder room 64.3
Rear shoulder room 59.3
Front hip room 62.3
Rear hip room 56.0

GENERAL SPECIFICATIONS

Dimensions, Ins:
  Length 226.4
  Width 80.0
  Height 53.7
  Wheelbase 122.0
  Track, front/rear 63.6/64.0
Luggage capacity .... N/A
Engine .... 455 CID V-8 (4-bbl)
  Optional engine(s) .... none
Horsepower .... 230 at 3800 rpm
Torque .... N/A
Transmission ..... 3-speed automatic
Brakes .... Power disc/drum
Fuel capacity .... 26.0 gal
Fuel economy .... N/A
Base price (excludes state and local taxes, license, dealer preparation and domestic transportation): $5305

MOTOR TREND Road Test

TORONADO, THUNDERBIRD, GRAND PRIX AND RIVIERA

You can get cozy with that "personal luxury car" if you've got $6000 to $8000/By Jim Brokaw

Back in the good old days of mosquitos, Sears' catalogues and frequent flat tires, Ford introduced a magnificent two-seater pseudo-sports car known to all as the T-Bird. In 1958, the Dearborn clay daubers added a rear seat to the 'Bird and it's been growing ever since. Regardless of whether two-and-a-half tons is *over*grown, Thunderbird kicked open a permanent slot in the auto market which tends to draw more competition with the passage of time. The 1973 roster includes Riviera, Toronado and maybe Grand Prix. Also Monte Carlo, Olds Cutlass S, Eldorado and Lincoln Mark IV, if you want to get tacky about it, but we're only testing four of them. The marketing term for this class of conveyance is "personal-luxury." Personal because they used to have distinctive styling, luxury needs no explanation.

Our annual glance at the 'Bird market produced a very pleasant surprise. The intrusion of stability-tuned suspensions and steel-belted radial tires have brought a measure of handling to these symbols of success.

Handling is a relative term not to be confused with handling in the sense of a Capri or a Lotus. With three of the samples lugging around two-and-a-half tons of plastic, rubber and sheet metal, getting around a corner at speed in one piece constitutes handling. All four cars are capable of blitzing moderately exciting turns if done in the correct manner.

To begin with, Thunderbird, mounted on standard steel-belted Michelin radials, heels over moderately on a corner, but once set maintains a steady attitude, returning to level with one solid movement on the straight. Oddly enough there is very little of the plowing normally expected from one of these big boys. Naturally, everyday driving is quite stable. There is one slight clinker though, tire pressure is critical. Our test car didn't have any tire pressure information, but yours will have a booklet in the glove box. We found that 30 psi gives the best handling, but there is penalty of harshness at freeway cruising speeds. The best compromise seems to be 28 psi. When, and if, you purchase any heavy vehicle with steel-belted radials, be sure you get tire pressure information from the dealer before you drive off the lot. It do make a difference.

Toronado is another welcome surprise. The suspension engineers at Oldsmobile have certainly done their homework. For those of you who didn't know, Toronado is a front-wheel-drive machine. With the size and bulk of domestic drive-trains, we naturally expected a heavy weight bias on the front suspension. Not so. Toro's 5110 pounds are split 60% up front and 40% in the rear. Thunderbird divides at 59% in front and 41% at the rear. Not that much difference. Part of the trick is the Toro's powerplant, which sits much further back in the engine compartment than any of its brethren.

There is, of course, a measure of technique required to get the Toro to behave. The time-honored method of backing off the throttle approaching a corner, then applying increasing power throughout the turn is very essential. If you should be more brave than smart and wind up trying to smooth out the wrinkles on the brake pedal going into a turn, the old girl will plow like a draft horse.

Riviera sets a different tone than Thunderbird and Toronado. Suspension is stiffer, giving it more stability. The undercarriage geometry enables it to ignore large bumps at speed, but shows some sensitivity to the short, sharp lumps. By tucking the nose to the inside of a corner, Riviera keeps its head all the way through.

Grand Prix is a bit of an enigma because we're not really sure it belongs in the upper stratosphere of the personal-luxury class. It is 500 pounds lighter than the others, with only a 116-inch wheelbase, compared to 120-plus for the competition. As you may expect, with the short wheelbase and traditional Pontiac attention to springs and things, the Grand Prix handles like the leading lady in a skin flick. All you have to do is point it and punch the throttle. Nimble and quick, the GP must pay the penalty of ride harsh-

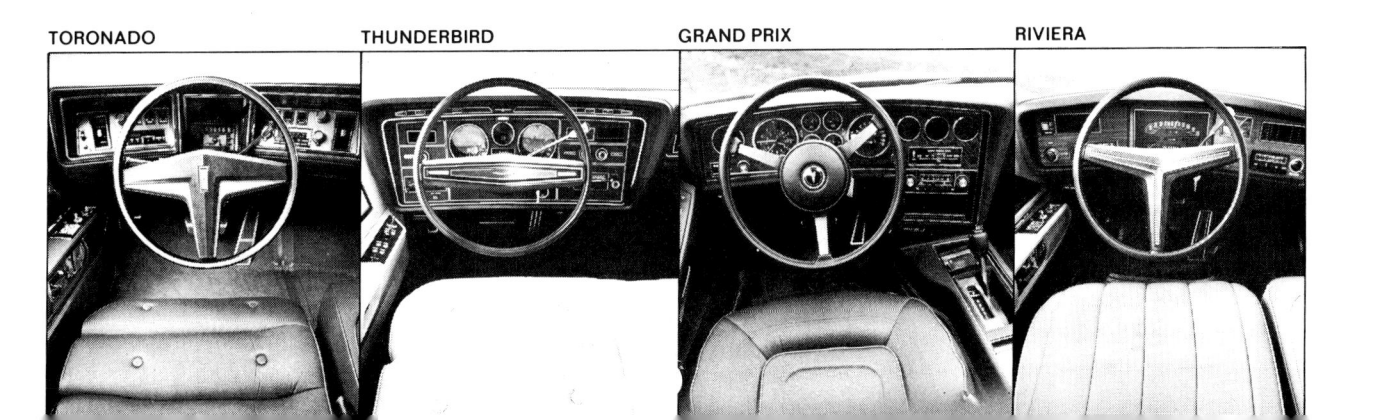

| TORONADO | THUNDERBIRD | GRAND PRIX | RIVIERA |

DOMESTIC ROAD TEST

ness. Relative to the other three of course. Stiffness is not of the kidney destruct variety, but it is a constant companion.

Interior comfort and decor is where it has to happen for these Wall Street sports cars. Seating arrangements are intended to accommodate two forward, however. All save the Grand Prix will permit a third person in front. Thunderbird and Riviera use the split-back bench with individual seat controls. Power controls for the right side are optional extras. Toronado employs a two-one split up front with a small individual seat for the driver and a wide section for passengers. Grand Prix goes the true bucket route with center console. All are six-way adjustable. Three passengers fit easily into all four rear seats.

Both Thunderbird and Riviera omit a specific lumbar support feature, which you may not notice, but I did. Toronado has the most firm seating with the best support. Grand Prix has the least comfortable. GP makes a gallant attempt, but overdoes it with padding under the thighs and too much convex curvature of the seat back center panel. Comfort is very much an individual thing, what pleases me may not please you and vice versa. However, I routinely spend two and a half to three hours a day on the road. Firmness and support count.

All three have the instrument panel clustered in front of the driver, with most of the gauges quite visible. Grand Prix has the best of all with oil pressure, water temperature, fuel and ammeter dials directly in front of the driver.

Riviera has a slight problem in the placement of the transmission selector lever. The right hand strikes the shift lever when reaching for the radio volume control knob. A change of angle on the shifter would help.

Toronado sports a cross-brushed gold dash panel that really gets the job done. Definitely uptown, unless you can't afford a Toronado, then it's crassly ostentatious. Another pleasing feature is the little row of toggle-switch accessory controls mounted along the upper edge of the dash.

Thunderbird's contribution to if-you-got-it-flaunt-it, is their cigarette lighter. It is four inches long with more stages to it than a Saturn V rocket and is more of an electric shish kebab than a mere lighter. If you threw it out the window in Belfast, you'd clear the streets in three seconds.

Upholstery varies from white leather in the Thunderbird and the silken smooth

MOTOR TREND Test Data

SPECIFICATIONS	GRAND PRIX	THUNDERBIRD	RIVIERA	TORONADO
Engine:	OHV V-8	OHV V-8	OHV V-8	OHV V-8
Bore & Stroke—ins.	4.152 x 4.210	4.362 x 3.850	4.312 x 3.900	4.126 x 4.250
Displacement—cu. in.	455	460	455	455
HP @ RPM	250 @ 4000	208 @ 4400	250 @ 4000	250 @ 4000
Torque: lbs.-ft @ rpm	370 @ 2800	338 @ 2800	375 @ 2800	375 @ 2800
Compression Ratio	8.0:1	8.0:1	8.5:1	8.5:1
Carburetion	4-V	4-V	4-V	4-V
Transmission	3 spd. auto	3 spd auto	3 spd. auto	3 spd auto*
	Torque converter	Torque converter	Torque converter	Torque converter
Final Drive Ratio	3.08	2.75	2.93	2.73
Steering Type	Variable power	Power	Variable power	Power
Steering Ratio	18.3-14.8:1	21.73:1	16.6-14.56:1	17.9:1
Turning Diameter (curb-to-curb-ft.)	39.9	43.0	41.7	45.65
Wheel Turns (lock-to-lock)	3.5	3.99	2.94	3.24
Tire Size	GR70-15	230-15X	HR70-15	J78-15
Brakes	Power disc/drum	Power disc/drum	Power disc/drum	Power disc/drum
Front Suspension	Coil springs stabilizer shocks	Coil springs stabilizer shocks axial strut	Coil springs stabilizer shocks	Torsion bar/ stabilizer shocks
Rear Suspension	Pivoted 4-link coil/shocks stabilizer	Coil/shocks stabilizer	4-link coil shocks	4-link coil/ shocks
Body/Frame Construction	Separate frame	Separate frame	Separate frame	Separate frame
Wheelbase—ins.	116.0	120.4	122.0	122.0
Overall Length—ins.	216.6	218.90	223.4	226.8
Width—ins.	78.7	79.7	79.9	79.8
Height—ins.	52.9	53.07	54.0	53.2
Front Track—ins.	61.9	63.01	63.6	63.5
Rear Track—ins.	61.1	63.09	64.0	63.6
Test Weight—lbs.	4425	5010	4950	5110
Fuel Capacity—gals.	25	22.5	26	26
Oil Capacity—qts.	5 (1)	4 (1)	4 (1)	5 (1)
Luggage—cu. ft.	(16.5 with space saver spare) 14.3	13.9	14.7	17.0
PERFORMANCE				
Acceleration				
0-30 mph	3.0	3.5	3.7	3.8
0-60 mph	7.7	9.0	9.6	10.6
0-75	11.2	13.7	14.2	15.7
Standing Start ¼-mile				
Mph	88	85	82	80
Elapsed time	15.8	17.4	17.2	17.7
Passing speeds				
40-60 mph	4.2	4.5	5.0	5.8
50-70 mph	4.8	6.0	5.9	6.8
Speeds in gears*				
1st . . . mph @ rpm	N/A	48 @ 4000	45 @ 4000	48 @ 4000
2nd . . . mph @ rpm		82 @ 4000	74 @ 4000	83 @ 4000
3rd . . . mph @ rpm		89 @ 3000	84 @ 3000	90 @ 3000
4th . . . mph @ rpm				
Mph per 1000 rpm (in top gear)	N/A	29.6	28.0	30.0
Stopping distances				
From 30 mph	34' 11"	33' 11"	31'	30' 10"
From 60 mph	165'	189' 9"	160'	155' 9"
Gas mileage range	10.0-11.1	10.2-10.9	10.3-11.2	10.1-10.6
Speedometer error				
Car speedometer	30 45 50 60 70 80	30 45 50 60 70 80	30 45 50 60 70 80	30 45 50 60 70 80
True speedometer	31 45 51 61 71 81	30 45 50 60 71 80	30 45 50 59 69 79	30 44 49 58 68 78

nylon of the Toronado to the Grand Prix's red plush scivvie cloth, the likes of which haven't been seen since Mrs. McCabe closed her Virginia City saloon. It is the brightest red in the industry.

Grand Prix sports the strongest power train of the lot. Highway response is quick and strong. Coupled with the nimble handling, the balanced package of power and control make driving almost a thrill again.

Thunderbird's 460 engine puts all of the muscle down at the low rpm range. We actually had to walk the 'Bird out of the hole at the Orange County drag strip to keep from spinning the rear wheels. Concentration of all that torque at the low end overcomes the ravages of smog equipment to give firm response with plenty left to run all the power goodies.

Riviera ran a close third in the power arena, with Toronado bringing up a leisurely fourth. Toronado feels very sluggish under full power even though the numbers are quite respectable.

Trunk space for those long weekends away from it all are quite adequate in the Toronado and barely adequate in the other three. Riviera sports massive seals on the upstream side of the trunk opening, indicating that a previous leakage problem has been remedied.

So much for the compliments, now for the complaints. Thunderbird made up for its overkill in the cigarette lighter by the inadequacy of the driver-side ash tray. The snubber is too small. Extinguishing a cigarette at night, at speed is a major operation and it shouldn't be. This can and should be easily corrected. Wind noise in the Thunderbird is very slight, but more than we have come to expect from Ford.

The glove box is very small, however this is a side effect of leaving sufficient panel space on the right side for the dreaded air bags if, and when, they become mandatory.

Grand Prix suffers from ashtray problems as well. The little plastic cover doesn't close properly and is difficult to open once it is closed. Not enough clearance on the hinge side.

There is insufficient room between the driver seat and the door. Reaching for the left side seat belt is a squeeze.

Our GP had a sun roof, which is a great option for fresh air, but not much for head room. I'm only 5-feet-10, but I brushed the roof even with the seat fully down.

To compensate for these ills, GP does have a superb steering wheel. If that compensates. Just the right size and spongy enough for a solid grip. It is also adjustable, as are all in this class.

Riviera has fewer difficulties. Partially open windows create excessive noise and there is a fierce breeze passing through the ventilation system at the lowest setting.

The design of the roofline inherently limits the vertical dimension of the back window, leaving rearward visibility only satisfactory.

The only two problems we noticed with the Toronado was the very slow recovery rate of the suspension on large bumps, giving a roller-coaster effect for a couple imparted by the front hood design. It is a bit boxier than the other three, leaving the driver well aware of fact that he best not blunder carelessly into tight places. It was a trifle intimidating.

All four vehicles do the job of imparting an image of prestige and attainment, with a small handling bonus for the driver. Toronado and Thunderbird do the best job. Thunderbird, the original, gets the edge. Riviera comes on less stately, but with distinctive styling. Unfortunately, the torpedo back is to pass into history with the 1974 model. Grand Prix is the least ostentatious, but the most fun to drive.

Price may help you with the final decision. Thunderbird is $8105, Toronado is $7862, Grand Prix is $6716 and the Riviera goes for $6516. Prices are without transportation charges and loaded. ■

Buick Riviera

Once big, flashy, fast and unique,
it is now simply big.

ROAD TEST

Faded glory. The aristocracy clothed in proletarian raiment, a stately old home reduced to middle-class necessity, the Queen Mary as a tourist hotel. The 1976 Buick Riviera, once the proud flagship of the Buick fleet, is now a gussied-up freighter.

It happened kind of quickly, it seems, because it was only a few short years ago that the Riviera was a car to be lusted after maybe even more than the Eldorado. It was a status symbol, to be sure, but it was a symbol unattainable anywhere else. The Eldo was a car for the idle rich, the country-club loungers, while the Rivvie was somehow more spirited, more red-blooded. For awhile, when it was styled with a kind of boat-tailed panache, it even upstaged the Cadillacs and Lincolns. But only for awhile.

And, now, in what seems certain to be the gray twilight of the kind of car the Riviera used to be, the almost baroque flair of the car has given way to a grudging conformist attitude, in which the Buick Riviera, ex-style leader, ex-heavy hitter, ex-statement car, is now just another GM CorpMobile.

All of which is not to say that the Big R isn't still big, or fancy, or expensive. It's all three: at 4800 lbs., with all the options you could want and a near-ten-grand price tag, it fulfills all the elements of its personality—on paper. But when you see it, sit in it and drive it, you can't help but miss that special aura a Riviera used to have. Considering the fact that Buick maintained that specialness for almost a decade, it would follow that there must be a reason for depersonalizing the car. And, although nobody from GM has laid down a piece of paper with the reasons for us (they're not likely to), we have some ideas.

First, the kind of style inherent in the Riviera may have been considered too openly flagrant for the times, its sweeping flanks and silly boat tail too gauche for an automotive era of relative conservatism. And second, the car may just have been a little too exclusive, and that, when every car sold is a vital buck needed, may have dictated a detuning of the personality.

Whatever the reason, driving the new Rivvie is hardly an exercise in feeling regal or powerful. It handles, accelerates, brakes and rides just like all its B-Body brothers, which is to say: sloppily, moderately, easily and softly, in order. You'll get to 60 mph in 12 seconds with the 455 4-barrel engine, get stopped in about 170 feet with a lot of fade and the de facto brake modulation of the GM no-lock brake system, and will achieve lateral-g figures of 0.67 on constant-radius turns. A big, softly-sprung car.

Assuming that you have just come out of a time capsule and have no preconceived mental picture of what a Riviera is supposed to do for you, the car is no worse or better than all the others in its price class. We even got it to gasp out 14.5 mpg on our driving cycle, even though a more realistic number would be found in the 10-12 mpg range, considering that few people can resist the thrust of a big engine fed by a four-barrel carb.

Comfort levels in the Riviera were of the highest GM quality throughout... which is to say, right up there with the Eldo and Lincoln and Imperial (now called the New Yorker Brougham). The seats were wide and soft, covered in our test car with the best imitation crushed velvet you could ask for, and, while the driver had the six-way power seat to help him get comfortable, the passenger didn't. This complaint of ours—that each front seat passenger should have at least reclining seats—is a familiar one to longtime readers, but it must be restated. The only real clues to the Buickness of the big car inside are in the arrangement of the dashboard, which has huge air conditioning vent openings (easily the biggest in the GM structure) and the typical silver speedometer face. Otherwise it could be a Pontiac, Olds, Chevy or even a Caddy.

As the Riviera has grown, so have its doors, until now they seem to weigh at least 50 lbs. each. Buick engineers have done their best to aid the passengers in opening and closing them, but their tremendous length doesn't aid the short people of the world, and more than once, as the huge door swung past center and accelerated to the closed position like the gates of Babylon slamming shut, we had to move fast to avoid a crunched limb. Now, we *know* about safety-beams, and we know about the sound of quality, but if Volvo, Peugeot, Mazda and Mercedes can build strong doors that sound good, why can't GM?

Part of it may be the electric goodies buried in the door; when you get electric door locking circuitry, electric window lifts, the window itself, a steel beam, and sound deadening all packed into a door the size of a small wing... well, it's just going to be *heavy*.

In a car with an overall length of 223 inches, you'd hope for some real sprawl-room in the back seat, but you'd be disappointed in the Rivvie. The rear seat area is wide, but legroom is remarkably limited for such a huge car, even with the driver and passenger scrunched forward. The trunk, at 15.1 cubic feet, is a wide, flat rectangular prism not too well suited to carrying big, bulky items.

But even when you try to be strictly consumerist about the Riviera, you can't help but feel like you're kicking a dog when it's down. The same day we picked up the car from the distributor we passed a '67 Rivvie on the highway and were astounded at the grace and sheer *style* of the older car. After nine years of exposure to the slings and dings of the outrageous real world, it still looked classy, and maybe more important, was *smaller* than the new car to boot. We wondered at our reaction (maybe we all just had a strange liking for older Rivieras) and began a concentrated program to see if anyone even recognized the car we were driving.

On the road, it simply blended in with everything else. People who would follow a Mark IV's progress past us wouldn't even look when we drove by. The car seemed to be no more attention-grabbing than the Caprice Classic we tested last year, which had to be the most invisible car we've ever driven. And every time we stopped and watched the reaction of people around the car, that feeling we had that it was invisible was reinforced.

Clearly, the last two years have seen the beginning of a trend to less personal cars, a trend brought home with great force by the *blah*ness of the Riviera. Perhaps it is the price we are paying for the restrictions the feds have poured onto Detroit; perhaps the automakers can't go on making individual models with specific identities because they need to amortize tooling costs more than ever.

But if, as now seems likely, big cars are going to stay around, it would sure be great if they all didn't have to feel exactly the same. ■

ROAD TEST DATA — BUICK RIVIERA

SPECIFICATIONS

ENGINE
Type	OHV V-8
Displacement, cu in	455
Displacement, cc	7457
Bore x stroke, in	4.31 x 3.90
Bore x stroke, mm	109.5 x 99.1
Compression ratio	7.9:1
Hp at rpm, net	205 @ 3800
Torque at rpm, lb/ft, net	345 @ 2000
Carburetion	1 4-V

DRIVELINE
Transmission	3-spd auto
Gear ratios:	
1st	2.52:1
2nd	1.52:1
3rd	1.00:1
Final drive ratio	2.56:1
Driving wheels	rear

GENERAL
Wheelbase, ins	122.0
Overall length, ins	223.0
Width, ins	79.9
Height, ins	53.0
Front track, ins	63.4
Rear track, ins	64.0
Trunk capacity, cu ft	15.1
Curb weight, lbs	4810
Distribution, % front/rear	55/45
Power-to-weight ratio, lbs/hp	23.5

BODY AND CHASSIS
Body/frame construction	separate
Brakes, front/rear	vented disc/drum
Swept area, sq in	384.2
Swept area, sq in/1000 lb	79.9
Steering	recirc ball
Ratio	16.6-14.6:1
Turns, lock-to-lock	3.0
Turning circle, ft	43.7

Front suspension: Independent, upper and lower control arms, coil springs, tubular shocks, anti-roll bar
Rear suspension: Live axle, four link control arms, coil springs, tubular shocks

WHEELS AND TIRES
Wheels	15 x 6.0
Tires	JR 78-15 Goodyear Steel Radial
Reserve load, front/rear, lb	526/1084

INSTRUMENTATION
Instruments: 0-100 mph speedo, trip odo, vacuum gauge, fuel level, digital clock
Warning lights: directionals, high beam, oil press, hot engine, alternator, brake, seat belts, cruise

PRICE
Factory list, as tested: $9100.00
Options included in price:
AM/FM stereo—$236; air cond—$512; vinyl top—$499; chrome wheels—$117; pwr seats—$126; custom interior—$123; cruise control—$79; frght—$421; plus $206 of other accessories and options

TEST RESULTS

ACCELERATION, SEC.
0-30 mph	4.4
0-40 mph	6.4
0-50 mph	9.0
0-60 mph	12.2
0-70 mph	16.8
0-80 mph	22.8
Standing start, ¼ mile	18.6
Speed at end ¼ mile, mph	73.8
Avg accel over ¼ mile, g	0.18

SPEEDS IN GEARS, MPH
1st (4200 rpm)	47
2nd (4200 rpm)	77
3rd (4000 rpm) (calc.)	112
Engine revs at 70 mph	2500

SPEEDOMETER ERROR
Indicated speed	True speed
40 mph	40 mph
50 mph	50 mph
60 mph	60 mph
70 mph	70 mph
80 mph	80 mph

INTERIOR NOISE, dBA
Idle	48
Max 1st gear	70
Steady 40 mph	60
50 mph	61
60 mph	63
70 mph	65

HANDLING
Max speed on 100-ft rad, mph	31.8
Lateral acceleration, g	0.67
Transient response, avg spd, mph	22.5

BRAKES
Min stopping distance from 60 mph, ft	171
Avg deceleration rate, g	0.70

FUEL ECONOMY
Overall avg, RT cycle	14.5 mpg
Range on 26.0 gal tank	377 miles
Fuel required	unleaded

RATING

Graph Of Recorded Data Expressed in Percentage of 100 (100 = best possible rating)*

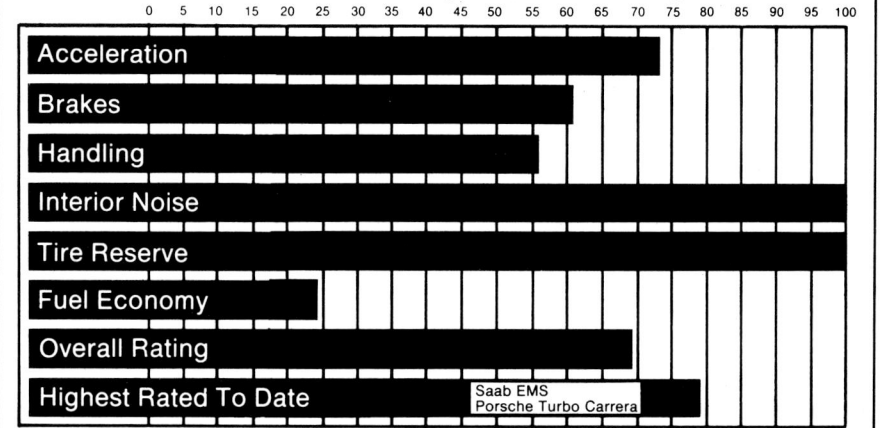

- Acceleration
- Brakes
- Handling
- Interior Noise
- Tire Reserve
- Fuel Economy
- Overall Rating
- Highest Rated To Date: Saab EMS, Porsche Turbo Carrera

*Acceleration (0-60 mph): 0% = 34.0 secs., 100% = 4.0 secs.; Brakes (60-0) mph: 0% = 220.0 ft., 100% = 140.0 ft.; Handling: skidpad lateral accel., 0% = 0.3 g, 100% = 0.9 g, transient response, 0% = 20 mph, 100% = 25 mph (average skid pad and transient response for overall handling percentage); Interior Noise (70 mph): 0% = 90.0 dBA, 100% = 65.0 dBA; Tire Reserve (with passengers): 0% = 0.0 lbs., 100% = 1500 lbs. or more; Fuel Economy: 0% = 5 mpg, 100% = 45 mpg or more. Test Equipment Used: Testron Fifth Wheel and Pulse Totalizer, Lamar Data Recording System, Esterline-Angus Recorder, Sun Tachometer, EDL Pocket-Probe Pyrometer, General Radio Sound Level Meter.

Buick Riviera

After some sweet-tooth pudginess and a session with Weight Watchers, the Riviera at last is lean, confident, and ready for anything.

ROAD TEST

It's beginning to wear its years well, the Riviera. Having gotten over the sweet-tooth pudginess of young adulthood, it is now striding confidently into its real prime with a new face and figure. Like an ex-football player who let his bigness and toughness go to fat but realized, just before it was too late, that it was now or never and so went off to Weight Watchers to shape up, the Riviera too has lived through its cycles. It has arrived in the Here and Now lean and tough and with the classy elegance that only comes with experience.

With the class come manners. It will never embarrass itself or you in any way; this is one car that knows how to arrive in style. Sure, the styling cliches are all there; the upright grille, opera windows, imitation velour upholstery, plastic wood dash. But picking those things as common threads running through all Motor City's offerings is tantamount to deciding upon one, two or three buttons as the sole criteria of a suit's style; obviously, some do it better than others. For instance, the Riviera's upright grille is remarkably un-Mercedes-like, being instead more a copy of the Parthenon, and while it may not make sense to drive around with an ancient Greek temple on your nose it is at least a classy, classic shape and a welcome relief from the boat-tail of a few years ago. The opera windows are bigger than

PHOTOGRAPHY: LARRY GRIFFIN

most—you can actually see something through these—the imitation velour upholstery is well done, comfortable and luxurious as an expensive sofa, and the plastic wood dash doesn't bend around corners in funny ways that real wood can't. In truth, a lot of the stuff on the Riviera is imitation, but *good* imitation, and in a world where *plastique* is king a good imitation isn't disagreeable in the least.

You have always been able to find sumptuousness in big American cars, but the rethink GM did when it put together the '77 B-bodies has added class to the luxury. You are no longer overwhelmed by low rococco decor everywhere. The GM rethink has resulted in a Riviera with the comfort of your living room without making the car one of the semi-mobile living rooms of the past. This Riviera is perfectly capable of being a car with no apologies for lack of a hideaway sofa or fireplace. You can see and touch all the instruments and controls, and the placement of the climate and sound functions in the center, where everyone in the front seat can reach them, is an improvement deserving of a red carpet welcome. Instrumentation is sparse, limited to speedo, fuel level and a clock *way* over there, but really, in a Rivvie, as long as you know the oil pressure is o.k. do you really care how much of it you have? Sparse on things perhaps you don't really need, clean and legible on the things you use a lot. Maybe not a favorite with the boy-racer purists and jocks, but perfectly suited for transporting your lady in style and comfort without mussing her gown or ruffling her feathers.

This transport-with-style business is helped along with the slick, leather-wrapped steering wheel, complete with a nice soft feel to it that is both comfortable and also allows you to get a good grip on things. With the opposite end of the steering column attached to GM's excellent power steering and the steering connected to the good results of the latest GM chassis thinking, the grip you get on things will be surprisingly good; surprising, that is, if this is your first shot at GM's idea of down-sizing. Because the '77 Riviera handles far better than anything bearing that nameplate in the past few years. In feel and ultimate cornering the Riviera isn't quite as good as the Le Sabre Sport Coupe with the optional handling package, but those accustomed to monstrocars will think they've transported themselves into the seat of something downright sporty. For American driving conditions (that's what we're talking about, right?) the Riviera has an excellent combination of those vague terms known as "ride and handling." To many, handling means something like low-effort power steering, but current GM products have us convinced that the calculator carriers in the engineering labs are more sophisticated than that. In times past, the Good Ride was characterized by an ill-controlled, softly wallowing motion down the road, with the passengers and driver isolated from *everything*. Soft? Yes. But Good? Definitely not, not unless your glovebox fare included Dramamine. No, the good ride of today as exemplified by this Riviera includes some firmness to the feel, control of the excess motion and suppleness over the ups and downs of highway life. Although firmer than former standards for "real American cars," the Riviera rides much better and in the bargain it steers better, corners better, and the subjective feel of the car is such an improvement over the faded days of past motion sicknesses that last year's offerings—or this year's from the competition—seem absolutely ludicrous by comparison; indeed, there *is* no comparison.

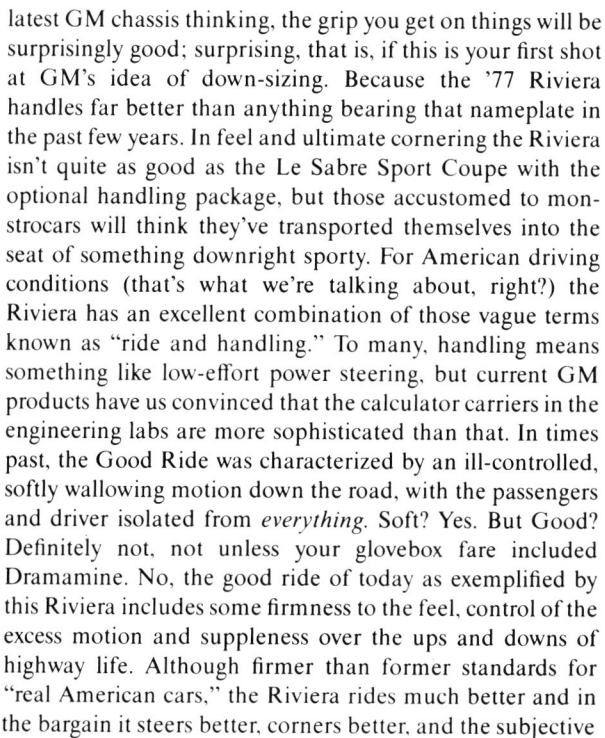

A classy conveyance works with style in all modes. This Riviera is no exception. All of this must be taken in context, of course, but for what it is, it is among the best. The brakes exhibited proper proportioning and reasonably short panic stopping distances. The huge engine, an Oldsmobile-built 403 that is now the standard 400-size engine for the Buick-Olds-Pontiac cars, pulled the car smoothly, quietly and quickly with no huff or puff at all.

Now, we know that a lot of you are unimpressed. If your life-style tends to follow either that of ancient Sparta or the Hell's Angels then this is not your kind of car. But if you've been through that, and you don't know where to turn because you want some comfort with style, but you also want something that drives better than the typical big car and you want something that handles, then the Riviera deserves more than a casual glance. Because the Riviera has been through all that too, from hard-driving jock to overweight retiree. It's been through the full run of it, just like you, and now it's ready to take you and your lady wherever you want to go in trim, controlled style—sort of like a good ex-halfback gone on to better things. ■

road test data

BUICK RIVIERA

SPECIFICATIONS

ENGINE
- Type: OHV V8
- Displacement, cu in: 403
- Displacement, cc: 6598
- Bore x stroke, in: 4.35 x 3.89
- Bore x stroke, mm: 110.5 x 86.0
- Compression ratio: 7.9:1
- Hp at rpm, net: 185@3600
- Torque at rpm, lb/ft, net: 315@2400
- Carburetion: 1 4-V

DRIVELINE
- Transmission: 3-spd auto
- Gear ratios:
  - 1st: 2.52:1
  - 2nd: 1.52:1
  - 3rd: 1.00:1
- Final drive ratio: 2.41:1
- Driving wheels: rear

GENERAL
- Wheelbase, ins: 115.9
- Overall length, ins: 218.2
- Width, ins: 77.2
- Height, ins: NA
- Front track, ins: 62.2
- Rear track, ins: 60.7
- Trunk capacity, cu ft: 19.8
- Curb weight, lbs: 4150
  - Distribution, % front/rear: 56/44
- Power-to-weight ratio, lbs/hp: 22.4

BODY AND CHASSIS
- Body/frame construction: separate
- Brakes, front/rear: vented disc/drum
  - Swept area, sq in: 384.2
  - Swept area, sq in/1000 lb: 92.6
- Steering: recirc. ball
  - Ratio: 16.1:1
  - Turns, lock-to-lock: 3.4
  - Turning circle, ft: NA
- Front suspension: Independent, upper and lower control arms, coil springs, tubular shocks, anti-roll bar
- Rear suspension: Live axle, four-link, coil springs, tubular shocks, anti-roll bar

WHEELS AND TIRES
- Wheels: 15 x 6.0
- Tires: GR 78-15 Uniroyal PR6 Steel Belted Radial

INSTRUMENTATION
- Instruments: 0-85 mph speedo, trip odo, fuel, clock
- Warning lights: directionals, high beam, oil press, generator, temp, fuel economy, brake, seat belts, rear defog, low fuel, cruise control

PRICE
- Factory list, as tested: $9948.85
- Options included in price: Electric door locks—$70; landau top—$244; auto. air conditioner—$621; rally ride & handling package—$18; 403 V8—$65; chrome wheels—$64; cornering lights—$44; lamp monitors, front & rear—$55; power seats—$276; two-tone paint—$185; tinted glass—$69; carpet savers & mats—$22; electric rear window defogger—$85; remote control mirror, right side—$19; lighted vanity mirror—$43; cruise control—$84; high-altitude emissions—$22; tilt steering wheel—$58; WSW—$43; fuel usage indicator—$27; power antenna—$42; AM/FM stereo 8-track—$341; speed alert—$20; bumper guards, front & rear—$38

TEST RESULTS

ACCELERATION, SEC.
- 0-30 mph: 3.3
- 0-40 mph: 4.9
- 0-50 mph: 7.0
- 0-60 mph: 9.4
- 0-70 mph: 12.9
- 0-80 mph: 17.5
- Standing start, ¼ mile: 17.2
- Speed at end ¼ mile, mph: 79.3
- Avg accel over ¼ mile, g: 0.21

SPEEDS IN GEARS, MPH
- 1st (4200 rpm): 51
- 2nd (4000 rpm): 82
- 3rd (4000 rpm) (calc.): 112
- Engine revs at 70 mph: 2400

SPEEDOMETER ERROR
Indicated speed	True speed
40 mph	43 mph
50 mph	53 mph
60 mph	64 mph
70 mph	74 mph
80 mph	85 mph

INTERIOR NOISE, dBA
- Idle: 49
- Max 1st gear: 70
- Steady 40 mph: 60
- 50 mph: 63
- 60 mph: 65
- 70 mph: 66

BRAKES
- Average stopping distance from 60 mph, ft: 153
- Avg deceleration rate, g: 0.79

FUEL ECONOMY
- Overall avg range: 13-15 mpg
- Range on 24.0 gal tank: 360 miles
- Fuel required: unleaded

HANDLING
- Avg speed on 100-ft rad, mph: 32.4
- Lateral acceleration, g: 0.70
- Transient response, avg spd, mph: 22.5

RATING

PERFORMANCE/ECONOMY
- *Acceleration: 4
- *Fuel Economy: 2

RIDE/HANDLING
- *Lateral Acceleration: 3
- Subjective handling: 4
- Predictability: 4
- Ride: 4
- Steering: 3

ENGINE/DRIVETRAIN
- Starting: 2
- Throttle Response: 3
- Noise/Vibration: 5
- Shifting Action: 4

BRAKES
- *Stopping Distance: 4
- Fade Resistance: 3
- Subjective Feel: 4

COMFORT/ERGONOMICS
- *Interior Noise: 4
- Controls/Instruments: 3
- Visibility: 3
- Entry/Exit: 3
- Front Seat Comfort: 4
- Rear Seat Comfort: 3
- Space Utilization: 3
- Interior Environment: 4

QUALITY
- Assembly: 4
- Finish: 3
- Hardware/Trim: 3

TOTAL: 87
Percentile rating: 70

*Denotes recorded data

5=Excellent, 4=Above Average, 3=Average, 2=Below Average, 1=Poor, 0=Unacceptable.

Test Equipment Used: Testron Fifth Wheel and Pulse Totalizer, Lamar Data Recording System, Esterline-Angus Recorder, Sun Tachometer, EDL Pocket-Probe Pyrometer, General Radio Sound Level Meter.

Buick Riviera 1977

The corporate weight savings program sweeping through General Motors has given Buick's Riviera a new lease on life. Seven hundred pounds have been pared away, so the engineers now have a proper base to build a road car in the early generation Riviera's tradition. Four-wheel disc brakes are newly optional, and the handling has been re-aimed more toward the needs of the serious driver. Front and rear anti-sway bars, springs and shock absorbers have been specifically tuned to this package. Power steering and brakes are standard equipment.

The only serious problem this revitalized Riviera has is styling: the sensuous sweeps and bulges of the mid-sixties are hardly comfortable next to today's upright grilles and rooflines.

Engine displacements have been trimmed in the interests of fuel economy, so now the choice is limited to a 350 or 403 cubic inch V-8.

Manufacturer: Buick Motor Division
General Motors Corporation
Flint, Michigan 48550

Base price: $7358
Vehicle type: front-engine, rear-wheel-drive
Body styles available: 2-door sedan

DIMENSIONS
Wheelbase .... 115.9 in.
Track, F/R .... 62.2/60.7 in.
Length .... 218.2 in.
Width .... 74.6 in.
Height .... 54.6 in.
Curb weight .... 3950 lbs.

SUSPENSION
F: .... ind, unequal-length control arms, coil springs, anti-sway bar
R: .... rigid axle, four trailing links, coil springs

BRAKES
F: .... vented disc, power assisted
R: .... drum, power assisted

ESTIMATED EPA FUEL ECONOMY
City .... 15 mpg
Highway .... 21-22 mpg

ENGINES / TRANSMISSIONS

Type	Displacement, cu in	Fuel system	Horsepower	Torque, ft-lbs	3-sp man	4-sp man	5-sp man	3-sp auto
V-8	350*	1x4-bbl	155 @ 3400 rpm	275 @ 1800 rpm				X
V-8	350**	1x4-bbl	170 @ 3800 rpm	275 @ 2400 rpm				X
V-8	403	1x4-bbl	185 @ 3600 rpm	315 @ 2400 rpm				X

*NA California **California only

Buick Riviera 1978

The spaceship styling that won the hearts and minds of the American people to the Riviera is gone. It went away last year as government-imposed fuel economy standards began taking their toll on GM's fleet of land yachts. But the high standard of luxury that distinguished the Riviera of old is still with us.

The car shed 700 pounds last year and became much more of a driver's car. Front and rear anti-sway bars, springs and shock absorbers have all been selected to bring you good handling. With such a major investment in redesign in 1977, changes for 1978 have been limited to trim alterations and new options including chrome wire spoke wheels. Power steering and brakes are standard equipment.

Manufacturer: Buick Motor Division
1051 East Hamilton Avenue
Flint, Michigan 48550

Base price: $8082
Vehicle type: front-engine, rear-wheel-drive
Body styles available: 2-door hardtop

DIMENSIONS
Wheelbase .... 115.9 in
Track, F/R .... 61.8/60.7 in
Length .... 218.2 in
Width .... 74.7 in
Height .... 55.0 in
Curb weight .... 3900 lbs

SUSPENSION
F: .... ind, unequal-length control arms, coil springs, anti-sway bar
R: .... rigid axle, 4 trailing links, coil springs

BRAKES
F: .... vented disc, power-assisted
R: .... drum, power-assisted

ESTIMATED EPA FUEL ECONOMY
City .... 14-15 mpg
Highway .... 20-22 mpg

ENGINES / TRANSMISSIONS

Type	Displacement, cu in	Fuel system	Horsepower	Torque, ft-lbs	3-sp man	4-sp man	5-sp man	3-sp auto
V-8	350*	1x4-bbl	155 @ 3400 rpm	275 @ 1800 rpm				X
V-8	403	1x4-bbl	185 @ 3600 rpm	320 @ 2200 rpm				X

*more power California, high altitudes

/ CAR AND DRIVER BUYERS GUIDE 1978

Buick Riviera 1963-1973

RETROSPECT Riviera

CROSS A ROLLS-ROYCE WITH A FERRARI...

by C. Van Tune
PHOTOGRAPHY FROM THE *MOTOR TREND* ARCHIVES AND COURTESY OF BUICK DIVISION

The late '50s were a tough time for Buick. Traditionally owning a loyal following of repeat buyers, the conservative, upscale division of General Motors suddenly found itself in dire financial straits. Due to a downturn in quality control and an upsurge of flamboyant styling (legend has it the '58 Limited wore more brightwork than any car in GM's history) legions of the Buick-faithful turned to other purveyors of luxury transport. Sales fell from 738,814 units in 1955 to a mere 241,908 just three years later; by 1960, the former rock-solid auto maker had slipped to ninth place in the industry—its lowest position since 1905.

In contrast to the boom many other manufacturers were seeing, this was tantamount to disaster for the car builder from Flint, Michigan. The performance era had arrived, and the industry was in flux. But Buick didn't have the engineering and financial strength of Chevrolet, the pure prestige of Cadillac, or even the youthful feel burgeoning within Pontiac (which was just emerging from its own identity crisis). So, with panic running rampant in the hallways, the question pressing hard on the minds of GM's brass: Could one of the oldest nameplates in autodom be rebuilt into a viable money maker, or had Buick's glory days simply come and gone?

The man brought in to save Buick was Ed Rollert. A brusk workaholic with a background in manufacturing, Rollert's *cause célèbre* was to reestablish Buick's reputation for producing high-quality cars. Many GM insiders thought the tri-shield division's new general manager was doomed before he began, but Rollert had a plan. After clearing out the dead wood from the previous regime, he ushered in a new management team with visions far beyond such bodyside tack-ons as ventiports and sweep-spears. Solid engineering would be its byword. And that philosophy paid off well. Rollert's first big success was the compact Special, which debuted to a small-car-hungry market in '61. In '62, with a new V-6 under the hood, it was named *Motor Trend*'s Car of the Year. But the best was yet to come.

In '63, a sleek, graceful, two-door luxury car emerged from Buick's well-shaken portals. The Riviera was born. In stark contrast to the massive, chrome-bedecked Buicks of just a few years before, the Riviera was a masterpiece of good taste. Resting on a 117-inch wheelbase, the 208-inch body was formed from some of the best-looking sheetmetal ever to leave an American factory. With the long-hood/short-deck design of a sports car, plus a four-place bucket-seat cockpit, 401- or 425-cubic-inch V-8s, beefy brakes, and supple handling, this was a luxury car for the Corvette set. Though targeted primarily at the hot-selling Ford Thunderbird, the Riviera also stole sales away from the more expensive Cadillac Eldorado. The new Buick's base price was $4333.

A world apart from the bloated, stodgy, Buick shapes of just five years earlier, the low and lean Riv captured 40,000 buyers in its first season, exactly the number Rollert had estimated. But this wasn't intended to be a mass-market car—it was an image-enhancement tool. And though annual sales never exceeded 65,305 in the Riviera's 31-model-year production run, this car was an invaluable part of the division's climb back to prosperity. No other GM line offered a similar-looking machine until Oldsmobile unleashed its forward-thinking Toronado in '66.

Ironically, the car that was to become Buick's most impressive model nearly missed its chance at success. Ned Nickels (a former protégé of the great GM stylist Harley Earl, and at the time a contributor to the design staff) originally intended the car to be a Cadillac—he called it the LaSalle II. But Cadillac, economically fat and happy with its existing crop of highway kings, wanted no part of a "little" car. GM styling chief Bill Mitchell showed the full-size clay model to product-hungry Rollert, who immediately took on the project as Buick's own. It emerged true to Mitchell's concept as "a cross between a Ferrari and a Rolls-Royce."

Buick ceased production of the Riviera in 1993, after close to a million had pointed their hood ornaments down America's highways. Though the model's original flair faded considerably after '73, things were far from over. The first front-drive Riv came in '79, replete with a turbocharged 3.8-liter V-6, and earned *Motor Trend*'s Car of the Year accolade. The inaugural convertible made its debut in '83, and a final platform downsizing took place in '86. This retrospect focuses on the Riviera's early performance years: 1963 to 1973.

The Buick Riviera Years

1963-1965

In an era when GM's only niche-market products were the Chevrolet Corvette and Cadillac limousine, the notion of a Buick with bucket seats and tire-burning performance must have seemed strange. Weighing in at 4192 pounds, the Riv was considered small by traditional luxury standards, though there was big-car cush inside. The test report in our April '63 issue found "comfortable seating for four passengers, with plenty of hip, head, and leg room both front and rear…craftsmanship was evident on the exterior, where all panels were perfectly fit, and on the inside, where detailing is top-notch."

The '63 test car was fitted with the standard 401-cubic-inch/325-horsepower V-8, but for an extra $50, you could opt for the healthier 425-cid/340-horse mill. A Dual-Range Turbine Drive automatic was the only transmission offered, though it responded well enough to move the Riviera from 0-60 mph in 8.1 seconds. For more go-power, our test driver suggested readers choose the 425 V-8 and combine it with axle ratios as low as 4.45:1. "With a little set-up work, this car could even be a real sleeper at the drags…you can almost bet that someone will show up at the Winternationals with a Riviera."

Handling was a pleasant surprise, even with the low recommended pressures used in the two-ply tires. "A stiff anti-roll bar at the front keeps the Riviera very flat. Once the driver gets acquainted with the light, quick power steering, the Riviera can be whipped over twisty mountain roads with the best of them."

The '64 Riviera was mostly unchanged, but a twin-four-barrel-carb version of the 425 V-8 (360 horsepower) was added to the option list. A minor facelift the following season debuted hideaway "clamshell" headlights, the Gran Sport appearance/handling package, and a three-speed Super Turbine 400 automatic. As his reward for effectively saving the division, Ed Rollert was promoted to GM group vice president.

Three years before the Olds Toronado was born, Buick tantalized America with its own personal-luxury car. Excellent performance and handling made the Riviera a luxo car for younger, style-conscious buyers.

1966-1967

A new fastback bodystyle and longer (119-inch) wheelbase gave the '66 Riviera room for six, while allowing it to share some components with the new Oldsmobile Toronado (though the Riv remained rear drive). The lead paragraph in the car's press release boasted "the biggest innovation in body ventilation in 32 years—the elimination of window vents." The clamshell headlights were replaced by more problematic units that recessed up into the grille…sometimes. Buick's advertising slogan that year was, "The Tuned Cars." Riviera sales jumped by nearly 30 percent.

Our test of the Riviera GS (Feb '66) noted the demise of the twin-four-barrel engine option, but added that "340 is still a lot of horses when all four barrels of the single big Rochester are open. Zero to 60 mph in 8.6 seconds and an 84-mph quarter mile in 16.4 seconds spell performance with a capital 'P.'" The car's roadability also continued to receive raves, with our writer effluviating, "On fast straightaways it tracks unswervingly, actually feeling better as speed increases.

"Comments such as 'sharp, wild, and sexy' were heard about its new styling. No one asked if it was a Toronado." The redesigned interior "uses real gauges plus a drum-type speedometer." There were few external modifications for '67, but Chief Engineer Lowell Kintigh's new 430-cubic-inch V-8 replaced the aging 425 "nailhead" V-8 (which had begun life back in '53 as a mere 322-cubic-incher).

The new mill delivered better breathing, smoother operation, and 360 horsepower. In *MT*'s five-way shootout against the T-Bird, Toronado, Eldorado, and Grand Prix (Aug. '67) the Riviera GS smoked 'em all.

The second-generation bodystyle was longer and wider, with less of a personal cockpit feel inside. A new 430cid V-8 debuted in '67, bringing 360 horsepower.

1968-1970

It takes a magnifying glass and field-spotter's guide to see the differences in the '68 and '69 Rivieras, but their changes from the '67 were much more obvious. Sharing basic body shells with the Eldorado and Toronado, the new-generation Riviera featured restyled bumpers, grille, tail- and turn-signal lamps, and revised rear suspension geometry. Hidden windshield wipers also made their debut in '68. The 430 V-8 carried over unchanged, except for the addition of government-mandated emissions equipment.

A five-car comparo test in the Feb. '69 issue pitted a luxo-optioned Riv against the Thunderbird, Toronado, Mercury Marauder X-100, and the hot, new Pontiac Grand Prix. In a shocking turn of events, everything but the Toro vacuumed off the Buick's chrome trim in short order (0-60 mph in 7.7 seconds for the Grand Prix; 9.2 for the Riviera). They should've ordered a GS. *MT*'s writer called the interior "a study in simple elegance," but noted the big three-across front bench seat "doesn't offer enough leg room for most men."

Styling took a turn for the bland in '70, as stodgy rear fender skirts arrived in Riviera-land. A GS package was still available, but few were ordered. All Rivs received the new 455-cubic-inch V-8, churning out 370 horsepower and 510 pound-feet of torque. This was the last year of the 10.25:1 compression engine, as all '71s were mandated to run on low-lead fuel.

The restyled '68 model (bottom) seems downright sporty compared to the fender-skirted '70 Riviera. But '70 brought a 455cid V-8.

1971-1973

The '71 model year got off to a slow start, because of a 67-day UAW strike, but once the production lines started, it was to be a record sales year for Buick. Jerry Hirshberg's extravagant "boattail" design of the Riviera created controversy at every level. Lee Mays, Buick's new general manager, hated the car and reportedly made every effort to rid it from his inventory. Part '63 Corvette, part '30s Auburn Speedster, the new Riviera was originally intended to be built on the smaller A-body (Skylark) platform. By moving it to the B-body chassis, it became too ostentatious. Hirshberg remembers it as "one of the more painful exercises I've ever been through."

Mechanically, the '71 Riviera received a revised four-link rear suspension and an optional traction-control system called MaxTrac. Though rudimentary compared to today's electronic systems, MaxTrac would reduce ignition spark if the rear wheels turned 10 percent faster than the fronts. Teenagers appreciated the system's on/off switch, which allowed them to do an occasional smokey burnout in Dad's Riv.

Though the beefy 455-incher was still alive, its output dropped to 315 horsepower in '71. Performance began to auger in by '72, with 0-60 mph taking 9.7 seconds. A real-world gas-mileage range of 10-12 mpg effectively sounded the death knell in '73 for the former king of the Buick dynasty. Riviera sales dipped from 37,336 in '70 to 33,810 in '71, and there seemed no stopping the decline. By '74, only 20,129 were sold, and the following year, sales slumped to 17,306. It was a time of gas rationing and panic buying of small, imported cars. A big behemoth like the 223-inch-long '73 Riviera suddenly was entirely out of place. **MT**

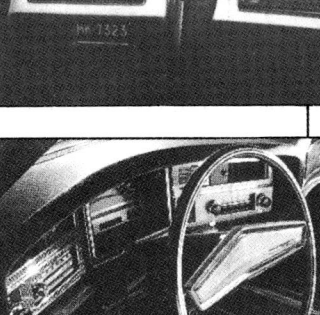

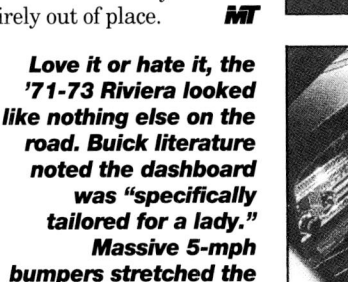

Love it or hate it, the '71-73 Riviera looked like nothing else on the road. Buick literature noted the dashboard was "specifically tailored for a lady." Massive 5-mph bumpers stretched the Riv's length to nearly 19 feet by '73 (below).

BUICK RIVIERA TEST DATA				
	1963	**1967**	**1969**	**1971**
Engine	401cid V-8	430cid V-8	430cid V-8	455cid V-8
Horsepower/rpm	325@4400	360@5000	360@5000	315@4400
Induction	4-bbl carb	4-bbl carb	4-bbl carb	4-bbl carb
Transmission	2-sp. auto.	3-sp. auto.	3-sp. auto.	3-sp. auto.
Curb weight	4192 lb	4420 lb	4358 lb	4363 lb
0-60 mph	8.1 sec	7.8 sec	9.2 sec	8.4 sec
1/4 mile: sec/mph	16.0/85.7	16.1/87.0	16.1/87.5	16.9/83.0
Price as tested	$5159	$6269	$6556	$6668

SPRING TIME ON THE RIVIERA

What's the best adjective for a '68 Riviera GS? Steven Myatt didn't need a dictionary to help make up his mind. Pix by Garry Stuart

'Pretty' isn't really a word that you would expect to include in a sentence about American cars – though, having said that, how else would you describe the Ford coupe on page 34?

You wouldn't describe many Fifties American cars as 'pretty', and it'd be the adjective furthest from your mind when it comes to Sixties muscle cars. I certainly can't think of any Buick that you'd call pretty – they tend to big, heft, almost brutal cars. Not until the coming of the Sixties Riviera, that is; one of the prettiest American cars ever.

Buick had used the name before of course, but the Riviera sport coupe was all new for 1963 (the year, by the by, that Buick sold all the tooling for their all-aluminium 215ci V8 to Rover – it had become too expensive for them to continue with, but is still being used in the UK now, 31 years on).

GM had conceived the Riviera as an alternative to the Ford Thunderbird; it was a luxurious car, sold with a distinctly upmarket image, and including many extras – such as two-speed wipers, an array of safety buzzers and warning lights, a 'smoking set', deep-pile carpets and deep-padded dash and a broad centre console – as standard features. It boasted power brakes and steering on all variants, and was an elegant, good-looking car – and above all, it looked fast.

It wasn't earth-shattering so far as its performance was concerned –

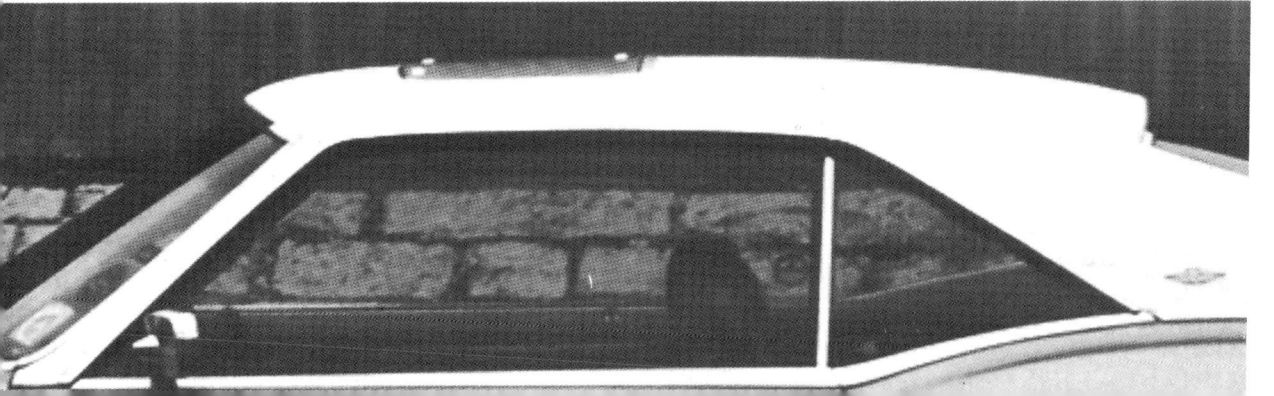

the Electra 225, and the Wildcat variant of the Invicta which sold for $3,850, the Riviera topped an impressive middle-market range of sporty four-seat two-doors.

Buick saw immediately that they were onto a damn good thing, and changed the Riviera very little for '64. They held the price, too, and total sales figures were only a tad under those for its launch year. For '65 the list of both standard features and options just got longer and longer, and a range of 'custom' interiors was also offered. Despite holding the price yet again, sales were down to around 35,000 and Buick decided that a revamped bodyshell was called for – though they were more than delighted with their top-of-the-pile sports coupe and the image they had created for it.

The '66 Riviera wasn't a radical departure from the earlier body shape, but was less razor-edged, still had a distinctive W-section nose, and was once again a very pretty car. The car had an updated interior but overall the biggest news was the new metalwork. The engine used was the 425ci unit, which produced 340bhp at 4400rpm, with a 10.25:1 compression ratio. All cars got a posi-traction diff, but there was a 'dealer option' on the motor which upped the power to 360bhp and used

indeed, 'sporty' would be a better word, with its bucket seats front and rear and its razor-edged styling. It cost $4,333 on launch day, undercutting the Ford car by a hundred dollars or so, and in its first year the Riviera's total production, at 40,000, was only around 3,000 less than the T-Bird – which by then was not a modern-looking car, certainly when set against the Riviera. At just over seventeen feet long it was a bigger car than it looked, but the clean and angular new Buick, with its distinctive W-section nose, was most certainly a very pretty car; a car that would appeal to both men and women, as the T-Bird had, and did.

The Riviera's immediate success helped Buick to touch one of its best-ever sales totals that year – 479,399 – and alongside its longer-running sport coupes like the $2,850 Skylark, the $3,070 LeSabre in its sport coupe version, the $4,300 coupe version of

SPRINGTIME C

dual four-choke carbs. In standard engine trim the 425 took the Riviera GS to 125mph, and it would run the standing quarter in just over sixteen seconds – by contrast, the livelier Skylark covered the quarter in a shade over 14 seconds, while the Wildcat GS (only available this year) thundered Zover the distance in almost a second less.

Buick took the price up by $100 dollars on the new-look Riv – but were rewarded with terrific sales; up over the 45,300 mark. A new grille was just about the only change for '67, and sales dipped only slightly – despite the broader range of Mustangs that were now available, and the Camaro coming on stream ... and bear in mind that the most you could spend on a hardtop Mustang or Camaro that year was $2,500. The Riviera was very much a luxury sports coupe, with a very appreciative ownership. The T'Bird, with which it was originally designed to compete, had got bigger and less sporty and had spawned a four-door model – but in two-door form it only sold 15,000 in '67 at a price very similar to that of the Buick.

1968 brings us to Nick Freeman's car, as you see here, and of that year's model Mechanix Illustrated magazine said it was '... just about the best of any 1968 car we've tested'. Price off the dealer's carpet had gone up to $5,245, but Buick came damn close to selling 50,000 of them. The front end was modified again, but the bodyshell was otherwise unchanged.

Nick's car is a real rarity; one of 2,905 Riviera GSs made that year with absolutely all available options loaded on; the uprated suspension kit, ventilated 10-inch discs, floor shift, power windows and quarters lights, rear 'screen defrost, and tinted glass – to mention just a few of the dozens of options on the car. NIck had the engine completelt rebuilt, which, with a few hiccups along the way – such as a cracked manifold and four split pistons – took all of eleven months. It was the first time the motor had been touched though, as the original factory-fitted

THE RIVIERA

gaskets showed.

He bought the car in '88, having gone to Billing in a Mustang II Ghia – and been offered a straight swap for the Riviera. He wasn't sure at first but a friend gee-ed him into it. Coming back home, Nick was stunned, first by the car's speed, and secondly by the fact that the throttle stuck wide open; he had to stick it in neutral and simply stand on the brakes – burning out the pads completely before pulling it up.

All suspension parts were replaced where necessary, and attention was turned to the body, which had a couple of dents as it had been too narrow for the previous owner's front gate. Nick got lots of parts from specialist supplier John Giles in Mississippi, who he says was very helpful. Tshe car needs some rechroming on the bumpers and Nick needs wheel centres after they were stolen off the car, but otherwise it's spot on and has done 1800 trouble-free miles since the rebuild. He says that the car handles really well with the GS suspension package; there's quite a lot of body roll but the wheels stay on the ground no matter what.

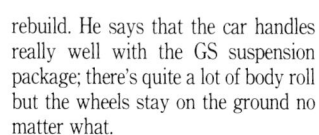

Nick did meet a guy with exactly the same all-spec model at a show a few years ago – finished in pearlescent white – but has heard that it's been sold and subsequently burned out.

He would very much like to keep the Riviera '... for ever and ever', but things have been tough in his line of work; if things don't pick up Nick would sell it for the right money. If he then went for another Buick it would be a 1970 GSX, he says. He used to race Triumphs and then sidecar outfits, and while he says that wouldn't go back to racing, he would like to go back to bikes; 'I'm 52, and that's far too old for racing. I am still a biker at heart though and I'd really like to own a Harley; I'd want a big twin, a 1340, something mean ... but I'd want the best of both worlds really – I want to run the Riviera *and* a Harley. Like I say, best of both worlds.' And who could ever argue with that? ∎

SPRINGTIM ON THE RIVIERA

VINTAGE STUFF
EDITED BY EDDIE ALTERMAN

1963 Buick Riviera

Almost a classic,

certainly a styling milestone.

BY ROBERT CUMBERFORD

Oceanside, California—

There's one thing you can always count on when you're driving a Sixties American V-8: No matter how big and heavy the car is, if you boot the throttle at the speed limit, you'll get a tremendous rush of speed, *right now.* This 1963 Buick Riviera, which is owned by collector Bill Colson, is no exception. Even with 126,340 miles on the odometer, even if its cylinder heads have never been removed for so much as a look at the valves, even if it weighs 4000 pounds. No matter.

The car rushes ahead and pins you back in the cushy red leather seats in a way no smaller-engined modern car can. Yes, a lot of fuel is consumed in the process of generating 340 bhp from the seven-liter engine, but in this country, who really cares how economical a collector car is?

Clearly the 1963 Riviera is worthy of collection. It's a superb sculptural object, perhaps the finest design from Bill Mitchell's reign as all-powerful GM styling chief and certainly one of Mitchell's own favorites.

The taut lines come from his appreciation for classic English knife-edge styling, interpreted into what he called his London Look. The initial design work was handled by Ned Nickles, one-time Buick studio head at GM styling, bar-side *bon vivant* at the legendary watering hole Topinka's, and all-around good designer when he put his sober mind to the task. It was he who put the twin grilles at the ends of the front fenders, grilles that looked much like those Mitchell himself had put on a pre–World War II La Salle. Called

La Salle II internally, the coupe design was shopped around and turned down by Cadillac and Chevrolet before being eagerly sought by both Buick and Oldsmobile. Buick won the car by making a far stronger presentation to the GM board.

For a Mitchell design, the Riviera was unusual in that it had very little excess decoration—only the fake scoops behind the doors and the knock-off-type alloy wheel covers were totally nonfunctional. If not exactly timeless, being fixed in the proportions typical of the late Fifties and early Sixties with what today we'd think of as too much rear overhang, it is a shape that has stood the test of time very well. In an era when Buick automobiles typified all the wretched excess that distressed import buyers, the Riviera was a car admired and even coveted by people who knew world-class machines. The interior is far more a period piece, with its minimal safety awareness, sharp edges and shapes, maximum use of chrome, and outrageously artificial wood trim.

On the other hand, if it looks a bit silly to us now, the interior is nonetheless quite comfortable for four people, and it incorporates a number of worthy touches, like the double interior door handles that allow people in the back seat to open the doors without crawling over the seatback. That is just as well, because the doors are positively huge. Colson's Riviera is equipped with a number of interesting optional features for the time, including a remote trunk-latch release in the glove box—although unlike today's electric solenoids, the operation was by vacuum from a separate pump, with a lot of piping and potential leak points. But it still works. A right-hand interior-control side-view mirror is fitted to the car you see here, although it is unusable from the driver's seat; there's no field of view. There are powerful horns with long trumpets under the hood and an optional lamp to light up the trunk—disconnected because, although it does work, it also drains the battery.

Buick engineers put a lot of effort into making the Riviera behave in a way appropriate to its tremendous power. It was a soft-riding luxury car, but it actually could go around corners quite quickly, and with its big-finned alloy-shrouded brake drums, it could stop pretty well, too. Uncle Tom McCahill, in those days the best-known automotive journalist in the land and one of the strongest critics of wobbly-chassis American cars, praised the Riviera to the skies, singling

The whole interior is a garish period piece, but it's also very comfortable, and the Big Ben instruments are easy to read. The thin-rimmed steering wheel beloved of Harley Earl was retained by successor Bill Mitchell.

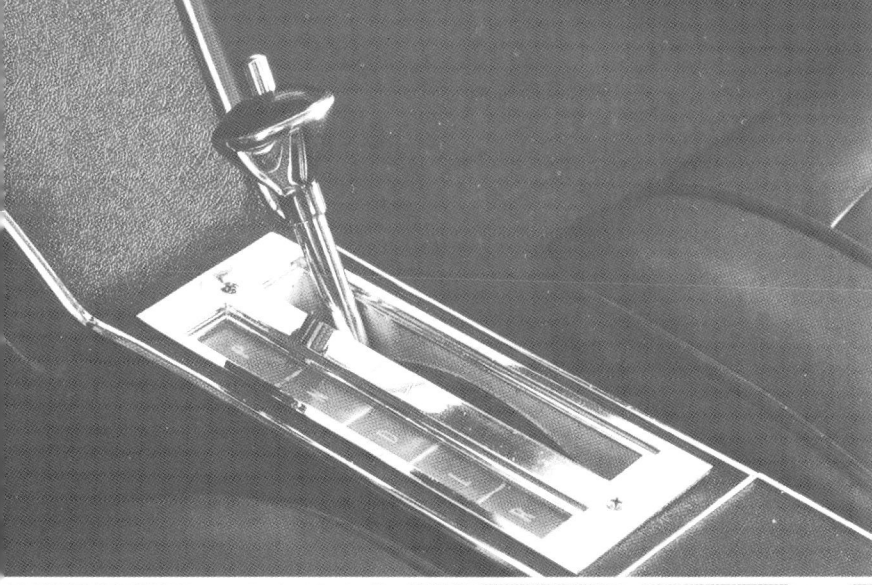

T**he Riviera was a car admired and even coveted by people who knew world-class machines.**

out the handling and roadholding in particular. Driving the car today, one is aware that the front end has worn a bit here and there, so there is play around the straight-ahead position, but the car is stable, its driver worry-free at 85 to 90 mph on an undulating two-lane blacktop road, and it would not seem like an adventure to take off for New York in the thirty-five-year-old machine—its condition is that good.

This car is amazingly original, with that indefinable patina that comes from caring for a vehicle for a long time without renewing or replacing every part, as is usual in restorations these days. Colson showed us a bit of foam-filled leather that he thought might be a factory extra but which I'm fairly confident was made up by an earlier owner. Its function is to cover the console speaker between the two rear seats, thus providing a hard but tolerable place for a third passenger in the back. Seatbelts were not required—and often not even available—in 1963, so this extra cushion might have been useful to someone long ago who wanted to carry a fifth person infrequently. In one of the few changes to the original specification, Colson has fitted racing-type seatbelts to the front seats. They're awkward to adjust, but once set they provide a bit of extra security and comfort, although regular seatbelts would be better for the sake of convenience and correct appearance.

The Riviera was available halfway through the 1963 model run, so there are not very many original coupes left, despite the "low volume" production run of 40,000 units. The standard Riviera engine was the 401-cubic-inch nail-valve V-8 that Buick had

The red air cleaner is the only really tidy part of the engine compartment. The chrome shift console is a thing of the past. The wheel covers were inspired by Buick Dynaflow torque converter castings.

introduced a decade earlier. It was rated at 325 bhp at 4400 rpm, that being an SAE gross figure, of course, and therefore highly suspect. Power was run through GM's Turbine Drive two-speed automatic transmission in early models, and later the Twin Turbine Hydra-matic.

A $50 option was a 425-cubic-inch, four-barrel-carburetor, 10.25:1 high-compression V-8 that was rated at 340 bhp. This was an impressive piece of machinery, with its bright red air-cleaner housing identifying it as a Wildcat 465. The name was likely a reference to the engine's torque rating of 465 pound-feet, but no doubt some owners thought it meant 465 horsepower. True to the period, the underhood area, apart from the air cleaner, is a typical cluttered, inelegant mess of pipes and wires going in every and all directions.

It's interesting to see the way the doors are made on the Riviera, with outer skin panels bolted to the inner framing. It looks for all the world like an early version of the current Saturn method of construction, except the skins are metal instead of plastic. But that's the only technical solution that stands out. The body-on-frame structure is pretty much standard for the period, there are no particularly unusual mechanical details, and in the final analysis one has to accept that the real touchstone of Riviera interest is the spectacularly successful styling. It has the same combination of hard edges, long horizontal lines, and voluptuous surfaces that manufacturers are offering today, without their pretentious marketing names. It's a beauty.

No aerodynamic concerns here. Blunt dragginess is overcome by sheer brute force—and lots of it. Four people could take all the luggage they wanted. No sedan today has as much trunk space.